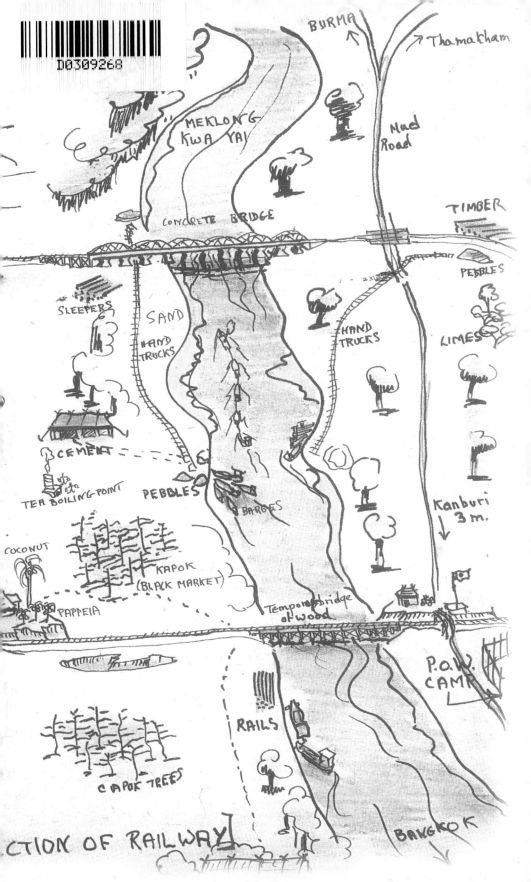

THE COLONEL
OF TAMARKAN

ALSO BY JULIE SUMMERS

Fearless on Everest: The Quest for Sandy Irvine

THE COLONEL OF TAMARKAN

Philip Toosey and the Bridge
on the River Kwai

JULIE SUMMERS

**SIMON &
SCHUSTER**

London · New York · Sydney · Toronto

A VIACOM COMPANY

First published in Great Britain by Simon & Schuster UK Ltd, 2005
A Viacom Company

1 3 5 7 9 10 8 6 4 2

Simon & Schuster UK Ltd
Africa House
64–78 Kingsway
London WC2B 6AH

www.simonsays.co.uk

Simon & Schuster Australia
Sydney

A CIP catalogue record for this book is available
from the British Library.

Hardback ISBN 0-7432-6350-2
EAN 9780743263504

Trade paperback ISBN 0-7432-6351-0
EAN 9780743263511

Typeset in Perpetua by M Rules
Printed and bound in Great Britain by
The Bath Press, Bath

Permission to quote from their books, letters and interviews
has kindly been given by Stephen Alexander, Brian Best, Kevin Brownlow, Peter N. Davies,
Bill Drower, Peter Dunstan, Charles Elston, Sibylla Jane Flower, Natasha Fraser-Cavassoni,
David Hamilton, George Holland, Yvonne Huntriss, ING Bank (London Branch), N.V.,
Peter Jones, Clifford Kinvig, Patricia Mark, Jonathan Moffatt, Mrs E. Poole,
Margaret Sergeant, Liz Shields, Gordon Smith, Ian Tod, the Toosey family,
Alan Warren, Charles Wylie, Christina Young, Dick van Zoonen,
the executors of Stanley Gimson, the estate of T. Newell
and the family of the late Norman Pritchard.

For William Arthur Denton Toosey

CONTENTS

CONTENTS

THE COLONEL
OF TAMARKAN

THE EXTENT OF THE
JAPANESE EMPIRE
JULY 1942

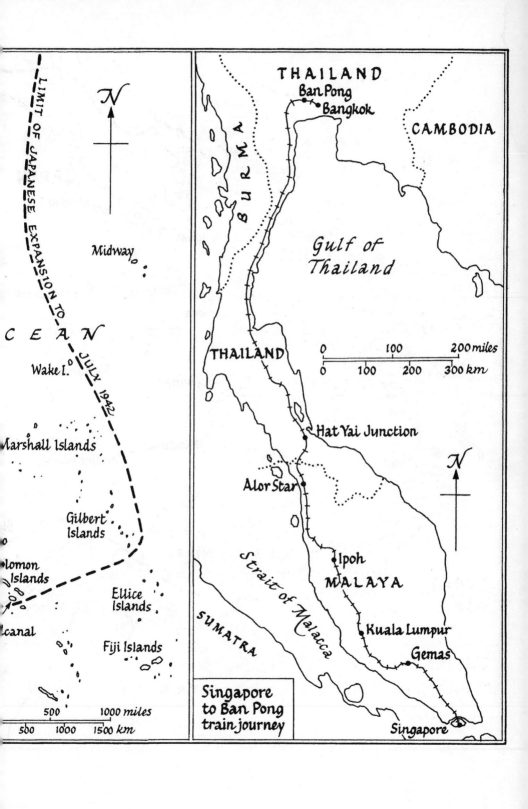

LIMIT OF JAPANESE EXPANSION TO JULY 1942

N

Midway

C E A N

Wake I.

Marshall Islands

Gilbert
Islands

Solomon
Islands

Ellice
Islands

canal

Fiji Islands

500   1000 miles
500   1000   1500 km

THAILAND
Ban Pong
Bangkok

CAMBODIA

BURMA

Gulf of
Thailand

THAILAND

0   100   200 miles
0   100   200   300 km

Hat Yai Junction

N

Alor Star

Ipoh

MALAYA

Strait of Malacca

SUMATRA

Kuala Lumpur

Gemas

Singapore
to Ban Pong
train journey

Singapore

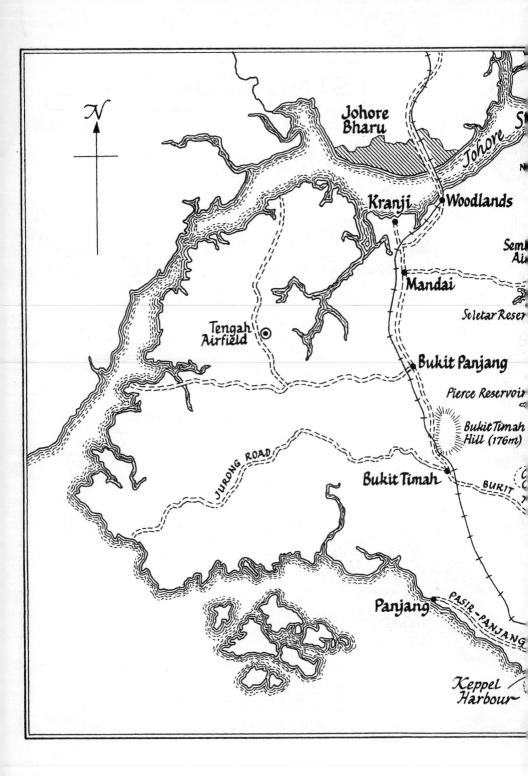

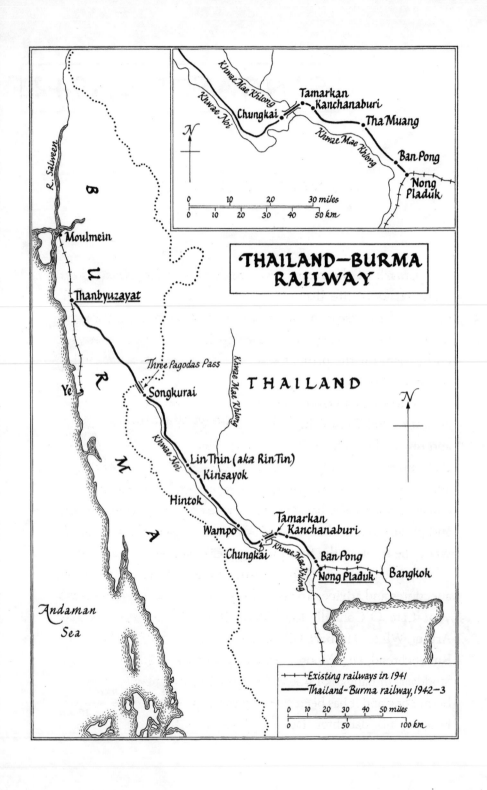

ACKNOWLEDGEMENTS

It is a mark of the respect in which Phil Toosey was held in many walks of life that I have been so fortunate, during the course of my research for this book, to find myself pushing at open doors. At every turn I have encountered generosity and enthusiasm for the project and enough anecdotes about him to fill two volumes.

For the most personal memories of all, I am indebted to those closest to Phil Toosey; his two sons: my godfather Patrick Toosey and my uncle Nicholas Toosey. They have allowed me to nudge their memories and have shared wonderful stories with me, allowing me to bring colour to the early part of his life. My cousin Erica Toosey has given me unstinting support as a reader and picture researcher and Giles Toosey, who challenged me to write the book in the first place, deserves a special thank you.

Many friends and Toosey family members have offered me anecdotes and advice. To all of them I give a very heartfelt thank you: Cate O'Connell, John Mare, Robin Eccles, Pat Bingham, Arthur White, Herbert Gilles, Ian Tod, John Prifti, Hilbree Hill, Ruth Behrend, Pegs Moore, Tricia Cox, Lila Ward, Doug and Tinker Stoddart. In Bangkok I was lucky enough to meet the family of Mr Boon Pong and it has been a great pleasure to get to know his sister Booppa, his daughter Panee Subhawat and his granddaughter

Amornsri Subhawat. Sri and I made a memorable visit into the jungle in May 2004.

Phil Toosey's business career at Barings spanned forty years and I have to thank many people there who worked with him and shared their memories with me: John Ashburton, who first met Phil Toosey in the early 1950s, Catherine Graves, who sewed a button on to his jacket at his leaving lunch; Jim Peers, Andrew Tuckey and Graham Cass. John Orbell put the Barings' archives together and this invaluable resource is now managed by Moira Lovegrove, Stephen Soanes and Julie Warr who have been very supportive.

Thanks are due to people who have helped me in various libraries and personal collections here and in Australia: Eileen Ward, Peter Winstanley, Ian Boumphrey, Neil MacPherson, Anthony Wilder, Joan Wilder, Lu Meredith, John Taylor, Sue Smart, Peter Jones. Thanks to the staff in the document and photographic archives at the Imperial War Museum in London who have been so generous and supportive during my many visits there. I should like to thank Rod Suddaby and Katharine Martin in particular.

Much has been written on the subject of the Thailand–Burma railway over the last sixty years and in recent times researchers and historians have looked at all different aspects of its history and construction. My thanks for their expert advice go to Sibylla Jane Flower, whose father was a great support to my grandfather and she has been an equal support to me; to Clifford Kinvig, Sears Eldredge and Jonathan Moffat.

Various people have been kind enough to read and comment on sections of text: Robin Ashcroft, Dr Geoffrey Gill, David Hamilton, Theresa Nicolson, Michael Swaine, Kathryn Wilkinson; Kathleen Lowe offered advice on post-war anxiety. Others who were kind enough to help me with questions and research were David

Smiley, Patricia Simmonds, Rose Denny, Petronella Ballard, Dick Shaap, Madzi Beverage, Ed Vermeulen, Ruud Spangenberg, John de Ramsay, Ruth Escritt, Margaret Sargent, Brian Best, Malcolm Ross, Philip Smiley, John Taylor, Herbert Gilles, Paul Cort, Sjoerd Wiegersma and Neil Westbrook.

Of the former prisoners of war who were prepared to talk or write to me about their experiences and about their memories of Phil Toosey, I would like to thank: Stephen Alexander, Johnny Anten, Dennis Bluett, Roy Bonnett, Tom Brown, Jack Chalker, Perce Curvey, Peter Dunstan, Charles Elston, George 'Dutch' Holland, Charles Letts, Esmond Love, Les Martin, James Noble, Norman Pritchard, Rowley Richards, Ronald Searle, Gore Sefton-Kenny, Gordon Smith, Mike Swan, Charles Wylie and Dick Van Zoonen.

Peter Davies, Professor Emeritus in the Department of History at the University of Liverpool, made a series of tape recordings over an eighteen-month period from February 1974 to the autumn of 1975 and these are now housed in the Imperial War Museum's sound archive. The tapes have formed the backbone of the book and without them the material would have been far less rich, particularly in respect of Phil Toosey's personal views and thoughts. I am deeply grateful to Peter for his generous support for this book and for the help and information he gave me regarding, amongst other things, the Japanese railway engineers.

My thanks to my agent Catherine Clarke and her assistant Michele Topham and to my editor Andrew Gordon and his assistant Edwina Barstow. I am enormously grateful for their support and encouragement. A grant from the Authors' Foundation made my travel to Thailand possible, for which I am most grateful.

Books do not get written without a cost to my family. They have been so patient and supportive, my youngest son even drawing me helpful pictures of the bridge being bombed. Thank you Chris, Simon, Richard and Sandy.

I owe a debt of thanks beyond all others to Rod Beattie. Rod has worked in Kanchanaburi for over a decade on the history of the Thailand–Burma railway. He knows every inch of its track, the site of almost every camp, the place of its most significant dramas. Single-handedly he cleared the railway above Nam Tok and with very little support he has built and created a magnificent museum and historical resource called the Thailand–Burma Railway Centre. Rod is untiring and unselfish. Every researcher, family member or interested person is greeted and treated with respect. I simply could not have written this book without his advice and expertise and I am profoundly grateful to him.

Two heartfelt and personal thanks remain: one is to Bill Drower whose remarkable story has touched so many people. Bill wrote to me in November 2003: 'I remember your grandfather warmly. He was the kind British CO who helped to keep me alive during a tiresome spell in the camp gaol, by intervention.' Since we met soon after our exchange of letters Bill has become a fast friend and this friendship I count as one of the great privileges of my life. The second is to Patricia 'Paddy' Mark whose father, Jim, was Phil Toosey's SMO at Tamarkan. Paddy has been a lynchpin between the past and the present. Her enthusiastic transatlantic emails kept me going in the small hours.

Finally I want to thank fully my mother and travelling companion, Gillian. We had a wonderful research trip to Thailand and Sri Lanka in 2003. Her support and enthusiasm have been a great source of strength. And we have had our laughs too.

AUTHOR'S NOTE

Spellings of place names along the Thailand–Burma railway are far from uniform. Our language has twenty-six letters with five vowels, Thai has forty-four consonants, thirty vowels and five tones so it is easy to understand how varied spellings for place names along the railway evolved. Furthermore, the prisoners of war might hear the Thai name for a certain place and adopt that name with their own pronunciation. This frequently came via Japanese or Dutch and the lingo that resulted was a form of pidgin which was uniformly understood along the railway but which is not easily understood by a general readership. For this book I have taken the spellings settled upon after years of research by Rod Beattie of the Thailand–Burma Railway Centre and agreed with the British historian of the railway, Sibylla Jane Flower.

The Pibul government officially adopted Thailand as the name of the country in 1939 but many prisoners still referred to it by its pre-war name of Siam. After the defeat of the Japanese in 1945 there was an 'interim' government led by Thawee Bunyaket which held power for seventeen days. One of the few formal decisions it took during this short period was to pass a decree that the country should again be internationally known as Siam. This nomenclature prevailed until 1949, when it reverted to Thailand.

I have taken the decision to use Thailand and Thai throughout the book, although where I have used a direct contemporary quote, the word Siam does occasionally appear.

Another area of possible confusion is measurement. The Allied prisoners used the imperial system, the Japanese metric. Rather than rationalise the measurements by adopting one system or the other I have elected to keep the different systems. The reader will find that the minutiae of everyday camp life such as bed spaces and hut sizes are measured in feet and inches whereas the railway, bridges, embankments, marches and other distances appear in metres and kilometres.

One final explanation concerns the name of my main character. His full name was Philip John Denton Toosey but anyone who addressed him by his Christian name called him Phil. Apart from his wife, who called him Philip, with a plosive 'p' on the end for emphasis. Of course, his men didn't call him Phil, they called him by his rank which by the outbreak of the Second World War was major, rising to lieutenant colonel in 1941, or sir. Although a merchant banker by profession, he rejoined the Territorial Army after the war and became a brigadier, so that introduced another name. Well, two. The Colonel became the Brig. His children called him the Captain. This was very confusing. In fact the full title they gave him was Captain Bush, who was a character with a fiery temper in the *Captain Hornblower* series. So in the end I decided to settle on his peculiar surname, Toosey, which would not have been out of character for the time in which the majority of this book is set.

I have had enormous help and encouragement in the writing of this book but I should like to state here that all conclusions I have drawn are my own and although I have been at great pains to strive for accuracy I take full responsibility for any errors I might inadvertently have introduced.

PROLOGUE

Three men squeezed into a telephone box. It smelled of stale cigarettes and urine. It was dusk and rain fell softly on the pavement outside. Nicholas Toosey towered over the other two. At over six feet he was head and shoulders above the young Japanese interpreter and Teruo Saito, a sixty-four-year-old businessman from Tokyo. During the war Saito had been a prison guard in the infamous camp where the Thailand–Burma railway crossed a great river, which was bridged using British and Dutch prisoners as slave labour.

This was Saito's second attempt to see Nicholas's father. Last time Phil Toosey had been recovering in hospital after major surgery to repair a heart valve damaged by three and a half years of malnutrition and bad treatment at the hands of the Japanese. Now Toosey was seventy, and frail. He did not want to meet Saito in person but he agreed to speak to him on the telephone and he asked his son to arrange it.

It was six o'clock when Nicholas picked up the phone and dialled his parent's home in Cheshire.

'Hello?' he heard his father's frail voice.

'Hello, Skipper. I've got Mr Saito here and he'd like a word with you. Shall I put him on?'

There was a pause.

'Yes, all right, put him on.'

Nicholas handed the phone to Saito who began to talk in Japanese. After a few moments he turned to the translator and offered him the receiver anxiously. The message was repeated in English.

'Saito san sends you his good wishes, Mr Philip Toosey. Saito remembers your kindness to him after the war and he wants to thank you for saving his life. He wishes he could meet with you.'

The young man translated Toosey's response.

'Please thank Mr Saito and tell him I am sorry I am not well enough to see him. Tell him that I believe he was fair to us under difficult circumstances.'

Saito was to have been investigated by the War Crimes Commission in September 1945, but Lieutenant Colonel Toosey and Captain Boyle had spoken up for him and Saito had been allowed to walk free.

Saito's eyes filled up. He began to talk very fast in Japanese. Then he began to weep uncontrollably and wave his arms around. The translator looked concerned. He put his hand on Saito's arm but Saito became more agitated.

Nicholas, squashed in the corner, was pushing ten pence coins into the slot of the battered black collection box. The windows of the phonebox were steaming up. The pervading smell of stale cigarettes and urine grew stronger. He could hear his father talking on the other end of the telephone but not what he was saying. The translator struggled to interpret Saito's garbled message of goodwill but it was not coming out right.

Nicholas could hear his father now: 'I want to speak to my son,' he commanded. 'I must speak to my son' and the phone was handed over.

'I can't do this,' he told Nicholas.

The conversation ended, Nicholas put the receiver back in its cradle and pushed the heavy door of the phonebox open with his shoulder. Saito pulled himself together and shook Nicholas by the hand. They exchanged brief greetings and went their separate ways, into the rain.

The next day Nicholas heard from his mother that his father's nightmares, which had faded over the years, were back with a vengeance.

1

THE BRIDGE ON THE RIVER KWAI: NOVEL, FILM, REALITY

Nobody else could have shot that picture as well as he did, let's begin with that. I remember the first screening of *Bridge on the River Kwai* was such a wonderful occasion for me that I hugged David.[1]

Sam Spiegel about David Lean

Between December 1942 and October 1943, 60,000 Allied prisoners of war and 177,000 Tamil, Malay and Burmese worked for the Japanese to build a strategically important railway through the jungles of Burma and Thailand. For nearly two hundred kilometres of its journey the railway ran alongside a river called the Khwae Noi or 'little river'. Around 12,500 Allied soldiers and more than 85,000 Asian labourers died during its construction and it became known as the 'Death Railway'.

In 1952, a French author, Pierre Boulle, published a novel called *Le pont de la rivière Kwaï*. It was based on the story of Allied prisoners of war who were working as slaves for the Japanese and forced to build a bridge for their captors. Much of the detail in the novel is accurate as Boulle had first-hand knowledge of the Far East, having spent a decade there from the late 1930s, although he was never a prisoner of the Japanese. The story told by Boulle is fiction and his aim was not to recreate the story of the Death Railway, or even one part of it, but to write a book about the madness of war. Boulle did not know the British Army officer in charge of the bridge camp, Lieutenant Colonel Philip Toosey, but he knew of him and certain stories in the book are based on stories of Toosey's experiences. The Japanese colonel in charge of the Boulle's fictional prison camp was called Saito and, confusingly, so was a Japanese prison guard, a sergeant major, in the bridge camp in Thailand in 1942 to 1943.

The novel tells the story of an English army officer, Colonel Nicholson, who is taken prisoner by the Japanese after the surrender of Singapore. He and his men are herded into a prison camp on the Burma border having made a seemingly endless journey by train right across Malaya and up through Thailand. On arrival at the camp Nicholson is ordered by his captors to build a railway bridge over a river. Time is short and the Japanese commander of the camp, Colonel Saito, demands that not only the men but also the officers work on the bridge. This, Nicholson tells Saito, is impossible. Under the rules of the Hague Convention the Japanese cannot insist that British officers carry out manual work. Saito is furious and threatens to machine-gun the officers on parade. The British doctor, Major Clipton, who speaks with the voice of reason throughout the novel, intervenes at the last minute and instead of shooting the officers Saito locks them up in shacks within the prison camp where they are fed on one salt-laced riceball a day. This goes on for three weeks, during which time Saito interviews Nicholson regularly to see if he has changed his mind.

During one such interview the British Colonel asks Saito how work is progressing on the bridge. This touches a nerve and Saito is forced to admit that it is not going well. On 7 December 1942, the anniversary of Japan's entry into the Second World War, and three weeks after Nicholson's arrival in camp, Saito announces an amnesty as a generous gift to mark the event. Nicholson is released and the officers do not have to work. During the next four days Nicholson inspects the bridge: 'It did not take him long to spot the outrageous mistakes intentionally committed by his men. [The other officers] could not suppress a cry of admiration when they saw the astonishing results of this activity.'[2] The Colonel, however, is not impressed: 'Do you think I'm pleased with this scandalous state of affairs? I am absolutely appalled by what I have seen this morning.'[3] He announces to his two officers that he will have to take the matter in hand and instil discipline and morale once again. He forms a plan in his mind to use the building of the railway to bring his men back from becoming savages.

The scene changes to Sri Lanka (then Ceylon) where a British sabotage group, Force 316, are planning to disrupt the construction of the Thailand–Burma railway. They have maps of the area and know all about the 60,000 Allied prisoners and their appalling working conditions. Colonel Green, the man in charge, chooses three men to carry out sabotage on a major target on the railway, the bridge over the River Kwai. They are Major Shears, an ex-cavalry officer, Captain Warden, a former professor of Oriental languages, and a young industrial designer called Joyce who had just completed a course at the Plastic and Destructions Company special school in Calcutta.

As Colonel Nicholson works out his plan to persuade Saito to let him build the bridge, using British designs by the engineer Reeves and crossing the river in a different place from where the

Japanese engineers had suggested, so Colonel Green instructs his sabotage team to plan the destruction of this bridge.

Colonel Saito is invited to a meeting in Nicholson's hut where he is presented with Reeve's design. Suffering a massive loss of face Saito has to accept that his own designer has been flummoxed and that the British design is better. Nicholson takes complete control from now onwards: 'You must realise, Colonel Saito, that we've got our own methods and I hope to prove their value provided we are free to apply them.' With that he hands Saito a list of his suggestions. Saito, with a mere nod, agrees to the whole scheme and departs.

The bridge is built in the limited time permitted using British soldiers, Japanese engineers, British officers and, to Dr Clipton's dismay, British sick, to the timescale set down by Tokyo. It is a masterpiece of leadership and organisation. Saito is duly impressed.

Force 316 plans its action with the same meticulous care that Nicholson and Reeves apply to their task. The climax comes on the day that the first train is due to cross the bridge. All night long the sabotage team has been laying explosives among the piles. As the Colonel makes his final inspection of the bridge in the morning he notices brown patches barely an inch below the surface of the water. 'That wasn't there two days ago,' he mumbles, 'the water level was higher, it's true. Probably some muck that's been washed up against the piles and stuck there. Yet . . .'

His suspicions are sufficiently aroused that he calls to Saito and the two men go down to the river bank to inspect. He spots an electric wire running along the shiny pebbles. Observing from the opposite bank is Major Shears. Joyce is hidden in the undergrowth close to Saito and Nicholson. Shears cannot make out what Nicholson is up to. The train in the background can be heard puffing and whistling. Joyce, realising his plans are in peril, leaps out from the undergrowth and fatally stabs Saito. As he drags himself out from under the body of the Japanese commandant he is confronted by Nicholson.

'Officer! British officer, sir?' Joyce muttered. 'The bridge is going up. Stand clear!'

There is no reaction from Nicholson and when Joyce repeats his shout more loudly Nicholson looks up:

'A strange light sparkled in his eyes. He spoke in a hollow voice: "Blow up the bridge?"'

As Joyce struggles to make his way back to the point where the detonator is hidden, Nicholson repeats 'Blow up the bridge?' with increasing comprehension. He turns and follows Joyce and falls on him just in time to prevent the bridge being blown up. Warden's report to Calcutta reads: 'Two men lost. Some damage done but bridge intact thanks to British colonel's heroism.'

Back in Ceylon a month later Colonel Green listens to Warden's testimony. Major Shears, on seeing that Nicholson wanted to prevent Joyce from blowing up his masterpiece, had swum across the river to try to kill Nicholson. He was intercepted by Japanese who were by now on the scene. The train meanwhile made it safely over the bridge only to be derailed by a bomb which Warden had placed on the trackside a little further on. It plunged down into the river killing men and losing stores. Warden had two injured men, Joyce and Shears, being led away by the enemy for probable interrogation. This was an impossible situation. Warden ordered his Thai support to launch a furious mortar attack, killing all three British men. 'The only proper action,' Colonel Green agrees.

Pierre Boulle was twenty-seven at the outbreak of the Second World War. Born in Avignon, he studied electrical engineering at the Ecole Supérieure d'Eléctricité in Paris. He worked as an electrical engineer in France before leaving his home country to become an overseer on a rubber plantation near Kuala Lumpur in 1938. In September 1939 he travelled to Singapore where he was mobilised and sent to French Indo-China. For two years he moved with his unit up and down the banks of the Mekong River waiting to be attacked by the Thais. His impatience to get back to Malaya was driven by the terrible news that came out of Europe in 1940 of the occupation of Belgium and Holland and the capitulation of France. By August 1941 he was back in Singapore where he enlisted in the Free France movement and was initially determined to get back to France to fight. This resistance movement, instigated by General Charles de Gaulle, who in June 1940 had been a little-known army officer and a junior government minister, grew slowly and eventually became an effective military force. However, the Free French in Singapore were thin on the ground and were unable to act effectively on their own. They therefore decided to offer to help British Intelligence. Their plan was to create a fifth column that would sabotage Japanese installations on the day they declared war on the Allies.

Pierre Boulle was invited to take a course at 'the Convent', a special training school for members of British Intelligence Service in the Far East, later to become Force 136 and the inspiration for Force 316 in his novel. The Convent was set up in a secret location in the Malayan jungle. Here Boulle recalled 'solemn gentlemen methodically instructed us in the art of blowing up a bridge, fixing an explosive charge to the side of a ship, derailing a train and also putting paid to an enemy sentry as silently as possible'.[4] These lessons later provided valuable material for his novel.

Over the next few months Boulle was to have the frustration of starting out but never completing several sabotage missions, including one to Indo-China where he was to have been responsible for instructing other young men in the art of demolition. He and his crew were called back just before they arrived at the coast and he returned to Singapore in November 1941 where the normality of life astonished him. How could this city ignore the fact that the Japanese army and navy were on its doorstep? Since July 1941 there had been tens of thousands of Japanese troops sent in to French Indo-China which meant that they were closer than ever before to Singapore and the Dutch East Indies, posing a real threat to the stability of the colonial powers in the Far East. While the British continued to sip *stengahs* and meet at their clubs, Japanese photographers, barbers and nightclub owners were eavesdropping politely on conversations up and down Malaya as well as in Singapore itself.

Despite the ever-increasing threat from Imperial Japan, the Governor of Singapore, Sir Shenton Thomas, was instructed to continue business as usual so as not to upset the population. Japan was coming under increasing pressure from America, an oil embargo being placed on her when Tokyo refused to rein in military activity in China. By October 1941 the government in Tokyo had resigned and General Hideki Tojo became Prime Minister. War with the United States suddenly began to look increasingly likely. On 1 December, Tojo advised an Imperial Conference that war was necessary to preserve the Japanese Empire. On 8 December 1941 (or 7 December east of the International Date Line) the Japanese declared war against the Western powers. They launched simultaneous attacks on Pearl Harbor, Hong Kong, Malaya and the Philippines. Two days later the two great flagships of the British Navy, the *Prince of Wales* and *Repulse* were sunk off Singapore.

In mid-January 1942, a secret agent, a British citizen from Mauritius called Peter John Rule, previously of French nationality, left Singapore to fly to Rangoon from where he drove along the Burma Road to China. During the next few months Rule, or Boulle as he really was, had a series of extraordinary adventures with the Free French which culminated in a journey into Indo-China through the jungle and down the Nam Na river on a homemade bamboo raft. The description of the early part of this journey, when he was helped over the border by indigenous porters, was rich material for the journey made by the saboteurs of Force 316 in the novel.

Boulle's aim was to get to Hanoi by raft and meet up with other people from the Free French but he was captured by Vichy loyalists and sentenced to a life of hard labour. He was imprisoned first in Hanoi and later in Saigon. Finally, after a dramatic rescue in November 1944, he was freed and rejoined British Special Forces. He was given a further disguise, an RAF uniform and was flown to Calcutta where his job was to interpret photographs of military targets in Thailand. It was there he is thought to have seen aerial photographs of a strategic bridge on the Thailand–Burma railway at a place called Tamarkan on the Mae Khlong river.

After the war Boulle went back to work on the rubber plantation in Malaya but he was restless and could not settle. Something had snapped in him during his long imprisonment and he realised he was incapable of holding down an ordinary job. He claimed that it dawned on him that, despite his scientific education, he had a role in life as a writer in which he would contribute to French literature. That decision taken he packed up his bags and moved first to the Cameroons and then back to France where he lived in a hotel in Paris and began to write. His first novel, *William Conrad*, was published in 1950. *Le pont de la rivière Kwaï*, published two years later, was followed by a further twenty novels including *La planète des synges* (Monkey Planet) in 1963 which was made into the highly successful film *Planet of the Apes*, starring Charlton Heston, in 1968.

So where did Pierre Boulle derive the inspiration for *The*

Bridge on the River Kwai? It is clear that he had personal experience of a great many aspects of events described in the novel, including sabotage and the intelligence services operating in the Far East during the war. However, Boulle was not out to write a history — this book is a work of fiction and the message he aimed to get across in the novel was of the futility and madness of war. The figure of Colonel Nicholson, he claimed, was based not on an English officer but on two French colonels he encountered in Indo-China. Initially they were Boulle's comrades in arms but after the collapse of France the two sided with Vichy while Boulle took up the struggle with the Free French. They eventually captured and imprisoned him for treason, apparently blind to the fact that it was they and not he who had swapped sides. Then, equally inexplicably, when it was clear that the Allies and de Gaulle would win, they switched sides once again and Boulle was free. This left him with a great bitterness and the scars of his two and a half years' imprisonment for treason ran very deep.

But why a railway bridge and why the River Kwai? Here Pierre Boulle was less than clear and he complained in his book *The Source of the River Kwai* of 'indefatigable snoopers [who] keep asking me where I drew the inspiration for this book, *The Bridge on the River Kwai*. For a long time I vainly tried to elucidate this mystery, which was as irritating for myself as for them. If the source of the *details* is obvious, where on earth could I have found the general idea, the background, which to me is essential? The background is likewise contained in a series of adventures.'[5]

John Sharp, himself a prisoner of war of the Japanese from 1942 to 1945, became an early bibliographer of books on prisoners of the Far East. When Pierre Boulle's novel appeared in 1953, Sharp wrote to him to seek more information about the inspiration for the book. Pierre Boulle wrote back what Sharp described as a very courteous letter informing him that the story was inspired, at least in part, by accounts of imprisonment which he heard from several planters he worked with in Malaya after the war, especially a man originally from the Orkneys called George Swanson. This man had been a member of the Malay Volunteer Force and had been a prisoner working on the Thailand–Burma railway. Swanson was killed in the subsequent emergency in Malaya in late 1948.

'I have listened', Boulle wrote to Sharp, 'to his stories for several long evenings, not knowing I would one day make use of the details in a novel, not even dreaming at that time of becoming a writer . . . I am certainly very much indebted to him.'[6] Other details, Boulle told Sharp, were taken from *Railroad of Death* by John Coast, a junior British officer, and *Behind Bamboo* by Rohan Rivett, an Australian prisoner of war and journalist. These books had appeared immediately after the war and gave graphic and detailed first-hand accounts of the treatment of the prisoners by the Japanese. Both Coast and Rivett had been imprisoned with Lieutenant Colonel Toosey in early 1945 when the Japanese separated the officers from the men and both had witnessed the incarceration of the camp interpreter in a prison dug-out, an incident Boulle picked up for use in the novel.

The Bridge on the River Kwai appeared in English, translated by Xan Fielding, in 1954 and the press took notice. It was described by the literary critic of the *New York Times* as one of the freshest and most unusual tales to come out of the Second World War. It was widely praised by other critics too: 'a terrific adventure yarn filled with action'; a 'thoroughly unusual novel – in every respect an admirable job' (the *Atlantic*); 'intelligent and thrilling suspense story' (*New York Post*). Almost everybody, it seems, was impressed by the book and nobody queried the source nor whether it was founded on fact or whether it was entirely fictitious. The book stood on its own as a great piece of story-telling.

The fact that the book was written by a Frenchman meant that the link between the story and the events on the Thailand–Burma railway nearly a decade earlier was slow to be made until it appeared in English. Even so, the book would probably have quietly been assigned to the dusty upper shelves of bookshops and libraries if not for the fact that it was picked up and turned into the screenplay for one of the most famous war films of all time.

The screenwriter of *High Noon*, Carl Foreman, who had been blacklisted by the communist witch-hunts, was working for Sir Alexander Korda's London Films where he read scripts. He optioned Pierre Boulle's novel and discussed with Zoltan Korda whether he might direct it. Alexander Korda, Zoltan's brother, eventually read the novel and declared that Colonel Nicholson was either a lunatic or a traitor and that they would be mad to make the book into a film.

Foreman then formed a partnership with the flamboyant producer Sam Spiegel who eventually sold the film to Columbia Pictures. Spiegel, who by 1954 had produced a string of successful films including *The African Queen* and *On the Waterfront*, liked to claim that he had chanced upon Pierre Boulle's novel when he was delayed on a flight from Paris. He was 'gripped by the story-line' and decided at once to buy the film rights. Whether true or not Spiegel believed he had landed upon a great story with potential. Zoltan Korda bowed out and his brother sold the rights to Spiegel, leaving Foreman and Spiegel to move the project forward. Spiegel invited Pierre Boulle to London to discuss the changes he and Foreman wanted to make in order to give the film the vital element that he knew it would require. The concern of the film-makers was to develop the story to include the usual box office ingredients such as sex, attractive-looking people, lovely scenery and an ending that would leave the audience with a warm glow. First, Foreman proposed introducing an American character, Commander Shears, who would be involved in the sabotage. In the book Shears is British and part of the sabotage team. Foreman wanted his American on the edge of the story where he could escape from the prison camp and become a hero. Secondly, Foreman intended to blow up the bridge. There are differing stories about Pierre Boulle's reaction to the changes proposed. The film's critics say that Boulle was against the plan and that he complained about it. However, Kevin Brownlow, in his biography of David Lean, maintains that Boulle told Spiegel he had wanted to destroy the bridge in the book but could not work out how to do it.

While Carl Foreman wrote the script Sam Spiegel began to search for a director. Having tried several he eventually offered the film to David Lean who later told Brownlow he thought the book funny and agreed to do the film on the advice of Katharine Hepburn who had worked with Spiegel on *The African Queen*. Hepburn told Lean: 'You'll learn a lot from him and he'll learn a lot from you.'[7] David Lean had previously worked with English actors on films such as *Great Expectations* and *Oliver Twist* but Spiegel's offer gave him the chance to move into the world of Hollywood. Spiegel saved Lean, according to film director Anthony Perry, 'from a bleak, intellectually unrewarding future, and made him the brilliant landscaper we will remember'.[8]

The Spiegel–Lean partnership was stormy but creative. Each had strengths that complimented the other's weaknesses. Spiegel's brilliance with the moneymen left Lean free to concentrate on directing the film. For all his reputation for flamboyance, Spiegel had an unerring eye and judgment. He knew instinctively what would work and he had a gut feeling about 'Kwai' which was to prove to be right.

Spiegel told Lean that Carl Foreman had written a great script and he invited him to New York to meet the renowned screenwriter. When David Lean read the screenplay he was horrified. It was insensitive both to Boulle's novel and to the British and Japanese. He was so disgusted with Foreman's script that he threw it away and wrote a long letter to Spiegel venting his frustration:

> War is not fun except in bad films and bad books. I haven't yet met a man who wanted to come face to face with the enemy and 'wouldn't want to miss it'. . . . these heroics are a positive disservice to youthful audiences who have no idea of war. War is the greatest plague on earth. I don't think this is the time to minimise its horror and film it in false colours. Those are my views as a private individual.

He went on to launch an attack on Carl Foreman: 'The subject is pretty tricky at the best of times. If it misses it will be a bad miss. To put it over, one has to have a real understanding of the British mentality or it will be offensive. Mr Foreman hasn't got the first glimmer and he is offensive. Monsieur Boulle, on the other hand, knows what he is talking about.' As David Lean continued the letter his thoughts about the way he wanted to treat the book developed and he concluded:

> If we can show this minor incident [building the bridge] as a miniature reproduction of the greater folly which is the War itself, we shall have a great film. That is why I want to treat Saito [the Japanese camp commandant] with dignity. I don't want to say that Saito is an uncivilised little Oriental. I want the Colonel to say it. I want the audience to see him as another human being not so unlike the Colonel.[9]

David Lean had no choice but to sit down and rewrite the script himself. He began by going back to Boulle's original novel. He worked on it during the spring of 1956 and it was at this time he had the idea of using the 'Colonel Bogey' theme when the men marched into camp. He knew it would not be possible to have the prisoners singing the soldiers' version – 'Bol-locks and the same to you' – but he thought if they whistled it the English audiences, at least, would understand the reference. Although both Carl Foreman and Sam Spiegel were against the 'Colonel Bogey' march David Lean won them over. Kenneth J. Alford, who had composed the march in 1914, was dead and his widow was initially against it being used in the film because of the words that had been put to it by British soldiers. However, she was eventually persuaded and in the end she earned a tidy sum from the royalties. When Malcolm Arnold came to write the score for the film he had just three weeks in which to do it. David Lean asked him to give the march 'grandeur and real swagger'. Arnold described how it was recorded:

> The whistlers . . . were a piccolo and seventeen members of the Irish Guards. They weren't handpicked; anybody can whistle. I said, 'Look, gentlemen, we all know both world war versions of "Colonel Bogey". But here, because of censorship, you've got to whistle it.' I had the piccolo to give them the pitch. And I'd already recorded the military band, so I had that over my ear and I conducted them to the picture and that was a nightmare – terribly difficult to fit.[10]

Arnold's arrangement of the 'Colonel Bogey' march became world famous. It was an immediate hit on the film's release and it is still one of the most evocative and readily recognised film theme tunes.

David Lean's production designer, Don Ashton, was one of the first men to be employed on 'Kwai'. Spiegel had wanted to make the film in Yugoslavia because it was close to London in comparison to other locations under consideration but Ashton looked further afield. After visiting Thailand and dismissing the area around Kanchanaburi, the site of the real bridge, as being too flat and not dramatic or jungle-like, and with a bridge already in place, he suggested filming *The Bridge on the River Kwai* in Ceylon, now Sri Lanka. His wife's family came from Colombo and he knew the island well. He proposed bridging a magnificent river close to the village of Kitulgala where the river cuts through a steep valley with thick jungle on either side. It was agreed. Sri Lanka had the added advantage of comfortable accommodation in the Mount Lavinia Hotel in Colombo.

The bridge seen on the film was one of two bridges constructed by a British engineering company called Husband and Co. The other bridge, a smaller service bridge, spanned a narrow valley and gave them the chance to practise their bridge-building technique. When the main bridge was under construction there was a storm which unleashed a great swell of water into the river which rose twenty feet over night and brought with it a mass of debris. This crashed into the piers and washed away part of one of them. Despite this and other setbacks the 425-foot-long bridge standing 50 feet above the river was finished by January 1957. It had taken five hundred workers and thirty-five elephants eight months to construct it, the same time it took the prisoners of war in Thailand to build the steel and concrete bridge at Tamarkan over the Khwae Mae Khlong.

The script was further reworked with input by Michael Wilson who arrived in Sri Lanka at the beginning of September 1956. He was the last in a line of scriptwriters who Spiegel had sent to work with Lean. Lean had complained that American scriptwriters made him nervous: they spoke well but wrote badly and they were 'so touchy'.[11] Michael Wilson understood instinctively what David Lean was after and the two worked feverishly in the last few weeks before the start of filming. Despite the fact that his and David Lean's script was much closer to Boulle's novel than was Carl Foreman's, Wilson liked the idea of blowing up the bridge. In the film the bridge is blown up, finally, when Nicholson, fatally wounded, stumbles backwards and lands on the charge, blasting the bridge to pieces and sending a train full of Japanese tumbling into the river.

As the script got closer to completion Sam Spiegel was still looking for his lead actor. If David Lean was not Spiegel's first choice as a director, nor was Alec Guinness first choice to take the role of Colonel Nicholson. Many, at that time more famous, names were put forward including Ralph Richardson, Charles Laughton, James Mason and Douglas Fairbanks Jr. The first time Alec Guinness was approached he turned it down. 'The first film script I saw (prior to becoming involved)', he wrote in April 1991, 'was utter rubbish, with elephant charges and hordes of seductive Burmese girls. The script that Lean and his writer turned out was infinitely superior but I could never make out the character of Colonel Nicholson and said so.'[12]

In the late summer of 1956 Sam Spiegel approached Alec Guinness once again. He was extremely persuasive over dinner, as Guinness recalled: 'I started out maintaining that I wouldn't play the role and by the end of the evening we were discussing what kind of wig I would wear.'[13] A few weeks later, on 9 November, Guinness flew out to Colombo where he was met by David Lean at the airport. According to Alec Guinness David Lean greeted him with the words: 'They sent me you and I wanted Charles Laughton.' David Lean denied this but Alec Guinness maintained it was true to the end of his life. True or not, it was not an auspicious start to their working relationship on the film.

Production began in November 1956 and was scheduled to take six months. The budget for the film was something Spiegel was consistently vague about but it was in the region of $2–2.5 million ($13–17 million in 2003). By the latter half of November the majority of the other actors had arrived in Colombo. Alec Guinness noted in his diary for 21 November that James Donald, who played the role of Major Clipton, was at the Mount Lavinia Hotel – as was Sessue Hayakawa, the Japanese actor who would play Colonel Saito. He was very Hollywoodised and grand, Guinness observed.

Filming was supposed to take twelve weeks but it ran well over schedule and the final shots, taken long after the actors had left Sri Lanka, were filmed in May 1957.

Colonel Saito and Colonel Nicholson in confrontation.

The making of *The Bridge on the River Kwai* was, by all accounts, a miserable experience for the cast and the crew. One of the main problems was the jungle conditions of Sri Lanka. The discomfort of the stifling heat and humidity was compounded by the threatening presence of snakes and leeches in the undergrowth. Most of the British team suffered from dysentery at one time or another. 'It was a sad picture in certain ways,' David Lean said later, 'I enjoyed some of it, but there was a bad atmosphere among the actors. They thought I was hopeless. A lot of the crew didn't think I was any good at all, either.' Although he had worked with Alec Guinness on six previous films they failed to agree on the portrayal of Colonel Nicholson. Alec Guinness wrote in a letter: 'I think he was meant to be sympathetic but to my way of thinking he emerged as a humourless fool.'[14]

Both David Lean and Sam Spiegel agreed that Colonel Nicholson had to be played straight and without the tongue-in-cheek approach that Alec Guinness wanted to introduce. There was tension between Lean and Guinness and Spiegel was called upon to act as the necessary intermediary. His biographer Natasha Fraser-Cavassoni wrote, 'Just as Spiegel was capable of infuriating people, he also had the force of character to be an effective peacemaker.'[15]

James Donald convinced himself and other actors, including Guinness, that David Lean was out to make an anti-British film. 'Consequently, David took an active dislike to the British actors,' Kevin Brownlow wrote. 'During a scene with Guinness on the bridge David exploded when Guinness queried why the camera was on his back and not on his face. Guinness had loved the dialogue for this scene and after debating the camera angle with David he took great care to time the speech to the setting of the sun. Instead of congratulating Guinness, David said, "Now you can all fuck off and go home, you English actors. Thank God that

I'm starting work tomorrow with an American actor. It'll be such a pleasure to say goodbye to you guys.'"[16]

William Holden was to play Commander Shears. His role had been completely rewritten from Boulle's novel. Rather than being a British intelligence officer with sabotage experience Shears is an impostor sailor from the USS *Houston* who stole a dead naval officer's uniform in order to gain the privileges of office in the prison camps. He is working as a grave-digger when Colonel Nicholson and his men walk in to camp and provides the cynical take on life in the camp to contrast with the stiff British Colonel. '[If] those new prisoners see us diggin' graves, they might all run away,' he jokes to his fellow grave-digger. Shears makes a successful escape and ends up being picked up by the British and taken to Sri Lanka where he recuperates on the beach in the arms of a beautiful WREN, adding the love interest that Carl Foreman was convinced the film needed: 'You give me powders, pills, baths, injections, enemas – when all I need is love,' he coos to Ann Sears. However, the British have seen through his deception and plan to employ him in the sabotaging of the bridge. At the time William Holden was the highest paid actor in the world thanks to the deal his agent arranged for him. He was paid $250,000 and received 10 per cent of the film's profits.

The role of Colonel Saito was played by a Japanese star of the silent movies, Sessue Hayakawa. In a career that spanned sixty years he played in eighty-three films and by 1956 he was already sixty-eight years old. He and Lean got on well although Lean was bemused when Hayakawa revealed that he had no idea he was going to die at the end of the film. Lean said: 'The real script was one inch thick. Sessue's was about an eighth of an inch thick. He'd gone through the script and put a cross at the top of every page where he had dialogue and he'd taken the script to bits, put all the pages with crosses together and thrown away the rest. So he just had his part. He didn't know he was going to get killed. And he was nominated for Best Supporting Actor!'[17]

Blowing up the film's bridge was a major event and attracted a lot of local attention. When David Lean announced the explosion was going to take place at 8 a.m. on 10 March 1957, a whole host of dignitaries came to Kitulgala to witness the event, including the Prime Minister, Solomon Bandaranaike, and his wife. A special platform complete with tables and umbrellas was constructed downstream and the guests, dressed in their finery, were treated to a VIP reception in full view of the bridge. It was an opportunity for Spiegel to thank the local dignitaries in spectacular style. Kevin Brownlow described the sequence of events: 'Ashton had designed a control panel, a wooden board consisting of light bulbs set in a circle, one for each of the five cameras, two for security and one in the centre which indicated that the engine driver had reached the entry point to the bridge, and had jumped from the locomotive. Each camera position was linked to the control by field telephones. It was agreed beforehand that David would not give the order to blow up the bridge until that circle of lights was complete.'[18]

When David Lean gave the command for the engine to start on its last journey across the bridge everyone was on edge. Sam Spiegel was terrified that something would go wrong and Don Ashton remembered him popping tranquillisers as he watched anxiously. The train came around the corner towards the bridge, the engine driver jumped clear, the lights from the camera positions lit up. 'One by one, the lights had come on – all but the last. David had three or four seconds to make up his mind. The fact that one camera was not working was immaterial; far more serious was the thought that the cameraman was not in his trench and might be exposed to the blast. The dignitaries were waiting to see one of the most spectacular and expensive shots in film history.

But the risk was too great. David cried, "Don't blow the bridge!" and Ashton and Best stayed their hands.'[19]

In his excitement one of the cameramen, Freddy Ford, had forgotten to turn on his light to indicate that he was safe. The train, now driverless, trundled safely across the bridge and ploughed into a sandbank on the other side of the river. Sam Spiegel had been right to be anxious and the dignitaries went back to Colombo disappointed. David Lean ordered the train to be retrieved and for things to be reset for the following day. Spiegel was furious with David Lean, who had dinner that night with Ford: 'You can't take the biggest idiot out to dinner to congratulate him for fucking up the scene.'[20] Lean had never been happy about making a major social event out of the bridge explosion.

The film crew appealed for help with heavy lifting equipment to move the train back on to the rails but none came. On enquiring as to why the Ministry of Works in Colombo would not lend them a crane Ashton was told: 'My wife and I were the only people not to have been asked to your party. I am very cross because I have looked after you since you have been here.'[21] The train had to be manhandled back on to the track a few inches at a time. It took them until 2 a.m. The following day everything went according to plan. All the lights went on, the cameras rolled, the bridge exploded and the train plunged into the river. It was witnessed by Sam Spiegel, David Lean, the film crew and a handful of locals. The bridge, which had been one of the most expensive movie props in history, rumoured to have cost as much as $250,000 ($1.7 million in 2003) was completely destroyed in the explosion.

In fact this figure was grossly exaggerated. The actual cost of the bridge was $52,834 ($358,000 in 2003) using local labour and elephants, but according to Natasha Fraser-Cavassoni, Spiegel liked to talk up the figure to make it seem all the more remarkable.

When the film opened in London on 2 October 1957 it was a box office hit. There was lavish praise from critics and audiences on both sides of the Atlantic. David Lean could not believe that the London critics were so positive. He was abroad and so witnessed its reception second-hand. When the notices finally caught up with him he was amazed: 'When I arrived here and read the notices it was I who had the fit. "Great! Shattering!" What happened to them all? I thought – in a few grandiose dreams – that the New York critics might pull out a few superlatives, but the *London* critics!'[22] The film was still playing to capacity audiences in the Plaza Theatre in London a month after its release.

The Bridge on the River Kwai won seven Oscars at the 1958 Academy Awards, including Best Picture, Best Actor for Alec Guinness in the role of Colonel Nicholson, Best Director for David Lean and Best Screenplay for Pierre Boulle. This was ironic. Sam Spiegel had credited Pierre Boulle with the screenplay although it had been written in the main by David Lean and Michael Wilson, based on Foreman's original script and Boulle's novel. There was acrimony over this for years. In the end the credits were revised in the 1980s and both Foreman and Wilson are named.

When the film was shown in Japan the title was translated as *Bridge in the Battlezone*. The Japanese were incensed by what they saw as a disparagement of their engineering capabilities. In an article published in English in 1981, Kazuyu Tsukamoto, a Japanese engineer, wrote: 'Colonel Saito, whose part was played by Sessue Hayakawa, by turning the story upside-down as both principal and auxiliary actor, however splendid his spirited performance, created a glaring error. We were defeated for the first time in a war, but we did not come off second-best in engineering so, categorically, we did NOT submit to the prisoners of war who constructed the bridge.'[23] The implication that the Japanese had to resort to asking the British to build a bridge for them offended them far more than other anti-Japanese aspects of the film.

Although the film opened in London in October 1957 it was not until the following summer that a special screening was organised for the British former prisoners of war. This was the first opportunity that most of the officers and men who had worked on the Thailand–Burma railway, and specifically on the bridges at Tamarkan, had had to see *The Bridge on the River Kwai*.

Japanese engineer Sugano's panoramic photograph of the completed bridge.

Like the Japanese they too did not like what they saw. First, they objected to the glamour Hollywood brought to their wretched prisoner-of-war existence and to what they saw as a wholly inaccurate account of the story of the construction of the bridge at Tamarkan. Secondly, they regarded the portrayal by Alec Guinness of Colonel Nicholson as a gross slur against the integrity of the man who had commanded the bridge camp at Tamarkan, Lieutenant Colonel Philip Toosey. Their greatest fear, however, was that the film would be accepted as portraying the truth of what happened on the railway.

Twenty years after the film was released John Sharp, who had corresponded with Boulle after the publication of his novel, wrote to Toosey: 'I have never ceased to object to the way in which the cinematic legend has overtaken and obscured the facts of what really happened on the Burma–Siam railway, and I have had letters published in *The Times* and the *Daily Telegraph* to this effect; but our culture is so entertainment oriented that it would be extremely difficult to make any effect on the image which the film has created.'

This book is about the real man and the real Bridge on the River Kwai.

2

AN HONEST BEGINNING

Perhaps your character gets improved by seizing the opportunity rather than being feeble and just not doing anything about it. I know that various things changed my life a great deal and made me more mature.

Phil Toosey 1974

Philip John Denton Toosey was born in Upton Road, Oxton, in Birkenhead, on 12 August 1904 in a little house with a beautiful garden. He was always very proud of his birth date because it marks the beginning of the grouse-shooting season, and shooting became one of his consuming passions. His wife, Alex, later complained that she had been married to guns, large and small, for over thirty years.

Phil, as he was known, was the second child and eldest son of Charles and Caroline 'Dotie' Toosey. In all there were seven Toosey children, born over a period of twenty-two and a half years, three boys and four girls.

In about 1910, the family moved to 20 Rosemount, a large

semi-detached house on a hill above Oxton with an uninter-
rupted view of the River Mersey. Oxton was then a village
surrounded by green fields. It has now been swallowed up by
Birkenhead although it still maintains its character as a village and
the heart of Oxton is little changed from a century ago.

Birkenhead is situated at the narrowest point of the River
Mersey and from the twelfth century was the crossing point
between the Wirral and Liverpool. In 1801 Birkenhead was a
hamlet with a population of 110 but by the 1830s Liverpool had
begun to spill over and the population of Birkenhead had
expanded to 2500. In 1837 the railway line to Chester was
opened and in 1843 docks and a tidal basin on the Birkenhead
side of the Mersey ushered in the industrialisation of the town.
In 1843 the town created history by purchasing land on which
they constructed the world's first publicly funded park.
Birkenhead Park was designed by Joseph Paxton and took three
years to complete. It was opened on 5 April 1847 by Lord
Morpeth and an estimated 10,000 people attended the ceremony.
Central Park in New York is based on Birkenhead Park.

The Toosey family lived at Rosemount until after the Second
World War. Although middle class and well respected in the village, the family was not wealthy. Dotie was always busy as, by the
standards of the time, she had little help. Charlie Toosey ran his
own cotton-broking business in Liverpool and he gradually made
a little more money so that the family could afford more help. By
the First World War there was a nurse for the younger children,
a cook, and a nanny for the older children. The nanny was known
as 'Oo Ow Ethley' because she was 'very efficient with the bristly
side of the brush', Phil recalled. The children adored her and she
stayed with the family for years.

Dotie was the dominant character of the Toosey family. Phil
Toosey once said she was really the great love of his life. Her own

mother was Irish and her father, Captain Percy, a good-looking man with a long forked beard that made a great impression on his grandchildren, had been the Governor of Dublin Gaol. He died young as a result of a bullet he got in the hip during the Afghan War but Phil remembered the impressive, bearded character who told exciting stories of his war experiences. Charlie Toosey was introduced to Dotie when she was just eighteen and Charlie thirty-two. 'She was an astonishing character,' Phil said later, 'she had everything against her, seven children, little money, a large house to run and yet she was always gay and always thinking of how she could do the best for us. She had something about her we all loved, she was an absolute darling.'[1]

Despite being petite she was strong both physically and emotionally. She had sparkling eyes and a captivating smile but she could be firm and stand her ground against her unruly brood. Dotie was forward looking in comparison to other women of the time and did not like the Victorian values of her mother-in-law. She embraced her children with warmth and affection and hugged them and loved them rather than scolding them and leaving them to the care of others. She taught the children about gardening, about furniture and about music. She was artistic and spontaneous and visitors to Rosemount recalled a house full of activity and laughter: 'Your mother and mine were the greatest of friends . . .' Phyllis Rimmos wrote to Phil in 1974. 'We used to see a lot of her and loved it, as we all seemed to be laughing most of the time.'[2] But Dotie also taught the children the importance of looking after others who were vulnerable. Initially this lesson was learned in the home as there were the younger children to care for but soon it was reinforced through the teachings at Sunday school.

Charlie Toosey was a different character from his wife. He wrote poetry and was contemplative but he also had a sense of

fun which came out in some of his less serious poems. One verse
of a poem he wrote for Dotie at Christmas 1912 reads:

> The kids have eaten all the food
> And still are in a hungry mood
> Excepting Phil, who's stretched out flat
> And covered with the nursery mat.

Charlie Toosey had been brought up in Birkenhead and had
followed his father and grandfather both in business and in religion. They worked as shipbrokers for a firm they called Ross
Schofield in Liverpool, a firm founded by Charlie's father in the
1840s. 'In those early days', Phil Toosey explained, 'they used
to get in their very small boats and row out into the Mersey
to try to catch the big sailing ships coming in before the other
brokers got to him.' The Tooseys could have made a decent
living, he believed, but for the fact that they devoted their
energies to their church rather than to business. As a boy Phil
got on well with his father. 'We used to go on holidays together,
alone, the two of us. He was a great walker and I loved walking.
We used to go to North Wales and walk about in those beautiful valleys, Llanrwst and so on. We lived in very simple digs and
that I enjoyed tremendously. But I found it very hard to get
alongside him as I got older, very hard.' The reason for this was
Charlie Toosey's entrenched views. He was neither broad-
minded nor inquisitive and this was not satisfying for a young
man who wanted to question and debate.

The overwhelming reason for Charlie's intransigence was his
religious faith. He was wholly devoted to a sect known originally
as the Catholic Apostolic Church, a religious community origi-
nating in England in the 1830s and extending later to Germany
and the United States. The liturgy was elaborate and much of the

symbolism and mystery was borrowed from the Roman Catholic Church, including devotion to the Virgin Mary.

This was not an appealing religion to young children, Phil Toosey admitted later, but the main problem for him was that he and the others were forced to attend this church three out of every four Sundays. Dotie was a Protestant and took the children every fourth Sunday to St Saviour's church in Oxton. She was as active in her church as Charlie Toosey was in his, becoming the head of the Mother's Union at St Saviour's. The church was run by a young parson, Canon Sayers, for whom Phil had the highest regard. He attended Sunday School there and found it interesting. The Catholic Apostolic Church, by comparison, was a harsh religion: 'It was run by ordinary men. For instance, the Archdeacon, during the week, was a stockbroker. The others were much the same type. Nevertheless they dressed themselves up in the most extraordinary bright robes and it was in a way very high church. It had a peculiar habit that it allowed members of the congregation to get what they called inspiration. You'd get somebody in the congregation suddenly bursting forth giving a long speech, it was usually so dull that one didn't understand it and gradually, slowly but surely, I got to dislike intensely the Catholic Apostolic Church, I mean really dislike it.'[3]

It was not only the pontificating participants that worried him. He sensed that the sect caused ill-feeling between his parents and that he instinctively disliked and mistrusted. One thing that exacerbated this was that the eldest children, Patsey, Phil and Arthur, were caught in the middle. Dotie never attended the Catholic Apostolic Church and Charlie never darkened the doors of St Saviour's. It was a strange arrangement and from a very early age it troubled Phil and he sensed it was the cause of a rift in an otherwise very happy family. It made him wary of organised religion for the rest of his life.

All the same he was influenced by his early experiences and throughout his life he came up against the question of how people dealt with their faith. His own belief was simple, he told Professor Peter Davies of Liverpool University, who interviewed him at length in 1974: 'I believe there is no life after one is physically dead. I don't believe in the physical resurrection because there wouldn't be room for us all to start with. But there is a sort of ghostly life left behind in this world which can still over years and generations continue to have an influence for good or for bad.'[4] As an adult he did not attend church, except on ceremonial occasions such as marriages, deaths and Remembrance Day services, but priests' sermons often angered him and he found himself wanting to stand up and tell them that he had seen what life was really like in the war: 'What inspired me both during the battle and in those camps was that I believe Christ set a standard to which I tried to live up.' He said later, 'The result, curiously enough, of that standard is that a matter of life and death becomes very much less important. You see I really didn't worry about whether I went on living or not, all I wanted to do was to be able, at the end of it all, dead or alive, either within myself or in people's memory of me to say "well done".'[5]

Apart from the question of church on Sundays, life at Rosemount was typical of the era. The children were taught at home by a governess before going to school at the age of nine. The dining room became the school room in the mornings and Patsey, Phil and Arthur were taught by a spinster called Miss Williams. 'She was very severe,' he recalled, 'but she was splendid and a very good teacher of the three Rs.' At nine Phil went to Birkenhead School where he was under the eagle eye of Miss Cox. He described her as 'an absolute terror'. 'We were all terrified of her but actually she was a great character, a great disciplinarian and a teacher of the simple things.' Miss Cox reinforced Dotie's message of developing a caring attitude and she added to that lessons about duty and service. This impressed itself on the young Phil Toosey.

Charlie Toosey bought a car but it was a while before he got the hang of driving it. 'It was one of those air-cooled Rovers,' his son recalled, 'a twin cylinder job with a kick like a mule when you started it. You could only start it by hand but I can assure you it practically threw you over the bonnet if you didn't get it right. My father was not a very cunning driver and he didn't really know quite how to stop it. I remember on one occasion he went past the front gate about four times before he realised how he could stop it. I stood at the gate shouting at him, "Turn the engine off!"'[6] Phil Toosey was never interested in cars, except as a means of transport. In fact his lack of ability in practical matters was a running joke in the family. He could not even change a light bulb and he could hardly read a map.

He learned that if he couldn't do something himself he would have to find somebody who could. Initially this was his mother and his older sister, Patsey, but later he learned to find others who could help him. It was not one-sided; he would be supportive and enthusiastic and do his best to be helpful in return. This turned into one of the traits that helped him more than any other in his life. Nothing was ever too much trouble for Phil Toosey and people knew it and respected him for it.

He spent just one year in the Senior School at Birkenhead, under Mr Griffin, before sitting Common Entrance. Dotie was determined that her children should all have the very best education they could possibly afford. Charlie had been educated in Birkenhead but he did not stand in his wife's way. When it came to choosing a school Charlie took the advice of his partner, who had a nephew at Gresham's School in Norfolk.

Gresham's was on the coast at Holt, a quiet market town with a Victorian seafront. One of Phil Toosey's strongest memories of school was the food they were given during the First World War. 'The bread had weevils in it and our major dish was ground rice with a tiny little bit of jam on the top. Ever since then I've loathed the sight of ground rice, I must say.' This was unfortunate given that during his captivity he was to eat 3500 meals of rice.

All the boys were known by their surnames and he became known from then on as Toosey. The boys had to have a cold shower every morning throughout the year and he complained that in winter there was often ice on the walls of the shower block. They were allowed one hot bath a week but the daily shower is what stuck in his mind. Corporal punishment was the norm and often carried out by the older boys. Toosey got a caning for pinching a boat and stealing the changing-room blind to use as a sail. Unfortunately the boat sank when they got too close to the weir on Letheringsett Lake and he and three others had to walk home without the boat and blind, although that was later recovered. He was quite sanguine about this: 'I don't think it did me any harm at all, in fact, I learned to be disciplined. If you were late you really caught it and we were also taught that if the food didn't suit you and you didn't eat it, you just went without.'

Toosey entered Gresham's in the autumn of 1916. His memories of the First World War were vague. France was a world away from Norfolk but he did recall the great sadness he felt at the growing casualty list as it was added to each Sunday in chapel. All the boys had to join the Officer Training Corps and there were visits from old boys who would come up to the school, dressed in their uniforms, and this gave the boys added incentive to take the OTC seriously. He remembered one old boy, who had joined the Royal Flying Corps, arriving at school in his Sopwith Camel, which he landed on the cricket field.

Toosey found the schoolwork hard. 'I happened not to have

a particularly bright brain and I was terribly bad at exams,' he said later. He tried hard and eventually got respectable marks in his Higher Certificate. Dotie wanted him to play the piano and so arranged for piano lessons at the school. Music at Gresham's was taught by a man called Walter Greatorex. He was an inspirational teacher and was affectionately remembered by many of the old boys from Gresham's, including Stephen Spender who had an otherwise unhappy time at the school. He taught music from 1911 until his death in 1949 and wrote a number of hymns in the hymn book including, in 1916, the school hymn, 'Lift Up Your Hearts!' Toosey showed no aptitude for the piano although he struggled on with it for two years, but Walter Greatorex was not going to be beaten, so he said to him: 'Toosey, it's no good, you'll never learn to play the piano. You've paid for this term so I will play you some beautiful music for the rest of your lessons so that you will know how to appreciate music in the future.'[7] This he did and it gave him a love of music that lasted all his life.

Toosey had a good voice and sang in the school choir, first as a treble and then graduating to tenor in his teens. School choir practices were a community singsong and later he encouraged this sort of singing in the prison camps as he knew it was a great morale booster. In fact, so much so, the Japanese banned certain tunes, such as 'God Save the King' and 'I Vow to Thee My Country' because they cheered the prisoners and raised their morale.

The headmaster at Gresham's was a man called J.R. Eccles, whose second cousin Toosey later married. J.R. Eccles knew that Toosey was not strong academically but he had a high opinion of him as a young man with potential. He very much wanted him to go to university but it was clear that he would not get in on his academic record. However, the school could propose sports scholarships for Cambridge and Eccles offered him one in his last

Phil Toosey in 1921 aged seventeen.

term at Gresham's. To Toosey's utter dismay, his father refused
to let him take up his place because he had arranged for him to
start an apprenticeship in a cotton firm in Liverpool. 'That really
was a great tragedy,' he said later, 'because I know I should have
enjoyed Cambridge very much. It would have broadened my
horizon. As it was I was really slightly parochial by the time I'd
finished at school.'[8]

Years later Graeme McFarlane wrote to Toosey about his time
at the school: 'Though, of course, you were two years senior to me
at Gresham's, I had the good luck to be in "Woodlands" with you
for two years, and your friendliness and example of courage and
cheerfulness, as well as earnestness in the things that mattered,
were a splendid help when I was at school and the happiest of
memories ever since. For these I have always been most grateful.'[9]

Toosey left Gresham's in 1922 with a record as a caring, active member of the school. He moved back into his old room at home. Rosemount was as busy as ever and the family now consisted of three girls and three boys. The last child, Elizabeth, was not born until 1924.

He joined a firm of cotton merchants in Liverpool called Newall & Clayton, one of the partners being his uncle, Philip Brewster Toosey. Having only one daughter, Philip Brewster saw his nephew as his natural successor and Charlie Toosey must have felt that his son had landed a very secure and sensible post. The nature of the business was to buy and sell cotton from growers all over the world.

Toosey hated the cotton business from the word go. He began a four-year apprenticeship in the summer of 1922 and was paid £150 for the whole period. He had to learn all angles of the trade, starting work in the office then moving on to sampling and selecting cotton. Selling the cotton came next and that is what he disliked most: 'I used to walk around the market with a parcel of cotton under my arm trying to sell it to unwilling spinners.' Later he was taught how to meet the cotton buyers and how to deal with the cotton spinners. By the end of the four years the partners in the company would have to decide which area Toosey was most suited to. In many ways he received a very broad education in a short period of time and he made many useful contacts in Liverpool. Like it or not, he had to admit it stood him in very good stead for the future.

There were two other apprentices at Newall & Clayton at the same time as Toosey: Derek Clayton, whose father was a partner, and Phil Glazebrook, whose cousin Fred he had been at school with. The three of them became good friends and they all played rugby at the Birkenhead Park rugby football club in their spare time. Toosey grew nearly five inches in the first year after school.

Now six feet and half an inch tall and weighing eleven stone ten pounds he was impressively fit and selected to play in the back row of the scrum for the club. He was devoted to the club and his enthusiasm was infectious. One friend, Bill Dennison, remembered him running down the touchline at Ampleforth in front of a row of belted monks and urging the Park Second Fifteen scrum with a battle-cry of 'For the love of Christ, chaps!' 'Ever since then', Bill Dennison wrote to Toosey, 'you have been a leader and an inspiration to all who have known and followed you.'[10]

Toosey's social life revolved around Birkenhead Park rugby football club. Founded in 1871, the pre-war club had an impressive fixture list that included a Boxing Day game against Leicester. A lot of beer drinking went on after matches and this led to some wild sessions involving the two older Toosey brothers, Phil and Arthur. They were known as the 'dreaded duo' and it was generally agreed that Arthur was wilder than his older brother. Arthur Toosey was very good looking and was described by one old lady as a 'bon viveur and a leading light in the revelry at Birkenhead Park'.

On one occasion the Park had beaten Blackheath at home, which was a feat as the London team had had an outstanding record of wins. After the match there was a terrific celebration. 'I'm ashamed to say I got very full of beer and very full of myself as well,'[11] Phil Toosey recalled. He just managed to catch the last ferry back to Birkenhead and was feeling very cheerful. He spotted a lifebelt and thought it would be great fun to try and hoopla somebody. This he did but, unfortunately, the lifebelt hit a local professional boxer called Ike Clark, who responded with a torrent of verbal abuse followed by a swift left hook that left him sprawled on the deck. 'Well, being a young and rather bellicose man, I got to my feet again and wandered round the ship and asked who had done that to me. Up came the same fellow again and laid me out stone cold.'[12] By this time the ferry was almost at Birkenhead docks. Toosey was last off the boat: 'As I staggered down the gangplank I was met by the men in blue at the turnstile. They arrested me and took me to the police station in Birkenhead where I spent the night in a cell. It was something of an embarrassment all round as my uncle, Philip Brewster Toosey, was not only the partner in the firm of Newall & Clayton, but he was also a town councillor.' However, the police were aware that Ike Clark was a bit of a nuisance so they let Toosey off with a warning and said he would be hearing from them in due course.

A few weeks later a letter arrived from the police which began: 'Dear Sir, re disorderly conduct on S.S. *Bidston*: if you will pay three guineas to the Widows' Sick and Benevolent Fund nothing more will be heard of this matter.'

Years later one of Toosey's oldest friends, Hubert Servaes, heard him criticising a young man for being full of himself and up to mischief. Servaes roared with laughter and reminded Toosey that in his youth he had been equally wild, recalling an occasion when he had clambered on to the roof of a moving tram and changed the sign from Shrewsbury Road to Tranmere. He was not caught on that occasion but his irrepressible enthusiasm was fuelled more by beer than malice. These episodes still made him laugh fifty years later.

His closest friends in Birkenhead at the time were John Bromfield, Hubert Servaes and Douglas Crawford, the latter two both rugby players and both businessmen in Liverpool. John Bromfield lost a leg in a motorbike accident in 1923 but he was very active playing cricket and shooting with Toosey both before and after the war. Hubert Servaes worked for the Liverpool stockbroker Tilneys, and Douglas Crawford, who came from the family that ran Crawford's Biscuits, went into the family firm. Both Servaes and Crawford were university educated and

Servaes, who had a great love of music, used to take Toosey to the Philharmonic in Liverpool and teach him about the classical composers. Another good friend at the time was Selwyn Lloyd, who, as a distinguished politician, played a key role in Toosey's life in the 1950s.

Liverpool's wealth had been built on shipping. By the twentieth century the culture of the city was one of philanthropy and public-spirited generosity. The first voluntary organisation Toosey joined was the Personal Service Society and he remained involved with it, in one way or another, including a long spell as honorary treasurer, until the end of his life. The Personal Service Society, or PSS, was established in 1919 to tackle problems in Liverpool caused by the slump after the First World War. The founders were all businessmen and they focused on the causes of the problems as well as the ways they affected the lives of people in the city. There was very little state support for the poor in Liverpool and the PSS fulfilled a vital role. Toosey was interested in the work of the society and became personally and actively involved. He learned from visiting people who were receiving assistance or advice. He took a great personal interest in them and followed through several cases over a period of years. Initially he could do little but observe and give his time but later he contributed expertise and contacts. He said that working for the PSS gave him an insight into how people lived under seemingly impossible circumstances. Whenever he travelled abroad he used his experience of the slums of Liverpool as a benchmark against which to measure what he saw.

The first few years of Toosey's apprenticeship were straightforward. He learned quickly and impressed the partners and other employees in the company with his grasp of the cotton market and by his ability to get on with people. One of these was a man called Rutherford who was the office manager. He always had a soft spot for Toosey and used to visit him in the late 1960s. He told him on one such occasion: 'I always thought you probably would do fairly well in life because I lent you half-a-crown when you were an apprentice, as I did to the others, and I may tell you that you were the only one who ever paid me back.'[13] Honesty and integrity were at the core of Phil Toosey's character. In general he was easygoing but if his honesty was questioned he would not take it lying down. On one occasion in 1927 one of the partners of Newall & Clayton accused him of not telling the truth. Toosey was furious and defended himself so loudly he brought business at the Cotton Exchange to a halt. The row was soon over but the echoes of it rang around the Cotton Exchange for a long time.

Newall & Clayton began to get into difficulties in the mid-1920s and there were two causes. The first was the general decline in the cotton mills in Lancashire, which had disastrous consequences for several cotton merchants in Liverpool, but the second had to do with their business activities in South America. Some time before 1920 the company had opened an office in Lima in order to be closer to the source of South American cotton. They were not the only company to do this but they were one of the smaller ones. By 1928 it became clear to the partners of Newall & Clayton that something was not right in Peru and they needed to send somebody out to investigate. Toosey was sent for. He was interviewed by the partners and asked if he would be prepared to travel to Peru to see if he could ascertain what was going on in the Lima office. He was somewhat daunted as he felt his business experience was 'very thin indeed' but the prospect of travel excited him. It would broaden his horizon and he would see a whole new world. In his mind he planned to settle in South America. He told the partners he would be happy to go and he sailed from Liverpool on the PSNC *Oroya* passenger liner in the summer of 1928 with a real sense of adventure.

Doc. 727

Toosey en route to South America.

When he arrived in Peru he was met by the manager of the Lima office, a Scot called Tulloch. He and his wife, Toosey discovered quickly, were serious alcoholics. They lived the high life in Lima with their two young children and paid little attention to what was happening in the office. Tulloch took him out to his house in the suburbs of Lima and, as Toosey recalled: 'There we sat for three days while he filled not only himself but tried to fill me with various sorts of gin.' In the end Toosey said to him that he had not come out to Peru to sit around drinking gin but that he wished to go and see the office. It was then that he realised Tulloch was not at all keen for him to do so. The outfit itself was run by a Peruvian who had no business experience and Tulloch did not want Toosey nosing about in the books. He immediately became suspicious. The Newall & Clayton agent responsible for Peru was a man called Stevenson. He was on leave in the UK

44

when Toosey arrived so there was nothing to be done but to try to find out for himself.

'To be quite honest I couldn't see anything wrong – I merely got fixed in my mind that there was something funny going on. I had not a clue how to set about it.' However, luck was on his side. There were half a dozen Liverpool cotton firms with offices in Lima, including the big firm of Alexander Eccles & Company, and as a result there was a thriving ex-pat community. Toosey was invited to the English Club and there he bumped into an accountant called Len White, who ran a small independent office. 'This man, I shall never forget him for the rest of my life,' he said, 'did me the best turn he possibly could have done. He said to me, "Look here, Phil, there's something very wrong in Newall & Clayton's set-up here. I don't know what it is and I'm quite certain that you yourself will not be able to find out because you haven't got the experience. I will help you."' The two of them agreed that White would charge Newall & Clayton the minimum fee and for that he would go through the books of the Lima office and try to establish what exactly had been going on.

He was true to his word and shortly afterwards was able to report to Toosey the disturbing news that by use of faked invoices Tulloch had got away with about £15,000 (over £550,000 in 2004). It was clear that he would have to go, so Toosey cabled Newall & Clayton in Liverpool and gave them a brief outline of the situation. He then had the job of telling Mr Tulloch that not only was he no longer wanted in the Newall & Clayton office but that he had to return to the UK with his family. Toosey booked him a passage on the SS *Orbita* and on the day of sailing escorted Tulloch and his wife and children onboard the ship. 'Tulloch', he recalled, 'was very tight, and his wife and I carried both his children on board and home he went.'[14]

The Liverpool partners then decided that Stevenson should be sent out to take over the Lima office and that Toosey should work under him. He was livid: 'This man had lived through all this scandalous behaviour and hadn't seen anything, so I'm afraid – I had a fairly acid temper in those days – I cabled home at once and said I flatly refuse to work under Stevenson. I either take charge or I come home at once.'[15] Whether they were impressed by this outburst or not the partners in Liverpool agreed to Toosey's request. Stevenson was sent straight back to Liverpool, having arrived in Peru only a few days earlier. Toosey took over the running of the office for the next ten months.

He adored Peru. He was enchanted by the beautiful countryside with its dramatic views of the great peaks of the Andes, snow-covered and towering above the plains. Lima was a buzzing city with an active ex-pat community. Peru had been colonised by the Spanish and the historic centre of Lima was famous for its colonial buildings and relaxed Spanish atmosphere. This suited Toosey and he could imagine spending the rest of his life there. He made many friends including a young man who worked for ICI called W.L.C. 'Dum' Tweedy, also known affectionately by Toosey as 'the peasant'. Dum Tweedy was far from that. He was a highly cultured man with a profound knowledge, understanding and love of South America. They became lifelong friends. He guided Toosey around and showed him the interior of the country as well as the sights of Lima. The expansion of the city during the 1920s and 1930s meant that the interior had opened up and trips inland on the new roads offered exciting opportunities to visit areas that had been barely accessible to the casual European visitor. They made trips out to cotton and coffee plantations. Toosey visited a snake farm and took photographs of the snake 'houses', strange earth mounds that looked more like beehives. On Empire Day, Toosey ran in the mile race and won it. Dum

Tweedy held his jacket and tie for him. He was presented with a large silver cup by Minister H.B. Bentinck.

Toosey's happy life in Peru was interrupted one morning in the summer of 1929. He received a cable with the news that the Lima office was to be closed down and he was to return at once to Liverpool. Unbeknown to Toosey, Newall & Clayton were in financial difficulties in Liverpool and there was not even enough money to pay for his passage home. The bank would not provide the fare so he was forced to sell the office furniture in order to pay for his ticket. He returned to Liverpool on board the SS *Orbita*. The same ship would bring him back from Rangoon nearly seventeen years later.

One day, soon after his return to Birkenhead, he heard from his brother Arthur that Alan Tod had asked to see him. At that time Alan Tod was the Liverpool agent for Barings Bank but he was also commanding officer of the 59th (4th West Lancs) Medium Regiment of the Territorial Army. Arthur was in the regiment but Phil Toosey, who had first joined the TA in November 1927 as second lieutenant, had resigned his commission when he went out to Lima. On hearing that he was back and unemployed, Alan Tod asked to see him.

Toosey went along to the meeting with Alan Tod with some trepidation. ACT, as he was known, was born in 1887 and was thus almost a generation older than him. A larger than life character, he was independently wealthy and a respected pillar of the community. He had the authority of a man who had fought in the First World War and had emerged with a good record. He was highly intelligent but had a brusque manner that made him feared as well as respected. Toosey recalled the interview clearly: 'I went to see him and he made a remark which I have never forgotten because I think it was only under those circumstances would I so willingly have joined him. He said: "I'm sorry to hear the position you are in Phil, how would you like to come and work *with* me?" Now, it was the fact that he said "with me" that really made me say right away that there is nothing I should like better.'[16] Toosey joined Barings on 20 October 1929, a week before the Wall Street crash.

Barings' Liverpool branch was based in 64–70 Cotton Exchange Buildings because their business at that time was principally the financing of cotton, grain and other commodities by means of bills of exchange.

ACT insisted that Toosey needed a grounding in every aspect of the banking business so that he would be of use to Barings. When Toosey asked him what he could expect to get paid, he got a predictably tight-lipped response: 'You will be extremely lucky if you get into a firm of this quality, if you take my advice, when you go up to the main London office, take whatever they offer.' He was offered £250 per annum, a cut in salary of £450. Toosey spent the first six months learning everything he could in the Liverpool branch and then he was sent down to the main offices in London for a year to learn about merchant banking.

There were those who thought that ACT was merely being kind to give Phil Toosey the job of Assistant Agent at Barings. However, ACT was thinking shrewdly about business. Raw cotton was an ideal commodity for financing by bankers because at all stages the bank controlled the cotton: from the purchase, via shipping documents, warehouse receipts etc. and cash on delivery. Risk was covered by the rate of exchange and cotton futures. The cotton people kept very much to themselves: after all they had been dealing in cotton on the floor most of their working lives and ACT knew he could make a good business if he could find an entrée. Being a very proud man, as his nephew Ian Tod explained, he would not be prepared to knock on doors looking for customers. This is where Toosey came in. He was the ideal partner. Toosey was everything that ACT was not. ACT had a brilliant business mind but he was an introvert and felt ill at ease seeking out new contacts. Toosey was an extrovert but he never claimed to be a great intellect. He delighted in meeting new people and making connections. The combination of his personality and contacts plus ACT's intellectual abilities married very well together. Toosey knew all the people in the cotton business and was well liked. They were delighted to see him back in Liverpool and he was successful in persuading many of them to move their business to Barings over the course of the next ten years. At all events, as Ian Tod recalled, whereas Lloyds Bank had previously financed 80 per cent of cotton, half of that amount had been transferred to Barings by the beginning of the Second World War.

ACT was strict with Toosey. He insisted on the rule that business was never to be discussed except in the office. Occasionally Toosey would bounce back from lunch full of ideas for this or that and ACT would call him into his office, ask him what had gone on and then put him straight. 'I've always said that Barings was the luckiest thing that ever happened to me in my life,' Toosey said. 'It literally made me. There is no question about it at all. Alan Tod was one of those extraordinary people who had the courage to let a young man have his head and he said to me, when I made a terrible mistake, "well, don't do that again or you will be sacked" but the point was, he always let me have another go.'[17]

It was the kind of education that he needed and it brought to him the secure knowledge that if he did not know the answer to a question, he knew a man who did. In the unusual circumstance that ACT did not know the answer, there was a long line of experts at Barings in London who could be approached for advice. Armed with this confidence, Toosey could concentrate on what he did best, which was dealing with individuals, while all the time learning the finer points of banking as he went along. To the end of his life, however, he could not read a balance sheet. But he knew a man who could.

Toosey moved to London in 1930. He rented a little basement flat near Marylebone Road and lived there for most of the year. It was cheap and convenient but he hated London and was lonely. The bank kept him busy and members of the Baring family were very kind to him. John Baring became a close friend and his father, Lord Ashburton, gave him his first directorship after the war.

When Toosey returned from London Alan Tod encouraged him to get a flat of his own rather than moving back in with his parents in Rosemount. In 1931 he met Muriel Alexandra Eccles, known to everyone as Alex. Toosey had had girlfriends before but this time he fell in love. He proposed to Alex at a dance in late 1931. He could not bring himself to propose to her in person so he wrote on the back of the dinner menu 'Will you marry me?' and Alex wrote 'Yes' and passed the menu back to him.

Alex was already twenty-nine when she met Toosey. Like his mother, Dotie, she was petite and very attractive. She was an excellent sportswoman and had played lacrosse and tennis for Lancashire. She was the daughter of Henry Eccles of the great cotton firm Alexander Eccles, and had had a very happy and active childhood. She had, however, a streak of stubbornness and prejudice that Toosey put down to her antecedents and in later life she gained a reputation for being difficult and speaking her mind.

They were married in Christ Church, Linnet Lane on 27 July 1932, and the reception was held at the Adelphi Hotel. This upset Toosey and Alex as they would have preferred to have the reception at home. He felt it was typical of his mother-in-law Muriel's Victorian approach to life that she could not accept that people would rather be entertained personally and in a warm manner rather than grandly and in a cold one. He would comment on this even forty years later.

Alex's father had at one time been very wealthy but he made a series of poor business decisions in the late 1920s and lost a personal fortune believed to have been in the region of £3 million. By any measure it was a colossal amount of money but he had settled a trust on behalf of each of the children that was immune from his business failures. Alex therefore had a private income that stood at £400 per annum. It was some time before Toosey's income matched hers.

When Toosey and Alex were first married they rented a flat in a house at 2 Aigburth Drive in Sefton Park, in Liverpool. It was a top-floor flat and he felt like a caged animal. He was a countryman and being cooped up in a flat did not suit him. They lived there until after their first son, Patrick, was born in October 1933, when they moved to Benty Heath Cottage in Willaston and then, in 1937, to a house called Heathcote, just outside the village of Hooton. Toosey asked Alex's uncle, who was an architect, to give his opinion and the recommendation was that it was a good buy at £2000. There was a good train service to Liverpool and, as they found out only after they had moved in, a noisy shunting yard that 'was an extremely busy place and the crashes and bangs that went on at night were shocking, absolutely unbelievable'. Next to the station was a waterworks 'that used to belch forth the blackest, filthiest smoke every six or seven minutes, which covered our garden with smuts'. Perhaps it is not surprising that the man who sold Toosey the house, Arthur Ratcliffe, was relieved to be rid of it.

Heathcote was built in 1910 in the style of an Edwardian villa. The house was set in the middle of a long thin garden that ran from the road to some fields at the back. Later Toosey acquired more land and this meant that the garden at the back could be extended and it was greatly improved. He was overjoyed to have a garden of his own and he spent most of his spare time tending it. He always pruned his roses on the Sunday after the Grand National and Gillian recalled him mowing and rolling the grass tennis court at the front with great care, only to be thwarted by a sudden downpour. Heathcote was to be the Toosey home for the next forty years.

At the end of 1934 Toosey was asked by Barings to make a trip to South America with a view to drumming up business and making an assessment of the state of the cotton market. He was pleased to be returning to South America but he was anxious at leaving Alex who was five months' pregnant and caring for one-year-old Patrick. He planned to be back by March 1935.

He arrived in Rio de Janeiro on 14 January 1935 and began a whirlwind tour of banks, cotton haciendas, coffee plantations, punctuated by visits to the British Embassy and various Brazilian ministries. Arthur Villiers of Barings' London office had asked Toosey to keep him informed of anything he observed in Brazil although the main purpose of the visit was to talk to the Brazilian banks about financing the growing of cotton. He kept a diary and wrote at least two letters a week to Villiers and ACT giving detailed accounts of everything he saw and impressions he formed. They replied with advice and comments but as the exchange of letters often took up to three weeks there were times when he had to guess what Barings would like him to do. In one letter he wrote to Villiers:

> During my stay in this country several points have struck me, particularly the fact that Englishmen, although they are liked individually, have not a good business reputation. There are many reasons for this. They keep too much to themselves, they do not learn the language, and the British shipping companies

have taken up somewhat uncompromising attitudes on the freight problems, and generally our business methods do not compare favourably with that of other nations, particularly with Germany, which nation is making every effort to get to know the people here they are dealing with and to assist them in every way. Many instances of this have been quoted to me, which I will discuss when I come home, but in my own judgement a number of these criticisms are true.[18]

In a postscript to the letter he adds: 'Please excuse some lapses in the typed letters. My secretary bursts into tears if she is corrected too frequently.' Toosey was an interested observer of human nature and had an appetite for political and economic information and gossip. He must have been exhausting to be with and the Brazilians got around this by giving him several guides.

At the end of January he made a week-long trip into the interior of Brazil. He wrote a letter to ACT giving his impressions. He travelled by rail and road in the company of Mr Moraes, who turned out to be a very energetic and interesting guide. They visited one cotton *fazenda*, or farm, where the cotton was being grown almost entirely by Japanese farmers. He commented: 'They are very efficient and capable when working for themselves but make very bad servants. I am told that the Japanese are cleverly pursuing the policy of peaceful penetration. The Japanese are wonderful farmers when they have their own land but as employees they are bad. They work night and day and live on nothing.'[19] This was Toosey's first very brief experience of the Japanese.

Letters from home brought his family to mind and he was often disquieted afterwards. He wrote most days to Alex and occasionally mentioned her in his correspondence with ACT. In one letter he said: 'Thank you for your messages about Alex. I have had a rather depressing letter from her which has rather disturbed me, but I am glad to hear from you that she is in good order.'[20] Alex would put on a brave face when Alan Tod rang her or dropped in to see her at Heathcote but in her letters to her husband she was more open about how she was not enjoying his long absence in South America.

Barings sent encouraging letters from both London and Liverpool, urging him to keep his ear to the ground and to watch carefully the business dealings of the Germans and the Americans. 'I am doing my best to acquire all the local gossip,' he assured Arthur Villiers, 'and report what I hear as well as the impressions I receive. Of course I am handicapped to some extent by not knowing the language.'[21]

One of the problems he encountered in Brazil, apart from the exchange rate difficulties, was the question of the cost of shipping. The impression he formed was that the British shippers, for some reason or another, were sticking to higher prices than those shippers delivering to the continent and in particular to Germany. He spoke to shippers and to brokers and realised that neither had bothered to listen to what the other side's concerns were. In typical Toosey fashion he decided that there was a simple way to put things right – and if things were right it would be better for Barings – and that was to get the two sides to sit down at the table together. He acted purely as an intermediary in this and once the differences had been aired he stepped back from the negotiations. He received warm praise in the next letter from Arthur Villiers.

Toosey liked the Brazilians. There were some he knew he could not trust and others he believed were as good as their word. It was this instinct for seeking out people who were trustworthy that ACT, and indeed others at Barings, found to be one of his most useful traits. ACT encouraged him in his opinions of people and urged him to get to know better those men his instinct told him were good. On 19 March 1935 he wrote to Alan Tod: 'In a new country things frequently occur which may seem to us difficult to understand but I am quite convinced that the people with whom I have been put in touch by Dr Numa [a South American cotton agent] are first class in every way. Dr Numa himself is very cautious about the introductions he gives me to people.'[22]

A natural listener, Toosey was adept at putting people at their ease and getting them to open up: in Brazil he gained a reputation as a man who could make things happen. People came to him for advice. There was Mr Colledge, an Englishman from Derby, who had come to Brazil to sell rolling stock to the São Paulo railway. When he arrived with his £500,000 consignment of railway wares he was told that the Germans had undercut him with a price that was 35 per cent below what he was asking. The man was in despair. He went to Toosey and learned how it was that the Germans, supported by their government, were able to offer such low prices. Negotiations were reopened with the São Paulo railway company and after several weeks of discussions Mr Colledge successfully clinched the deal and returned home in triumph.

Towards the end of his stay Toosey was invited as guest of honour at the Portuguese Club where he met Mr Perreira Ignacio Snr, the head of Votorantim, a company with which Barings was anxious to do business. Toosey wrote of his visit enthusiastically, 'I feel that I leave this country having established at any rate very friendly connections with our various clients, even if no business results.'[23] His experiences on this trip had been varied and one of the things that had most bothered him was the Germans. He wrote to ACT towards the end of March:

> You will by now have received a number of letters from me regarding the cotton situation and the German competition. It

is all very disturbing and unpleasant, and one wonders what is going to be the outcome of all these various difficulties. The German situation in Europe has caused a great stir in São Paulo, and everybody is talking very foolishly about war in the near future. I dined last night with Mr Morse and three other Germans, and they found it difficult to conceal their esteem at Herr Hitler's latest demonstrations of German strength. They still remain in many ways a very arrogant people and are not really popular here, although there are about 10,000 Germans in São Paulo alone.[24]

Toosey sailed back to England on 25 March 1935 and arrived in London on 11 April, just a fortnight before the birth of his daughter Gillian. He would not return to South America for over a decade and the events of the intervening years were to change his life completely.

3

SPIKE THE GUNS
AND SAVE THE PERSONNEL

When my grandchildren ask me what I did in the War I shall tell them that I ran like hell. Twice. The second time we ran out of land.

Phil Toosey 1974

Toosey's career as a Territorial Army soldier got off to a bad start not helped by the fact that, for reasons never made clear, his father, Charlie, was very much against his sons joining the TA. 'In those early days I disliked it intensely,' Toosey said, 'I didn't know what I was doing, I didn't understand it and I felt it was absolutely bogus to be an officer without any training.'[1] The selection process was straightforward enough, he explained. A recommendation was made: 'The commanding officer took a look at your face and if he liked the look of you, you were accepted and your commission came through, which is what happened to me. But to show you how bogus one could feel, the first time I went on parade in uniform the No 1, that is the sergeant in charge of one of my guns, walked up to me, tapped me in the ribs and said, "Excuse me sir, but your spurs are on upside down", which just shows the height of my military knowledge.'[2]

On his return from Peru in 1929 Toosey did not take up his commission and it was only once he began to work for Barings that ACT asked him whether he had rejoined the regiment. He replied in the negative and ACT turned to him and said sharply: 'Bloody well do it, and do it straight away. There is a drill parade tonight.' Barings encouraged their employees to undertake some aspect of public service. They then backed volunteers, allowing them time off to meet their commitments. For instance, Toosey had a full extra week's leave so that he could attend the two-week summer camp and still have a week in hand to spend with his family. Apart from annual camp, he had to attend at the drill hall two evenings each week for training and lectures under ACT where they were taught about all aspects of gunnery.

During the inter-war years the Territorial Army was a substantial and focused back-up to the regular army. It recruited civilians in full-time jobs and trained them towards deployment on active service should the need arise. Toosey's regiment, the 59th (4th West Lancs) Medium Brigade RA (TA), was a unit with a high reputation within the TA. 'There was no doubt', Sir John Smyth wrote in 1972, 'that the personal interest in the Brigade shown by its distinguished Honorary Colonel, Lieut.-Gen. Sir Hugh Jeudwine KCB, KBE, TD, was a source of inspiration to all. At a levee in March 1933 five officers of the Brigade were presented by the Hon. Colonel to the King.'[3] Three of the five were Hubert Servaes, Douglas Crawford and Phil Toosey. In due course, John Smyth continued, all five became brigadiers which must be unique in the annals of the TA.

The TA became an absorbing interest for Toosey from the

mid-1930s. Every summer the regiment would spend a fortnight at one of the major artillery camps. There was Redesdale in Northumberland, Trawsfynydd in North Wales and Salisbury Plain. They alternated each year to prevent them getting used to the targets. The equipment the 59th trained with in the 1930s was the same equipment that had been used during the First World War, but with one significant improvement – the iron tyres were replaced with rubber ones as experience had shown that travelling over the *pavé* roads in France had shaken and damaged the weaponry. Progressively, horse-drawn transport gave way to the internal combustion engine and this was phased in with dramatic and, at times, amusing results: 'Now that was a chaotic business for the very simple reason that they took two bites at the cherry,' Toosey recalled. 'They first of all mechanised the guns, they were pulled by Fordson tractors, and left the officers and some men, particularly the signallers, on horses. Well, when on parade the Ford tractors started off with a roar and every single horse bolted.'[4] The first tractors were more or less useless as they would rear up on their back wheels as they set off because of the weight of the guns, whereas a team of eight horses could pull a gun and move along at about 6 to 8 m.p.h. Then the army introduced the Scammell, a much more robust tractor which could pull anything anywhere.

The Ranging Cup, rewarding accuracy of aim, was presented at the annual camp. Toosey's 236th Battery won the cup more than any other and he was proud of that achievement. There was friendly rivalry between himself and Douglas Crawford for the summer cups. Archie Crawford, Douglas's brother, was a subaltern in Toosey's battery. He wrote:

You must first picture the intense competitive spirits of the best kind which existed between the four Batteries of the

59

pre-war 59th. The officers had in most cases known each other all their lives, and off-duty there was complete identity of outlook and interests. On duty, and especially at Practice Camps, the only aim was to bring one's own Battery to the highest pitch of excellence. This was not done in any selfish spirit but the Battery was the team in those days and this was the best way of ensuring that the 59th would be acknowledged as the most efficient gunner unit in the TA.

Phil would be the first to agree that he was not the most profound technical gunner, but he more than made up for this by his ability to evoke the maximum response from his team by his own infectious enthusiasm and dedication. And yet it was all such fun! We never started as favourites for the Ranging Cup, which of all the cups competed for was the one which mattered most, but Phil took us by the scruff of the neck and somehow produced performances from the Battery, of which we had never thought ourselves capable, to win it several years in succession.[5]

Pat Bingham, a member of Toosey's battery at the end of the 1930s, still remembers his obsession with accurate firing. Bingham did not like loud bangs and Toosey caught him with cotton wool in his ears which he made him remove immediately. There were no half measures with Major Toosey.

In 1935 Toosey's battery was selected to represent the regiment in the final of the King's Cup, a competition between four field batteries which was held at the end of September. There was intensive practice during the month before the event and a real sense of excitement as the great day approached. On the morning of Saturday 28 September the battery went into action. Toosey was crawling to his observation post when he was struck by an attack of lumbago. He was supposed to keep completely out of sight but he could no longer crawl: 'It was agony,' he said, 'so I had to say to the umpire "I'm awfully sorry but I can't crawl any longer. Will you imagine I'm crawling and let me walk?"' Fortunately the umpire did. Their accurate firing, and their concealment despite the lumbago attack, meant that the battery narrowly defeated the 71st Battery from the West Riding.

The congratulations poured in from all sides. The importance of the battery's achievement was underlined by the presentation in London on 26 October by the Adjutant to the Forces, General Sir Harry Knox, at the Guildhall, when everyone who had taken part was on parade. It was an unforgettable day for Toosey and his men.

But it was not the rivalry of gunnery and competitions which absorbed the TA officers and men for much longer. Overhead were the dark clouds of war. On 1 April 1939 the War Office ordered all TA units to double their numbers, forming additional regiments. At that time the 59th Regiment's strength was 25 officers and 458 other ranks. 'We have always been extremely proud', said Toosey later, 'of being the first artillery regiment in the country to double up completely.' This was achieved in five weeks and they formed the 68th Regiment. He was convinced this was due to the high reputation of the 59th.

In July 1939 a practice camp was held at Redesdale. In spite of almost incessant rain and mist continuous operations were carried out day and night. The King's Cup was cancelled for that year but there was a regimental cross-country race which Toosey won. Not bad for a thirty-five-year-old major. There was no doubt that war was imminent. The question was when.

On 31 August 1939 Toosey was dining at Heathcote with Alex and her brother, Ommy Eccles, when a telegram arrived summoning the two men to HQ. They got up from the table and left the house. That was the last Toosey saw of Heathcote, apart from a brief visit in 1940, for six and a half years.

The two men made their way to Grange botanic gardens in Liverpool, which was the headquarters of the regiment. There they gathered until they were ordered to move to Tarporley in Cheshire where the officers were put up in the Swan Hotel in the main street and the men occupied two large houses, Bow Mere and Gardenhurst, both of which had been requisitioned by the army.

Over the next few weeks their equipment began to arrive. As a Territorial Army unit they had only ever been equipped for camp so much of what they now received was new to them. They had to learn how to use the wireless sets as well as paint the equipment. All lads aged eighteen and below were sent back home and were replaced by regular army reservists. These changes concentrated the men's minds and they were fully occupied during their three weeks in Tarporley. Some of them were nervous about the war now that it was obvious they were going into action, Toosey remembered. 'One night a young gunner fired his rifle in the billets when all the men were in, then he ran for it. Luckily no one was hit. We sent a search party out to find him. He was scared of going overseas. I did not punish him but gave him a piece of my mind. He turned out to be a good soldier.'[6]

Although Tarporley was less than thirty miles from Hooton he did not go home to see Alex and the children. The men had no leave during their time in Tarporley so he took none himself. He kept in touch with Alex by telephone and she came over to see him at the Swan Inn once or twice.

Major Toosey and his men left for France in the last week of September 1939, just three weeks after mobilisation, to join the British Expeditionary Force. They were the first Territorial gunner regiment to leave the country. He described their departure: 'We were played to the local station by the band of the Second Line of the 68th Medium Regiment. In many ways it was a thrilling moment. We had no idea what lay in store for us.'[7]

What lay in store was the Phoney War. After the invasion of Poland in September 1939 many in Britain had expected a major calamity but for almost seven months there were no great battles and a period of anxious waiting ensued. The British Expeditionary Force, established after the Boer War in case Britain ever had the need quickly to deploy a force to take part in a war overseas, was sent to the Franco-Belgian border. It was considered a formidable fighting unit that would help France to defend its 200-mile-long frontier against the Germans. The Allied governments and high command spent much time over the next few months discussing offensive plans against Germany but, as Liddell Hart wrote in his history of the Second World War, the plans constituted, 'a wonderful collection of fantasies – the vain imaginings of Allied leaders living in a dream-world until the cold douche of Hitler's own offensive awoke them'.[8]

Having landed at Cherbourg Toosey's men were deployed to Lille and found billets in the two villages of Herrin and Chemy. There they learned the hard way how to fend for themselves. 'It was a pretty painful experience; before this we had always had permanent cook houses at camp and I well remember the many cooking problems and getting used to the atmosphere of living in the field.'[9]

The winter of 1939–40 was bitterly cold and the men living in the barns had a hard time. Toosey kept them busy digging huge pits for the guns and building command posts on what was an extension of the Maginot Line, France's main fortification stretching along its borders to the east.

Even at this stage Toosey was concerned that they were following the static defences which had been found wanting in the 1914–18 war. He felt certain this was not how modern warfare would develop but he was not allowed to mount any mobile exercises, something he later described as 'in retrospect unthinkable'. 'The winter was very hard indeed,' he wrote. 'The frost breaking up the *pavé* roads and heavy guns and vehicles would have completed the job and probably made them unusable. At any rate, this was the reason given. We had to light fires each night below the buffer system of the gun to prevent the oil from freezing.'[10]

Not only were the tactics dated but so was their equipment. True, they now had solid rubber tyres on their transport but they were armed with the same equipment as had been used in the First World War. This worried Toosey. So did a visit from their Corps Commander, General, later Field Marshal, Alan Brooke, Churchill's Chief of the Imperial General Staff. He talked to the officers and told them exactly how he thought the campaign would develop. 'It was very depressing in view of the sort of training we had so far been doing. How to counter these tactics no one appeared to know at that stage.'[11] Toosey was impressed by this analysis and he wrote later that he had been, of course, completely accurate in his assessment of how the Germans would attack. He went on to write: 'I am quite certain Brooke was the first British General to foresee the Blitzkrieg.'[12]

Spring followed winter and the feeling of unreality was in danger of sapping morale. Toosey's response was to step up all aspects of training and fitness in the knowledge that it was bound to come to a fight.

Two events happened on 10 May 1940 that changed the course of the war. Hitler's forces broke through the defences in the west and Winston Churchill became Prime Minister in place of Neville Chamberlain. The German invasion was devastatingly efficient. Using both the Luftwaffe and armoured forces they caused confusion and alarm in neutral Holland which surrendered after only five days.

Toosey's battery crossed into Belgium, at the request of the Belgian high command, and was warmly welcomed by the locals. Despite this he was troubled: 'On the other hand,' he wrote, 'we met the first trickle of refugees blocking the road and carrying all their possessions either on their backs, in perambulators or in wheelbarrows, and to see this for the first time is a very sad sight indeed.'[13] This was made worse by the sight of some Belgian soldiers bicycling at high speed in the wrong direction.

On top of that came the usual spate of fifth column scares. The atmosphere was not nearly as pleasant as they had first thought. One incident Toosey witnessed illustrates how jumpy everyone was: 'In the middle of the night we came out of the house and saw a blue light flashing about 500 yards away in front of the Belgian Headquarters. There was immediate panic by all the Belgians and they said, "There you are, there is somebody signalling telling the enemy exactly where we are." So at my suggestion, four or five of us, heavily armed, stalked this light to discover it was the reflection of a full and very bright moon on the top of a glass frame. Such was the state of mind.'[14]

Toosey's recollection of the next few days, leading up to the evacuation from Dunkirk, focuses more on the sights he saw around him than on the bigger picture of the battle. He and his battery arrived in their gun area at Berthem where they were going to deploy. 'This lovely little village was a sad sight. Empty houses with meals still on the tables, unfed animals and, in particular, unfed cows making an appalling noise. Fortunately one member of the Battery was a trained milkman and so the animals were relieved and we lived on good fresh milk.'[15]

They were bombed for the first time by a German Dornier flying at tree-top level. It was an awesome sight but they had no anti-aircraft guns so no means of responding. It was not until they arrived in Templeneuve some days later that the battery went into action. One of his men was hit and received a nasty wound in the back. It was the first time that the battery had come under fire and Toosey was reassured by how well they stood up to it. It was, after all, what they had been training for in the TA but people were unpredictable in real warfare. One of his junior officers was his old school friend Fred Glazebrook. Toosey remembered sending him off to look for stores to add to the rations: 'He was probably the oldest subaltern in the Royal Artillery and always imperturbable. He returned later covered in mud from head to foot with some useful stores. I asked him what had happened and he said he had been blown off his motor bicycle by a German shell. He did not seem to think this was anything unusual but he did confess to having a slight headache.'[16]

In Templeneuve Toosey was standing talking to a man called Doherty, an NCO, who had fought in the First World War and who in peacetime worked in the Liverpool sewers. As they were talking a shell landed close to them. Toosey immediately fell flat on his face and when he stood up, to his embarrassment, Doherty was still sitting on his motorcycle, quietly smoking a cigarette. 'He said I really must get used to this sort of thing; he had been in the 1914–18 War and knew exactly where those shells were going to land.'[17] The shell you don't hear, Doherty told him, is the one that is going to kill you. It was a useful lesson and later he earned a reputation for bravery during shellfire in Singapore.

The BEF was in full but orderly retreat to the English Channel and preparations were in hand for the most ambitious seaborne rescue operation in British naval and military history. From Templeneuve Toosey was ordered to withdraw to Flers. He had no doubt at this stage that they were heading for a humiliating withdrawal and he felt this keenly. 'From Flers we went to Neuve Eglise on 26th May; the roads an absolute nightmare of refugees, dead horses and abandoned French and Belgian equipment. We were dive bombed several times. I spent an uncomfortable quarter of an hour in a roadside ditch filled with stinging nettles. The Stukas with sirens attached to their wings were frightening, especially since we appeared to have no air force at all.'[18]

The atmosphere among the Territorials was one of dismay. But Majors Toosey and Crawford had agreed between themselves that whatever they did, they would keep their men together and operate as an efficient unit. At Flers they had come under the command of Major General H.R.L. Alexander, later Field Marshal, Lord Alexander of Tunis. He ordered the following: 'When you are behind the Canal, personnel only will be evacuated to England, therefore if, owing to road blocks, you are unable to get across the Canal before you are surrounded, spike your guns and save your personnel.' The Majors agreed that during the withdrawal Crawford would lead the regimental column and Toosey would 'whip in' at the back on a motorcycle. It was an excellent piece of teamwork as Crawford was a much better map reader than Toosey. They drove the men hard and succeeded in getting all but one of their guns across the Canal before the bridges were blown. Toosey was determined to rescue this last gun that had fallen into a ditch and he urged Ommy Eccles, who had been driving the gun, to go back and fetch it 'because I wished to finish with the total complement of guns in the battery. He did not seem to like the order so eventually I went back with him and we got the gun out safely.'[19]

At Givelde they were once again in action and here Toosey witnessed several casualties. They did not know where exactly the Germans were but the men had injuries from shells, splinters and rifle fire. It was frightening and he described the area with characteristic understatement as being 'a pretty hot spot'. His guns were in the middle of a field of abandoned French vehicles, which he thought was a good ploy as it would be difficult for the Germans to work out whether the guns were live or not. However, a little while later he reassessed the situation and felt less comfortable with it so moved the guns 300 to 400 yards from the 'car park'. This proved to be 'an outstanding success and demonstrated the value of an alternative position because whenever we fired from the new position they shelled our old one'.[20]

It was here that Toosey first saw the RAF in action and he witnessed 'some splendid dogfights'. He saw three German aircraft and one Spitfire being shot down. A parachutist from one of the German planes landed in a ditch close to his position so he and a few others 'made a dash to try and capture or help whoever it might be'. It turned out to be a good-looking young German pilot who told them they should surrender now as they would soon be captured. Toosey found him arrogant but also a sad case. He kept shaking his hand which was covered in blood. When he asked him what the trouble was the young man replied that in peacetime he was a professional pianist and that he would be unlikely ever to be able to play again as he had a gaping hole right through the middle of his right hand.

Meanwhile all units were moving west. On 31 May Toosey received an order to thin out. That afternoon with great sadness he and his men destroyed their old guns and the new Scammell vehicles that had so impressed him and had given such good service. That night they marched to Dunkirk. For the first part of the journey he travelled with Lieutenant Colonel Servaes but when the column of marching men halted he insisted on getting out. He wanted to walk 'with the men who had served me so splendidly throughout the withdrawal. They were all very tired and I thought it wrong that I should travel in a vehicle whilst they trudged along the road.'[21]

Exhausted, one or two of them lay down and fell asleep on the side of the road whenever the column came to a stop. Toosey had the greatest difficulty keeping them moving and a young bombardier, who had fired over 150 rounds and was completely worn out, kept falling asleep: 'I always had to wake him up and finally with considerable irritation I gave him a tremendous crack on his backside with the back of the spade. He turned round to me and he said: "Bugger you, sir", to which I replied, "Let us wait and see until we get home to see who does what to whom."'[22] The man later apologised but Toosey had nothing but praise for him: 'He was a splendid man and typical of the sort of Lancashire troops we had in those days.'

On arrival in Dunkirk they discovered that the French had occupied the area designated for them so they were told to march into the sea in the hope of being picked up by a boat and taken home. Practical as ever, Toosey put John Tilney at the head of his column as he was the tallest officer. He remained at the back and checked that all his men were in line. 'It was a most eerie sight at Dunkirk; this long column of men standing patiently in the sea waiting for someone to pick them up.'[23]

The boats came. All shapes and sizes, little boats, sailing boats, barges and tugs. Eight hundred in total. Men scrambled aboard and were borne away to the larger vessels waiting off-shore. The boats came back to pick up more men. Eventually, at about 2 a.m., the last of the men had been safely picked up and Tilney told Toosey that he should come too. He was hauled into an old Thames barge that was already three-quarters full of water and they chugged out to the minesweeper HMS *Lyd*. On the way over to the ship the Thames barge was taking on alarming amounts of water and had to be baled out. Toosey was in a state of

Men standing in the sea off Dunkirk waiting to be evacuated.

exhaustion so Tilney organised the baling, getting men to use their tin hats. 'I was so dazed', Toosey recalled, 'that I did not get on with the job until he gave me a great thump on the back and shouted at me "Bale, you bugger, bale!"'[24] So he did. They came alongside HMS *Lyd* and began to board. As the last man clambered up the ladder on the side of the minesweeper the barge gurgled and sank.

Once aboard ship the sailors took the soldiers' soaking wet uniforms. When Toosey's was returned it was without buttons. The sailors had kept them as souvenirs. But, as he said later, he would have given them a great deal more than that as they had saved his life. In all 330,000 men, including some 95,000 Allied troops, mostly French, were rescued from the beaches of Dunkirk. The British called it a miracle.

Landing at Margate on the morning of 2 June they were welcomed as heroes. Toosey felt like anything but a hero and was only too glad to board a train, destination unknown, to put behind him the humiliation and horror of the last three weeks. 'We were', he concluded, 'still enthusiastic amateurs.'[25] Amateur or not he took a strong stand on matters of discipline, as Archie Crawford observed:

One of the reasons why men willingly followed him has always seemed to me that he was human. He could be hard (as when on return to England he paraded three men, who had 'slipped away' on the beaches in the general chaos before the order had been given, in front of the whole Battery) but was always aware of human frailty, particularly among the rank and file if they hadn't received a lead from their officers (as when he gave the same three men a second chance to redeem themselves in the Battery – a chance they all accepted). He never spared himself and he felt passionately that those who had the privileges accorded to an officer must return this manifold in service to the men; and woe betide any junior officer who fell down on this.[26]

Later that day they arrived at Ashton-under-Lyne, just east of Manchester. Toosey phoned Alex to say that he was safe but he was concerned as to whether she had heard from her brother Ommy, who he had last seen in France a few days earlier: 'Yes, you idiot,' Alex replied, 'it's you that we have been worrying about. He has been here for 24 hours.'[27]

Although the unit was only an hour from Liverpool the men were not entitled to leave. Toosey thought that this was most unfair so he discussed the situation with his officers and they decided to give the men leave on their own initiative. He spoke to them before they left: 'I told them that I was taking a risk as we were not allowed to do so but I trusted in them and sure enough not one man failed to return on time.' Toosey did not go home. He phoned Alex and they arranged to meet in Manchester for dinner: 'This, I think, was one of the most vivid contrasts of the whole war – the night before standing up to my neck in the sea at Dunkirk with not a great hope of ever getting home and the next night having a very good dinner in the Midland Hotel, Manchester.'[28]

Hubert Servaes, who was with Toosey in France, wrote an assessment of his actions after the war: 'During the winter Phil commanded his battery really magnificently. It was only in the operations ending in Dunkirk, however, that I really realised how good he was. He is one of those fortunate people who thoroughly enjoy being shelled or bombed, the nearer the better, and I had considerable difficulty in preventing him taking on the German Army single-handed. Of course his inspiration and example to his men were tremendous, and he and his battery put up a really fine show.'[29]

The first phase of Phil Toosey's war was over. He personally did not feel that he had covered himself in glory.

He had very little time for leave in 1940–41 but he did manage to get to see Alex and the children once and that was the first time he saw his youngest son, Nicholas, who had been born in February 1940. Gillian remembered him picking the baby up and putting him on the mantelpiece in the hall at Heathcote to have a good look at him. Alex was horrified and shrieked at him.

The process of regrouping and developing a new role for the battery was a tedious business and after a number of moves they ended up, now properly equipped, in Sussex. Here there was a change. Hubert Servaes, who had been their commanding officer up to this point, was promoted to another corps and Douglas

Crawford took over as the commanding officer with Toosey as his second in command. It was during his time in Sussex that Toosey attended staff college and emerged with an excellent report.

By now he was judged ready for greater responsibility. He had impressed the senior officers to the extent that he was offered the command of a regiment in his division. It was very flattering. He might have taken the position except that Brigadier Servaes heard of this development: 'Shortly afterwards I went to the 18th Division as Commanding Royal Artillery (CRA) and found that one of the Regiments had got into a very bad state and needed a new commander. I applied quickly for Phil, and only just in time, as General Osborne had also applied for him, so I had another battle royal. By pulling every string I knew of, I managed to secure him (to the chagrin of Osborne!) and he came to us about two months before we started our ill-fated trip abroad.' Servaes offered Toosey command of the 135th (North Herts Yeomanry) Field Regiment, RA, which he accepted with enthusiasm.

Toosey described this East Anglian regiment as a very aristocratic set-up. He joined them at Macclesfield in Cheshire where they had been posted following a chaotic training exercise in Scotland. Among the officers were 'several members of the House of Peers and some very distinguished gentlemen as officers and very fine too. They sniffed round me like dogs looking for a fight.'[30] Initial impressions were not favourable on either side. 'I met my new adjutant at the station who was one of London's most successful stockbrokers called Malcolm Northcote and he (which worried me at the time) smelled heavily of scent.'[31]

Toosey took over from Lieutenant Colonel Hudson whose style of leadership was more laid-back than his. The first morning after his arrival Toosey had breakfast with the men. One young gunner, Tom Brown, recalled standing in the breakfast queue when he heard a commotion behind him. He turned round to see the new colonel talking to the regimental sergeant major. 'You don't need to queue here, sir,' RSM Coles said to him. 'That's all right, Sergeant Major,' Toosey replied, 'I just want to know what the men are having for breakfast.'[32] His presence was felt from the top of the regiment to the bottom and some did not like it. A small number of older officers left and Toosey had under his command a unit with which he had to prepare for posting overseas within weeks: 'There was magnificent material,' he said, 'but it was quite obvious that the standard of training was exceedingly low.'[33]

They went to the Royal Artillery practice camp in Trawsfynydd in North Wales where he put them through their paces. 'All that happened was that during the whole day's firing we succeeded in hitting two villages outside the ranges and very rarely any of the chosen targets. The results were disastrous and it was clear that a great deal of training was needed, and needed as quickly as possible.'[34]

The trouble was: how to communicate this message in such a way that it would drive home the seriousness of the situation. It was normal after such exercises to have a debrief but on this occasion Toosey was not certain what he should say. 'One could do nothing but criticise and this, I do not believe, would have done any good. So I got up on the platform and said to them: "Look, if men like you cannot do better than this, we shall lose the war", and left the room.'[35]

He waited with some trepidation for a reaction. A short time later the senior battery commander, Major Osmond Daltry, came to see him. He invited Toosey to join them after dinner for a glass of port. Toosey went along and listened to them. They knew there were significant weaknesses but, they concluded, 'Under your leadership we will learn and work as hard as you like.'[36] Stephen Alexander, who was a subaltern in the regiment, remembered the result: 'With Toosey's arrival the feeling of fiddling while Rome burned left us . . . His bearing went down well with the troops, and the officers soon found that they could take it or leave it. The older ones departed, and everyone else now felt Toosey's keen dark eye upon their successes or failures.'[37]

The training was hard but Toosey was unrepentant. He was determined to turn the regiment into an efficient fighting unit and in this he was judged by Servaes to have been successful. In a letter to Arthur Villiers after the war, Servaes wrote: 'How he achieved his results so quickly I shall never know, but in six weeks he changed a lazy, feeble and rather scruffy rabble into a keen, efficient and really fine regiment. My General, Beckwith-Smith, whose standards were extremely high, was most delighted with him. The Brigadier to whose infantry brigade Phil was attached (a regular of 30 years' service) told me he thought him the best officer and the best fellow he had ever met.'[38] They became known at their next destination as 'Toosey's boys' and it would seem that he had succeeding in inspiring them with a dose of what later became known as the Toosey magic.

Six weeks later, on 28 October 1941, Toosey sailed from Gourock in Scotland aboard a Polish vessel called the *Sobieski* for an unknown destination. The only clues were the guns and vehicles which were all painted sand colour and the packages labelled Basra.

The *Sobieski* was a small ship and she bounced around on the Atlantic waves like a little tub. Conditions for the men below decks, where they were forced to sleep tightly packed in rows of hammocks, were uncomfortable. Toosey made sure they got as much air and exercise as possible. Getting up in the mornings in their gym kit and doing twenty minutes exercise caused quite some grumbling.

Toosey often went to the bridge to talk to the Polish captain who kept alluding in mysterious terms to a 'powerful friend' that they would soon be meeting. He was not sure what the captain meant but one morning he looked out of the porthole of his cabin while he was shaving and saw an aeroplane with a white star on its wings. He dashed up on deck and saw what looked to him to be 'most of the American Navy. There was certainly one cruiser, one seaplane carrier and at least eight destroyers, which had been escorting a convoy to England and had then taken over and took us back to Halifax in Newfoundland.'[39]

This was October 1941 and nearly two months before America entered the war. He recalled: 'Their behaviour was entirely different from the behaviour of our ships. They dashed about all over the place, they depth-charged whales and put on a terrific show, but it was all very reassuring.'[40]

On arrival in Halifax they transhipped on to American passenger vessels that had recently been converted into troop-ships. Toosey and the 135th sailed on the Mount Vernon, originally named the SS Washington, along with an entire brigade group (some 3000 men). He was with the 53rd Brigade under the command of Brigadier Duke which itself was part of the 18th Division under Major General Beckwith-Smith. Their two and a half month voyage went smoothly; there was good food and the ship was well run by the American sailors. Duke was a veteran of the First World War where he had developed a reputation for bravery. One officer wrote: 'Members of his brigade like to recount how he . . . appeared to be quite oblivious to enemy fire. The snag was that none of his staff could take cover unless the Brigadier did – which was hardly ever!'[41]

The major problem Duke and Toosey encountered on the voyage was overcrowding, and once again they found it a struggle to keep the men physically and mentally fit. There was a programme of physical exercise for the men and lectures for the officers and senior NCOs. However, with the lovely weather and the lack of space to do any real training, the journey felt to everyone more like a peacetime cruise than a journey to the battlefront.

While the *Mount Vernon* continued its voyage the news coming from the Far East was ominous. Until the middle of 1941 the general belief among the Allies was that war with the Far East was unlikely and that all efforts should be concentrated on Europe and the Middle East. By the autumn this had all changed and there were real concerns about the rise of Japan.

The late nineteenth and early twentieth centuries marked Japan's imperial expansion. 'Rather than risk Japan becoming another plaything of the west,' Alan Warren wrote, 'the Japanese ruling class set out to modernise their country. Rather like Great Britain, Japan had the tremendous natural advantages of a common language, ethnicity and culture, combined with good communications, basic education and a large population in a compact land mass. The pace of change proved extraordinary.'[42]

Japan's ambitions were made public on 2 July 1941 when the Imperial Conference in Tokyo agreed to 'construct the Greater East Asia Co-Prosperity Sphere regardless of changes in the world situation'.[43] They began by expanding their military strength in French Indo-China and soon set their sights on the lands to the west, namely the Dutch East Indies, Malaysia and the Philippines. The attraction of these countries was their wealth of natural resources, which they would require to supply the young expanding empire.

The British had not ignored the threat from Japan and reinforcements had been sent to Singapore and Malaya but these were fewer in number than had originally been requested by the command in the Far East. As an example, by the end of 1941 there were 158 aircraft in Malaya with a further 88 on reserve even though it had been estimated that 566 would be required to defend the peninsula.

By late autumn 1941, relations between Japan and America had deteriorated. America's embargo on Japan was having the effect of strangling her development. Before the embargo the USA had supplied 80 per cent of Japan's oil but had stopped after the Japanese had refused to curtail their military activities in Indo-China. Japan believed she was facing collapse. On 1 December 1941 Prime Minister General Tojo announced that 'war was necessary to preserve the Japanese Empire. Subordinate headquarters were sent orders to confirm that hostilities would commence on 8 December (or 7 December east of the International Date Line).'[44]

Toosey was with Duke in the Captain's cabin on 8 December 1941 when the news of the surprise attack on the US Pacific Fleet at Pearl Harbor came through. 'It was most interesting to me to get the immediate American reaction,' he wrote, 'and it was quite simply, "You are all right now, we are in it, we shall win the war."' A few days later came the shattering news of the sinking on 10 December of the Royal Navy's battlecruisers *Repulse* and the newly commissioned *Prince of Wales* off Singapore. They had been diverted to Singapore on Churchill's instruction and against the advice of the Admiralty. Toosey described the news of their loss as a body blow: 'Nobody could believe that two such great ships – one very modern – had gone down without putting up any fight at all. They had no air cover and this taught a lesson which later was to pay great dividends, but it was a very expensive and very demoralising way of learning it.'[45]

Back in London the news of the loss of the two great battleships was greeted with dismay. Churchill wrote in his memoirs: 'I put the telephone down. I was thankful to be alone. In all the war I never received a more direct shock . . . As I turned over and twisted in bed the full horror of the news sank in upon me.'[46] Churchill had met Roosevelt on the *Prince of Wales* in August 1941.

On receiving the news of the sinking of the two ships Duke immediately began to practice withdrawal exercises. This caused a drop in morale and Toosey questioned the wisdom of this. His natural optimism would not allow him to contemplate defeat. Duke was more of a realist and he saw the bleakness of the position his brigade was likely to face if, as he thought probable, they were to be diverted to Singapore. His greater experience told on this occasion.

The morale on board ship was lifted when, on 14 December, they arrived at Cape Town. They were given a rousing reception by the local population. Almost all the men found themselves treated as guests by local families who fed and entertained them. Toosey made himself unpopular by insisting that the men should be made to march around Cape Town and get themselves fit during their few days on land. He was determined not to let this opportunity slip by but there was mumbling and groaning among the men. He attended a meeting where General Smuts spoke to the officers: 'He made the most extraordinary statement, but one can now see the wisdom of it,' he wrote years later. 'He opened his speech by saying, "Thank God for the Japanese, they brought the Americans in and now we shall win the war."'

They left Cape Town two days later. 'This was the last glimpse of real civilisation for four years, though we did not realise it at the time,' Toosey wrote.

The man in charge of the defence of Malaya was Lieutenant General Arthur E. Percival. He had been appointed General Officer Commanding Malaya in May 1941 and he had under his command disparate units, some more experienced than others but few with any knowledge of warfare in the Far East and none with experience of fighting the Japanese.

The news coming out of Malaya reached the ship and it was gloomy. Every day brought details of another withdrawal. As the convoy reached Madagascar they stopped and 'a long boat was rowed from the *Exeter* to our ship the *Mount Vernon* and took off the Commodore of the convoy and put him on board another ship. We ourselves immediately set out for Singapore at top speed completely unescorted.'[47]

There was a change of mood on board, a sense of heightened tension and expectation. Brigadier Duke organised drills of every kind – anti-aircraft drill, fire drill and boat drill. Toosey remembered sailing through the Sundra Straits between the islands of Sumatra and Java. 'Here again I heard a typical pithy American comment: "Boy, did you hear that door clang shut behind us?" How true it was.'[48]

The *Mount Vernon* arrived in Singapore harbour in thick cloud and heavy rain on 13 January 1942. The men had spent less than six days on dry land since September of the previous year. 'A less suitable preparation for jungle fighting could scarcely be imagined,' wrote Lieutenant Stephen Alexander, 'and every day the radio brought news of more "strategic withdrawals" down the Malayan peninsula. The Dutch presence was increased by the battlecruiser *De Ruyter* and more destroyers – the *Tromp* and the Australian HMAS *Vampire* – and finally by three Dutch minesweepers. All this attention made us feel we were nearing the moment of truth; after weeks of fattening we were being politely but firmly shepherded – "After you, Gentlemen!" – to the slaughterhouse.'[49]

As the men disembarked in Singapore the news from Malaya hundreds of miles to the north was demoralising. Units of the 11th Division were retreating southwards from Jitra after a heavy defeat. Worse was to follow.

Toosey kept a diary of the following month which was kept

safe until the end of the war. It records his and his regiment's battle for Singapore rather than offering a picture of the overall battle.

He and his men made their way to a transit camp in a rubber plantation at Nee Soon, about four miles south of the Naval Base. They could hear Japanese aircraft above the clouds but they could not see them. The camp provided an unpleasant welcome to the tropics. The heat and humidity were overwhelming. Every movement made them sweat. Their shirts were constantly soaked and their tropical clothes felt unfamiliar and clammy. All around them were strange insects and creatures making eerie noises.

The following morning Brigadier Duke called Toosey to attend the 28th Indian Brigade conference at midday. Toosey was offered sufficient guns to equip his regiment (his own guns were on a separate ship that had not yet arrived in Singapore) but far too few vehicles. This was a predicament and he knew that he could not operate without the means to deploy his guns. So he made his way to the command headquarters. 'Here I saw a scene that really did surprise me. The whole place was still running on peace time lines – everybody was smart and tidy, glasses of cold water alongside their desks and no awareness that the Japanese were only a few hundred miles away.'[50] He made his demand for vehicles and was told to come back in twenty-four hours. This he did but there was still not sufficient for his needs. He was told to come back again the following day. Toosey got the bit between his teeth, as Stephen Alexander recalled:

> Toosey, with his guns still in Basra or perhaps Bombay, now had to battle not with the Japs but with the local ordnance store to get hold of some 25-pounder field guns. They proved elusive, and a less zealous CO might have been content to wait in the fleshpots of Singapore until they materialised. Stuart

Simmonds . . . accompanied him on his almost daily journeys to Ordnance, whose staff learned to dread their approach. After many abortive visits they arrived one day to find the office empty and an uncanny silence reigning.

'That's funny, sir! Doesn't seem to be anybody here.'

'I smell a rat, Simmy. Let's comb the place.'

They looked in cupboards and behind partitions and at last found the warrant officer in charge cowering under a spare desk. The guns were collected a couple of days later.[51]

Toosey's other concern was that he had received an order for one of his batteries to be used as infantry because there were not sufficient towing vehicles. This, he was convinced, was a terrible waste and he railed against the order: 'I knew perfectly well that there were sufficient guns available and the only thing lacking was transport and this could very easily be made up of civilian transport. I got his (the Corps Commander's) blessing and a note to go to Flagstaff House to demand the necessary vehicles, which I did with a certain amount of vigour. In the end we managed to collect a most extraordinary mixture of vehicles including refuse carts, had them all painted green and they did perfectly well as towing equipment for the last battery'.[52]

The role of his regiment, which had now come under the command of General Key, Commander of the 11th (Indian) Division, was to support the infantry as 'Flank Guard on the West Coast Road for the main body which was withdrawing down the road through the centre of Malaya'.[53] After weeks of training and months of waiting he was determined to put up a good show. 'In order to simplify the picture my orders were to string out the troops of my regiment at various intervals on the coast road back to the Singapore causeway. It was a sensible order because it was possible to pin point exactly the position of the guns and also where the enemy was by the milestones on the road.'[54]

By 24 January Toosey and his four batteries were on the Malayan peninsula. His headquarters were at a place called Pontian Kechil where the 11th (Indian) Division had also established their forward HQ the previous day. They were all prepared for the word 'Go' but there was trouble with their radios. Whether it was due to the thick jungle or their inexperience with the sets, or a combination of the two, they were forced to rely on telephone lines for communication. The following day, a small section of his men were ambushed outside Senggarang. The section commander and all other members of the party were killed. 'It was our first taste of battle and it was pretty unpleasant,' Toosey wrote in the diary. He went up to Senggarang to see what had been going on. It was there he saw his first Japanese soldiers. They ran across the road in front of him: 'I let them have the full contents of my Tommy gun but unfortunately missed. This was a great pity.' A day later one of his officers (from the village next to Hooton), Ben Bolt, and several men were killed. It was Bolt's twenty-first birthday.

Over the course of the next few days Toosey witnessed the Japanese push down the mainland towards Singapore Island. While efforts were made to impede their progress the Japanese were more experienced in jungle warfare and more mobile than the Allies. On 27 January Toosey's rear headquarters withdrew to Singapore Island and on the following day he learned that his own guns and transport had arrived in dock. He was relieved to hear these would be ready for use. Meanwhile the Japanese attacked Pontian Kechil but were driven off: 'We believed they were using their usual tactics of getting behind us through the jungle,' Toosey wrote. 'This had been their trump card and we had no idea how to cope with it at that time – the lesson was not really learned until very much later in Burma.'

Four days after the first men had begun their retreat to the island of Singapore Toosey finally left the mainland. He went with his second in command, Major Pillings, to inspect the positions he had chosen for the guns, which were well hidden in the middle of a rubber plantation. Toosey believed they were not discovered until the capitulation. He moved his headquarters to the dock-yard area on the north of the island and east of the causeway where Brigadier Selby, the Brigade Commander, was positioned. It turned out to be a wise move as he was able to liaise closely with the infantry.

At about that time Brigadier Servaes and the remainder of the 18th Division arrived in Singapore. 'Everyone there seemed to be talking of this fellow Toosey, how he was going after the Japs single-handed with a Tommy gun and other similar exploits, and what a splendid show he and his regiment were putting up,' he wrote after the war. 'My General sent for him, and personally congratulated him not only on the part his regiment had played, but on his own personal showing, and told him how proud he was of him. I cannot describe to you the state of things at Singapore at that time but to come out as he did in that atmosphere of defeatism, panic and complete loss of morale seems to me very fine.'[55]

By now it was the first day of February and the battle for Singapore Island, which lasted only a fortnight, was about to commence. Toosey spent two days inspecting his observation posts and checking on his men. In addition he had been put in charge of the 21st Mountain Regiment, which consisted of two batteries of light guns and four 6-inch howitzers. He visited their observation post and was dismayed to find that the men, who were all Sikhs, were despondent. 'I asked them if they had done any firing and they said "No", which seemed to me quite ridiculous so I pointed out a target to them and told them to have a go. They hit the roof with their third shell. This completely restored their morale and when I left they were roaring with laughter. I had to speak rather harshly to the young white officer in charge for lack of initiative.'[56]

By the morning of 4 February all his batteries were in operation. They had received useful information as to Japanese positions from a group of retreating Australians and so were able to register their guns with greater accuracy. Meanwhile he had got a message from his battery commander in an observation post in a water-tower that he wished to evacuate as he was being heavily shelled: 'The approach was pretty dicey but as I was going up the water tower it received a direct hit – whilst I was climbing the ladder inside – and it made no impression whatsoever. When they saw me appear and knew the tower had been hit their morale improved immediately.'[57] These men felt safe but one of the other observation posts was not so secure: 'It received one or two direct hits and the OP officer's bed was set on fire but', Toosey added wryly, 'he was to lie on harder things than concrete before he finished.'

For the next five days they shelled the Japanese and the Japanese returned fire. On 9 February Toosey and his men spotted a reconnaissance party of eighteen Japanese engineers examining the gap in the causeway. 'We had registered this gap as one of our targets and let them have a couple of rounds from the whole regiment. All but one disappeared and were never seen again; one single man was seen swimming back to Johore Bahru.'[58]

Shortly after this he was ordered to withdraw to an area near the golf course, north-east of Singapore town. The battle at the Naval Base was now over. Brigadier Selby told him after capitulation that he learned from the Japanese that the reason they had not attacked the Naval Base direct was because of the weight of artillery fire they received once they attempted to move into the area. Toosey noted with great pride: 'This came almost entirely from my regiment.'[59]

By 13 February the regiment had sorted out its positions around the golf course. They had their regimental headquarters on the outskirts of the city while the HQRA was in the city itself. Toosey was shocked by the state of affairs: 'Panic had clearly broken out in Singapore. The Japanese had cleverly dropped a number of fire crackers into the city and caused everybody to think that this was rifle fire.' His driver, a Yorkshireman, turned to him and said: 'The trouble with this show is that everybody is afraid of their own bloody shadow.'

A day or two before the surrender the high command decided to evacuate a small number of officers and men. They were to be selected as the most valuable people to the army and Britain as a whole. Toosey was summoned to divisional head-quarters on the evening of 13 February for a meeting with General Key who informed him that he would be evacuated to India. He had been selected on the basis that his experience and enthusiasm could be used elsewhere. Toosey refused. General Key was taken aback but Toosey would not budge. 'I could not really believe my ears but being a Territorial I refused.' He explained later, 'I got a tremendous rocket and was told to do what I was told. However, I was able to say that as a Territorial all orders were a subject of discussion. I pointed out that as a gunner I had read the Manual of Artillery Training, Volume II, which says quite clearly that in any withdrawal the command-ing officer leaves last.'[60]

General Key refused to give in and sent Servaes off with Toosey to talk some sense into him. Servaes appealed to his old friend to listen to reason. In 1945 he wrote to Arthur Villiers describing this meeting:

> The General said to me: 'I don't care who you send as long as Toosey goes.' I told him there was not the slightest hope of persuading him to leave his men; however, he said it was an order and must be obeyed. I tried my hardest to convince Phil that it was in the country's interest for him to go, and thought I had succeeded; but next morning he came jauntily walking into my headquarters never having had the slightest intention of obeying us. He was also, I learned, top of 11th (Indian) Division's list to go.[61]

The next morning Toosey agreed to send Osmond Daltry, his senior and very able battery commander. When Daltry was at the docks waiting to be evacuated he was hit by a blast from a Japanese bomb and was badly wounded, losing an eye and a leg. 'He was carrying a letter to my wife, trying to explain why I had decided to stay behind. I got it back weeks later heavily blood-stained . . . We were still fighting. How would the men have reacted if their CO had walked out and left them? It was a very ill thought out order.'[62]

He kept the letter he wrote to Alex throughout the next three and a half years:

Darling,

I have been offered the chance of leaving here alone, in order to train another Regiment in India. I have refused: I know you will appreciate my actions. I could not have done anything else. It may be hard on you, but, tradition is so important in war time that I felt it would be wrong to do otherwise; and know that you will agree. I could not possibly leave these chaps, who have done so brilliantly. Again, I know you will agree.

My very best to you all and be good, Philip

The following day the regiment was back in action. The Japanese had raised a barrage balloon as an observation post and had a good view of Toosey's position. 'Naturally we were heavily shelled. We did our best to bring it [the balloon] down by taking a cross bearing on the string which held it to the ground. Every time we fired the balloon was pulled down so we must have been fairly close to it, but it was very soon up again.'[63]

At this stage Toosey's position was close to a civilian camp full of thousands of Malays and Chinese who had fled from the Malayan mainland. The Japanese shells would often miss his batteries and land in the refugee camp. 'It was too appalling for words. I went in to see if there was anything I could do to help and a child climbed round my neck. I couldn't get rid of it – it had its leg blown off and this was swinging around. It was a terrible tragedy, seeing civilians killed all the time.'

General Percival's troops had been forced to retreat from the coast and move closer to Singapore city. Meanwhile the infrastructure of the island was causing concern. The water supplies had been badly disrupted and civilian deaths in the city were mounting. On 14 February Sir Shenton Thomas, the civilian Governor of Singapore, urged Percival to surrender. Meanwhile, morale among the troops was running low. 'All imaginable excuses being made to avoid returning to the line,' wrote one officer in his diary after witnessing deserters in Singapore, while Brigadier Ballantine of the 44th Indian Brigade claimed 'that for every man who wanted to fight there were two who did not'.[64] The Japanese kept up the pressure on the British perimeter, and

Death of civilians in Singapore.

by dawn on 15 February 1942 Percival had arranged for a commanders' conference at Fort Canning for 9.30 a.m. 'The 18th Division's General Beckwith-Smith could not attend but he sent a report saying that his formation had been unable to contain the infiltration of its front during the night. Brigadier Simson, Singapore's Chief Royal Engineer, told the assembled officers that the piped water supply might not last into the next day.'[65] Percival raised the subject of continued resistance. Others argued against it and General Heath, Percival's second in command, was particularly concerned that a failure to appreciate the true situation 'and face up to it would have been a deplorable blot upon the Empire which it would take more than a subsequent victory in the World War to expunge'.[66]

With great reluctance Percival decided to accept the advice given to him by the senior officers and capitulate. 'It was decided to ask the Japanese for a ceasefire from 4 p.m.'[67] Accompanied by

Major Wild and Brigadiers Torrance and Newbigging, Percival met General Yamashita at the Ford Motor factory near Bukit Timah village at 5.15 p.m. They shook hands and sat down to work out the terms of the proposed ceasefire. General Percival tried to negotiate keeping a 'thousand of his men under arms to keep order in the town'[68] but Yamashita was impatient, thinking Percival was using delaying tactics. He banged his fist on the table and demanded: 'Is the British Army going to surrender or not? Answer YES or NO.' He used English for emphasis. By 6.10 p.m. Percival had agreed to Yamashita's demands and the ceasefire was set for 8.30 p.m. that day. Percival issued the following statement to the 18th Division:

> It has been necessary to give up the struggle. But I want the reason explained to all ranks. The forward troops continue to hold their ground but the essentials of war have run short. In a few days we shall have neither petrol or food. Many types of ammunition are short and the water supply, on which the vast population and many of the fighting troops are dependent, threatens to fail. This situation has been partly brought about by hostile aircraft and military action. Without the sinews of war we cannot fight on. I thank all ranks for their efforts throughout the campaign.

The *Syonan Times* of 16 February 1942 published an editorial which ran:

> The death knell of Singapore has been tolled, the much vaunted Imperial Force has surrendered. The fortress of the Lion City has fallen like a thunder-smitten oak. The gateway to the unlimited treasures of the East has been forever slammed on the British. The gigantic doors of the prison-house of all Asiatic

peoples have been thrown open. The trumpet call of liberation of the Asians have been sounded. The rule of the White man in Greater East Asia has begun to end . . . Like a mighty dragon shaking itself after a long and heavy slumber, DAI NIPPON has shown the world what an Eastern people are capable of when roused.

The surrender of Singapore was the worst defeat in British military history.

4

AN ODD AND CURIOUS PARTY

Anger, disappointment, frustration, helplessness, hopelessness, shame, resignation or relief – whatever a man's
feelings happen to be in the first moments of becoming a
POW, they are not likely to last long. Prisoners of war may
know about the Geneva Conventions, but they can never be
sure that the men who hustle them towards the enemy rear
know about it also. . . . For the majority of POWs, the
question of status never arises. To suggest that they had any
status at all would be calculated at best to raise a ribald laugh.

A.J. Barker in Behind Barbed Wire

For Toosey the day of 15 February 1942 began with shellfire. By
the end of it he was ordered to blow up his guns, which his men
did immediately and spectacularly – a piece of shell going through
the window of HQ. Later he received a counter order to carry on
fighting. For a few hours confusion reigned and then soon after
7 p.m. he received confirmation of the order to surrender.
Toosey was one of nearly 90,000 British Empire servicemen who

became prisoners of war of the Japanese. 'Perhaps the only consolation I had personally during that ghastly period was that I had been given the Distinguished Service Order in the field by General Key,' he wrote.

Later, in captivity, Toosey received a note from General Beckwith-Smith: 'Dear Toosey, there seemed little chance of seeing you to congratulate you on a DSO, deserved many times over in a very short space of time. I would, however, like you to know what real pleasure this award brought to me.' Toosey regarded this decoration as a tribute to his regiment, which had fought so well. The regiment also received one Military Cross and a Distinguished Conduct Medal. In all the 135th had sustained 122 casualties including 37 dead, 38 wounded and 47 missing.

In the curious silence of Singapore after the firing had ceased Toosey and his men waited for two days before they met any Japanese. Determined they should all go into captivity together as a unit, Toosey ordered all his men back from Cemetery Road, where they had been directed to gather by their own high command. This proved to be greatly to the benefit of the men in the future. They were exhausted and most of them fell asleep, some lying in the open, for anything up to twelve hours. Over the next two days they sat and lay in the sweltering tropical heat and waited as the reality of the defeat sank in. The worst defeat in British military history. It was a profoundly depressing time and there was little Toosey could do to cheer them up. They were crushed and dejected and it was scant consolation that his men had put up a good fight. The uncertainty about the future weighed on everyone's minds.

Toosey received the order from General Percival that officers were not to attempt to escape but to stay with their men. 'This was a novelty, for sure,' wrote Captain William M. Drower, 'for

King's regulations instructed all ranks to do their utmost to escape in the event of being held captive.'[1]

Some men disobeyed and tried to escape. In the confusion that followed the surrender they formed small parties commandeering boats, junks and launches. The distances to safety were enormous and as Europeans they were easily recognisable. Only a few attempts were successful. Many parties were quickly recaptured by the Japanese. Some men were later executed to demonstrate the futility of trying to escape. One success story was Major Geoffrey Rowley-Conwy, later Lord Longford. 'He had been given a very sizeable motorboat,' Lieutenant Charles Elston recalled, 'he said that if Singapore fell he would use the boat. At the time there were very few officers for 1200 troops and I felt I should stay with my men. As it happened the Japanese segregated the Indian troops and it wouldn't have made any difference.'[2] Geoffrey Rowley-Conwy and almost 160 officers and men of his 30th Anti-Aircraft Battery got to Ceylon after adventures at sea, having left just after the surrender.

The most senior officer to escape from Singapore was Lieutenant General Gordon Bennett, the Commander in Chief of the Australian Imperial Force (AIF). 'On the evening of 15 February, after he had destroyed his papers and packed a few belongings, Bennett handed over command to his divisional Chief of Royal Artillery, Brigadier C.A. Callaghan. Bennett did not inform General Percival or any other senior officers of his intention to leave Singapore.'[3] He wrote a farewell message to his men at 9.30 that evening in which he thanked all units for their loyalty and wished them good luck for the future. Bennett reached the coast of Sumatra three days later and eventually reached Australia, having flown from Java, on 2 March 1942. His decision to leave his men was questioned by many of the British, as well as by his own men. On his arrival in Melbourne he was told by General Sturdee, the Chief of the General Staff, that his escape had been "ill advised".'

On 17 February the Japanese made contact with Toosey's regiment. At first they were frankly amazed at the appearance of the Japanese soldiers. Not only were the Japanese on average smaller than Allied soldiers but they fought with what the British regarded as obsolete weapons – rifles with fixed bayonets. Their clothing confused the men too. Some of the Japanese had been issued with rubber boots that were divided at the toe, making them ideal for tree climbing and therefore for jungle warfare. Like most Westerners, they were imbued with the innate racist belief that the Asiatic soldier was a lesser opponent. One of the British senior officers had even suggested that the Japanese had poor night vision and would not be able to fight in the dark. Toosey was as bemused as everyone else.

To the Japanese mind they had captured a disgraced army, representatives of the decadent white race who did not have the courage to fight to the last and die honourably for their country. It was inconceivable to the Japanese that they should have allowed themselves to be taken prisoner. On 8 December 1941 the Imperial Japanese Army had issued an order forbidding soldiers to surrender. Some of the Japanese soldiers had even gone so far as to stage their own funerals before they left Japan.

The soldiers who first approached Toosey and his unit were polite, even affable. He was surprised. He learned later that the Japanese had been given a hard time by his guns and had suffered many casualties as a result of their precise shelling.

That afternoon the unit was ordered to march to Changi, some twenty miles north-east of Singapore town on the far eastern tip of the island. Toosey and his men were already five miles to the east of Singapore. The Japanese provided two lorries for the heavy gear but there was no transport for the men so they had to carry all their kit and march the fifteen miles. 'We started off from our last position soon becoming one unit in a vast procession of tired figures trudging through the tropical midday heat. We trudged past shelled villages, past bodies still lying in the roads, a defeated army in the hands of an Eastern Nation.'[4] They reached Changi at dusk.

Toosey and his men found themselves in Roberts Barracks along with thousands of other Allied troops, British and Australian. The barracks had been built to house 8000 men and was at this moment groaning under the strain of accommodating over 40,000. The place had been bombed during the fighting and there was neither running water nor sanitation. There was chaos, confusion and overcrowding and everywhere was the smell of death.

The Japanese left the prisoners alone to fend for themselves. They supplied no food. In fact there was plenty of food in Singapore, both native food and tinned European food. It was estimated that there was enough food in the stores to last the population of Singapore Island, including the army and the large number of refugees, for twelve months. The captured army had no access to these stores and had only been able to take with them what food they could carry. It was sufficient, the quartermasters calculated, to feed the men in Changi on normal rations for a couple of weeks. However, there was no indication that the Japanese were going to supply any food so the high command decided that the stores, such as they were, would have to be eked out. On reduced rations they estimated they could feed the men for eighty days.

In the first few days at Changi the menus were still standard army fare, although the quantities were minute. Food became an all-consuming topic. 'What we want is food,' Charles Steel, an NCO in the 135th Field Regiment wrote in the first of 183 unposted letters to his wife, Louise: 'We are very hungry.'[5] He noted the menu for 24 February 1942:

Breakfast: 1 teaspoon sardine, 2 biscuits, 1 pint tea
Lunch: 1 pint tea
Evening: Dessert spoon stew, 3 biscuits, 1 pint tea

Australian soldier Roy Whitecross wrote:

As the days went by, each 'meal' only served to aggravate the hollowness between ribs and backbone. It was the first time many of us had really been hungry. What I had previously thought to be hunger, I realised, was just a healthy appetite. We went to the kitchen starving, and after eating the bare mouthful of food issued we were assailed by a feeling of hopelessness; the next mealtime was hours and hours away, and with nothing to occupy our minds we just brooded on our empty stomachs. At night it was worse. I found it impossible to sleep for the pain in my stomach, and my imagination presented an endless vista of vast quantities of food.[6]

Just as things were getting desperate the Japanese began to supply the prisoners in Changi with rice. The army cooks had little experience of cooking the rice and Whitecross recorded this:

It was awful. Upon the heads of the 'bloody cooks' were heaped the combined curses of the unit. But what could they do? Rice is tricky stuff to cook properly. A tablespoon of rice to go with the family's curry at home requires an entirely different technique to the cooking of 100 pounds of rice for 180 men. The cooks tried hard, but at one meal the rice would be a slush of liquid, at the next practically raw. Sometimes it was both raw and burnt. It was months, sometimes over a year, before the cooks got the right rice cooking equipment and turned out well cooked rice.[7]

The Japanese now issued the prisoners with rations every fifteen days. The bulk of the diet was rice but they also added small quantities of flour, tea, sugar and milk, meat, salt, fat and occasionally wheat. The amounts were tiny and the men were living on starvation rations.

The menu had changed so Charles Steel recorded the new day's diet for his wife, Louise:

Breakfast:	Boiled rice, spoon of milk, tea
Tiffin:	Boiled rice, tinned herring mixed together
Evening:	Boiled rice and a little stew

The first side-effect of eating such quantities of rice was on the kidneys. Men found they had to get up and relieve themselves several times a night. A far more unpleasant effect was on their digestion. Some could not take it and suffered from chronic diarrhoea, others from constipation. Whatever their individual complaint, the men took weeks and sometimes months to adjust to their rice diet. One prisoner counted that he had, during his three and a half years of imprisonment, 3680 meals of rice.

If the predominant concern in Changi was food, the second was hygiene. It was six weeks before the water and plumbing were restored. In the intervening time, latrines had to be dug as well as malarial drains in order to keep disease at bay. Dysentery broke out and men, in their weakened state, succumbed quickly to disease. Men fainted on parade and it was not long before the vitamin deficiency disease beri beri was diagnosed. By early

March 1942 the whole of Roberts Barracks had been turned into a hospital and Toosey was ordered to take his men to some sandy ground above the swamps in order to camp and make way for hospital cases.

One of the problems that the British medical officers had was lack of knowledge of tropical diseases. There were a number of doctors within the Malay Volunteer Force who had had extensive experience of tropical medicine and their help, when it was listened to, proved to be invaluable. One such man was Dr P.E.F. Routley who had lived in Malaya before the war. He succeeded in convincing Toosey of the importance of hygiene in the tropics. Toosey organised for Dr Routley to visit his and other units to lecture them on this important issue. 'You may remember', he wrote to Toosey years later, 'that I with my particular local and tropical experience, was posted to 18th Div in Changi. It was difficult, as all units had to be gently, but firmly, inured to the concept of prevention, tropically, of unnecessary ill health.' As a mere captain in the Royal Army Medical Corps, Routley was looked down upon by some of the British high command at Changi despite the fact that his experience of containing tropical disease was so valuable and important.

As the prisoners were left to themselves initially, the British Army high command took over and re-established the Army Act, the act passed by Parliament on a bi-annual basis to give the military a legal code. They felt it was essential to ensure that discipline was maintained to prevent anarchy breaking out. It was necessary but unpopular, particularly among the Australian troops who felt that the British had foregone any right to preserve the officer/other ranks status. The Australians were a unit of new recruits, many of them having had only a few weeks' training before they were thrown into Singapore and their resentment was keenly felt. Moreover, the departure of General Gordon Bennett had caused a drop in morale and deepened further their feelings of anger towards the senior Allied officers.

After six weeks at Changi, the news came that the Japanese planned to make use of the huge and unexpected pool of labour. Initially, work involved small parties of men going into Singapore to unload supplies at the docks. Sometimes they would be unloading equipment, petrol drums and even bombs but on other occasions they were fortunate enough to handle consignments of food and looting was possible. Stealing was a risky business as some of the Japanese were prepared to turn a blind eye to it whereas others meted out vicious punishment beatings. Nevertheless men were always prepared to take the risk because they were so desperate for food. On their way to and from the docks they were reminded constantly of the Japanese attitude to the captives. Decapitated heads of Chinese 'dissidents' were mounted on poles as a warning to the civilian population and, by extension to the prisoners, that the occupying power would brook no dissent.

Within Changi there was boredom. One man described it as 'a perpetual TA Camp, with no chances to get out or satisfy one's hunger'.[8] The high command at Changi had made efforts to keep boredom at bay, establishing a university at which all manner of subjects could be studied, with faculties for modern languages, English language and literature, history, geography, mathematics, economics and theology. Each faculty had a number of lecturers and lectures and seminars were held regularly. Toosey was too busy with administration to attend lectures but he did go to a talk by Lieutenant General Heath who spoke about the reason for the fall of Singapore. That interested him and he kept a copy of the notes for the talk throughout captivity. He also had notes from a lecture on the heavy artillery dispositions on Singapore Island.

One of the things that shocked him in Singapore was the

treatment of the Chinese. He watched how the Japanese rounded them up and drove them down to the beaches where they massacred them with machine guns. If he needed any reminder of the brutality of his captors later he had only to reflect on this, he said, when asked whether he had ever considered refusing to work for the Japanese.

In March the order came from the Japanese that Toosey and his men would be moved to a new temporary camp near the golf course where they would build a shrine to commemorate the 3500 Japanese who died during the battle for Singapore. The move came, finally, on 5 May 1942. They marched the twenty-four miles across the island in the full heat of the tropical sun. The Japanese forced the march through the crowded streets of Singapore in a deliberate attempt to humiliate them further. Several noticed hostility on the part of the inhabitants but there were some who evidently felt sorry for the prisoners and offered them little bits of food and drink. Many men, already suffering from malnutrition and deficiency diseases, struggled to march. As they trudged up the hill into the bombed-out RAF camp the march became a shuffle.

'This Camp (no. 2 Camp) was situated close to Singapore on the site of ex-RAF HQ Far East', Toosey explained in his 20,000-word camp report written for the Allies in September 1945, 'and consisted of wooden huts with attap [palm leaf thatch] roofs which had been seriously damaged during the battle. All the buildings were damaged, there was no electric light and no water supply, and the whole area was filthy with the aftermath of a battlefield which included many dead British and Japanese Troops, in most cases only partly buried.'[9]

Number 2 camp at Bukit Timah comprised 3000 prisoners made up of 800 Australians, 500 officers and men from Toosey's 135th Field Regiment, and the remainder being members of the

18th Division from the Suffolks, Norfolks and the Royal Army Service Corps. The camp was under the command of Brigadier Duke. Toosey was on the camp staff as was Lieutenant Colonel Robertson AIF who had responsibility for the Australians and Lieutenant Colonel Mapy of the 2nd Cambridgeshires. Duke ordered a wholesale clean up, which was necessary and distressing. The half-buried bodies of soldiers, often horribly maimed, had to be dug up and reburied before the area could be declared fit for habitation. Charles Steel described one episode when a man from the regiment came in with a soldier's pay book that he had found in a pipe in the ground. 'I went and found that the stick was stuck into a ditch partially filled in. I had two men dig and quickly came across the remains of some poor fellow who had been partially blown to pieces. The head was separate and the skull quite clean, but the body had been foolishly buried in a ground sheet and had not decomposed. We buried as many parts as could be sorted out and held the customary service. We buried him as I. Cambs. His hometown was in Stowmarket. How futile war is! A simple country lad like this – his home amid the cornfields of Suffolk, dragged to the other side of the world, butchered, and put in a hole under rubber trees so far and foreign from his own lovely countryside!'[10]

Toosey was not a man who liked to reflect on the horrors of war. However, in a letter written on 19 September 1942 to Alex he gave some clue that he too had struggled to maintain his positive frame of mind, perhaps more than he himself liked to admit:

Darling,

There is just a chance that Osmond Daltry may be repatriated, so I am writing this in the vague hope that it may reach you one day. I shall not say much because it might be subject to censor and in any case Osmond will give you all the latest news. This is an odd and curious party. I have a great deal to be thankful for. I am alive and well and well fed which is more than can be said for a great many other people in this horrible war. At first I thought I should go mad because it is not in my nature to be locked up. But now I feel much better and, thank God, my mind has been acclimatised to being a prisoner. It is hell of course not hearing about you and the children, but again other people are suffering worse than that. The greatest boon of all is that we are not separated from the men and so have plenty to do looking after them; and at times they need it, poor devils. On the whole we have been very well treated, much better than any of us ever expected.

Hubert [Brigadier Servaes] has left us with the other senior officers and I shall not see him again until after the war. He was not a good prisoner, poor chap. He doesn't like hardship at all.

I hope you got my post card. I will tell you about my D.S.O. when I get home. I was pleased to get it, particularly under the circumstances.

My best love to you all, darling, and I feel quite happy that all will be well at home in your hands. I miss the children and would give a lot to see them again. Pray that this war will soon be over and again my very best love.

Philip

That letter never reached Alex. Osmond Daltry was not repatriated. He spent the rest of the war in Changi. Toosey got the letter back from Daltry when he visited him in Changi some weeks later and kept it with him until the end of the war.

The site of Bukit Timah camp, standing as it did on the crest

of a rubber plantation with views down the valley to a pictur-
esque Chinese farm, was lovely. They were reminded of English
parkland by the golf course with its clumps of trees and the view
to the north-east was of the MacRitchie reservoir stretching away
to wooded hills 'holding the tropical jungle at bay'. The prisoners were left to roam on the golf course on the days that they
were not working on the shrine. Many of them wrote of the natural beauty of their surroundings: 'When one looks across the
lake one sees a mighty growth of trees. One often sees monkeys
swinging about from branch to branch. But what takes one's eyes
are the great patches of colour provided by flowering trees. The
flowers are huge, creamy yellow as buds, turning to fiery red at
maturity. Against the green of the vegetation they are a wonderful
sight . . .'[11] There were magnificent butterflies that caught their
attention: brightly coloured and some with a wingspan of 8
inches. It was not only their surroundings that surprised them.
The attitude of the Japanese guards was not brutal. Sick men and
those without boots were not forced to work and the conditions,
Toosey observed, 'approached more or less normal standard for
POWs. Also we were learning how to adapt ourselves to an
entirely new mode of life.'[12]

The food was an improvement on the provisions survived on
in Changi and, as they were a smaller group, Toosey was able to
keep a much closer eye on what happened. 'After a starvation
diet at Changi rations improved immediately on arrival at this
Camp and remained quite sufficient for the whole of our stay. We
got meat, vegetables and rice every day in sufficient quantity, and
for the last month of our stay in the Camp we received a good
supply of Red Cross rations sent from South Africa in a ship
exchanging civilian internees.'[13] This view of the food at Bukit
Timah was not shared by others. They found themselves short
and continued to despair over the preparation of the rice, which

they found unpalatable and at times disgusting. The ration scales for the food at that camp were generous by the standards of what was to come later but at the time they did not know that and felt very hard done by.

A typical meal in June 1942 was described by Charles Steel in one of his letters to Louise:

Breakfast: rice, 2 spoons stew, tea
Lunch: fishcake, cucumber, tea
Supper: rice 'meat pie', 'apple turnover', tea. Largely rice and ersatz[14]

The food at Bukit Timah improved when regular working parties started and pay – little as it was – began to come in. 'Even so we were always hungry,'[15] one officer complained. In camp the command maintained separate quarters for the officers and men. The officers slept and ate separately from the other ranks and petty jealousies were not uncommon. The officers' mess was a comfortable hut with a mosquito-netted verandah with a view over the golf course. 'Living regimentally may have been good for morale', wrote Stephen Alexander, 'but it made for an incestuous society.'[16]

It was during this relatively peaceful time that the prisoners worked out a means of survival. Dr Stanley Pavillard, who was in a camp nearby, observed how it worked: 'We had to re-shape and re-direct our whole outlook: life became a game of make-believe and we acquired the knack of turning our attention entirely away from personal discomfort and deprivation. Together with a sense of humour this psychological technique saved morale and life as well.'[17] Some did not adapt and these men, Dr Pavillard noticed, became morose and gloomy. When they became ill they more often than not died. Another prisoner wrote later of the need to maintain civilised behaviour towards others in order to survive. To be selfish and individual did not work to the good of the community: 'It cannot be too strongly stressed how, in those days, the individual had to subordinate his desires to society rules if that society were to survive. The three things that could, at any time, kill us all off were work, disease and starvation.'[18]

The guards at Bukit Timah were regular soldiers from the Imperial Japanese Army who treated the prisoners with disinterest and kept their distance, a far cry from the brutality they were to suffer later. The man in charge, Lieutenant Matsuzama, dealt directly with Duke and Toosey and it was only later that they understood this to be unusual. In future Toosey and other camp administrators would have to deal with the convoluted workings of the Japanese hierarchical system that took months, if not years, to sort out. 'We had few incidents in this camp though we were introduced to the traditional method of Japanese punishment, which is a severe beating with a bamboo or any other implement available at the time,' Toosey wrote. 'The only serious case was that of one British driver who had an altercation with two Japanese officers, who attacked him severely and broke one of his arms with a metal crowbar. We also met for the first time the various other punishments, such as standing to attention for hours in the sun holding baskets of earth, etc., above our heads.'[19]

When the prisoners were first taken captive the administration of the camps was run by the Allies. It was not until six months after the surrender of Singapore that the Japanese set up a separate POW administration. Toosey explained in his report:

The organisation inside the camp [at Bukit Timah] was entirely British and Australian; the Japanese did not interfere at all. The camp was partially surrounded by a single row of dannert wire and in the initial stages we provided our own guard, but subsequently we handed over to Sikh and Japanese guards. These guards never entered the camp and in no way interfered with our domestic arrangements. With the exception of the Sikh traitor guards who attempted to assert their authority, the guards were well behaved.[20]

The fact that Toosey spelled this out is important. One of the troubles he was to endure later was the free access Japanese and Korean guards had to the prison camps in Thailand. The situation in Bukit Timah accorded more closely with international law than any other he was to encounter.

Improvements to the camp continued. By the end of May there was electricity in the huts. Someone had discovered a sub-station within the perimeter of the camp and a squad of men had rigged up electricity not only for the officers and men but also, at their request, to the Japanese guardroom. 'Fired by success, the squad went on to develop water services from some old mains, and an improvised pumping station,' Stephen Alexander recalled. 'In them, and with equipment scrounged from the golf clubhouse, a more sophisticated system for a twenty-four hour water supply was established, and showers and water closets installed. So successful did this become that a bill was solemnly presented by the water company through the Japanese, solemnly accepted by us, and forgotten by everyone.'[21]

With time on their hands, the men and officers wanted entertainment, especially in the evenings. Two of Toosey's officers, Malcolm Northcote and Bill Peacock, laid down a racecourse on the concrete floor of one of the bombed-out huts. Wooden horses were carved and numbered and colours were made up for the jockeys. 'The course was floodlit and Bill and Malcolm sat at a table throwing dice, one for the horse and another for the moves. The whole camp flocked to the meetings, sweeps were run for the hospital and even the Nip guards used to sidle up and ask us to place bets for them.'[22]

Despite the congenial view given by this and other accounts, Bukit Timah was a prison camp. The biggest risk that the prisoners took was in their desperate search for news from the outside. It was a risk that brought with it severe penalties if found out but this risk never deterred a number of brave men from trying to supply the camps with information. In Bukit Timah this was run, again in the account of Stephen Alexander, as follows:

> In the flurry of electrification a new secret radio had come into being. The adjutant of the 2nd Cambridgeshires, John Becket, and one of his signallers, Corporal Rogers, smuggled out of a dump – under the eyes of the guards and concealed in the grassbox of a lawnmower or disguised as refrigerator parts – metal valves, condensers and resistors, together with a complete radio relay cabinet. In spite of the confusion in colour coding between Australian, American and British parts, they installed a working set in the roof of a washhouse. It was used sparingly and only for BBC headlines, to reduce risk of detection, and news was passed on imaginatively as though it had come from civilian contacts.[23]

Toosey was always careful about news dissemination. He had good reason to be. First he realised that more of the Japanese than ever admitted to it could understand English. Careless talk might lead to the discovery of the source of information and this would, and indeed in one case did, lead to the death of those directly involved. Toosey, who was to become Commanding Officer in the camp, would have been one of the first to be held responsible and punished. However, there was another reason for holding back the information. During the summer of 1942 the news headlines from the BBC were depressing. They spoke of defeats and withdrawals, as well as some Allied successes, and Toosey sensed that no news for the men was better than bad news. Gossip, speculation and rumour was rife and he felt, on balance, that a healthy degree of speculation was probably better at this stage than too much focus on what was known to be the truth.

Shinto shrine by Will Wilder.

The shrine they were building was on an island in the middle of the MacRitchie reservoir on the golf course. It had Buddhist archways and a red lacquered sacred bridge. They also had to dig up the fairways and lay ornamental roads leading to the shrine. Toosey wrote: 'The work was not hard though the hours were very long, from 0800 until 1900 hrs. We were normally given one holiday per week. All officers and men working received 10 cents per day. Sick and non-workers were not paid.' Some of the men used their civilian skills, such as carpentry, but the majority had to work as simple labourers, breaking stones or digging earth and shovelling it into baskets to move it from one spot to the next.

It was while doing this work that they first came across the Asian tool that replaces the European spade, a chunkel. 'You see, my dear,' Charles Steel explained in a letter to Louise: 'spades are no good in a country where the peasantry doesn't wear boots! The chunkel – like a large Dutch hoe – is therefore used instead. It is raised above the head and then brought down smartly into the earth.' [24] By the end of October 1943, 4 million cubic metres of earth would have been dug out by chunkel and been moved in baskets.

The Australians at Bukit Timah felt resentful of the Allied command and showed little respect for Brigadier Duke. Things reached a climax on 11 June 1942, when the Japanese called a parade and held the first formal count. Discipline almost broke down and the Australians began to roar abuse as the adjutants stepped forward to Brigadier Duke to report the number of men on parade. This spread to the British ranks who joined in the shouting. Duke restored order but it was an unsettling episode. A few days later the Japanese announced that all officers of the rank of full colonel and above would be sent to Japan. Rumours of the move had been flying around for several days so that when Brigadier Duke left Bukit Timah in mid-June he did not expect it to be for good.

Major General Beckwith-Smith, who had awarded Toosey the DSO after the battle, got special permission from the Japanese to visit Bukit Timah a few days before the senior officers left for Japan. Toosey asked him to pass on a letter to Brigadier Duke for the two had not had a proper chance to say goodbye to one another. On parting Beckwith-Smith shook Toosey warmly by the hand and said: 'I've seen what you are doing, Phil, just carry on like that until the end of the war and God bless you.' It was the last time he saw him. Beckwith-Smith, who was one of the best loved and respected of all the senior officers, died of diphtheria in 1944.

The next day, Duke wrote to Toosey thanking him for all he had done adding: 'I have at times only been depressed at the thought of what I missed by being flung into this predicament. Anywhere else we could have put up some sort of show and I could (or would) have gone into battle confidently with your regiment in support. Many thanks for your help in the no 2 camp and I couldn't leave it in better hands than yours.'[25]

The balance of power now changed and the men felt that without their senior officers they would have less leverage with the Japanese. The higher the rank, they had observed, the better the bargaining powers they had. However, life at Bukit Timah continued satisfactorily through the summer and the main concerns of the men were for food and news. The heat and humidity of Singapore, which had been such a shock to many of them, was another recurring theme. Major John Coombes wrote: 'Those days were a constant procession of fierce heat, when movement, even in the shade, was always an effort, and the nights a purgatory of sticky breathlessness, relieved about once a day by rain storms of tropical intensity.'[26]

In August there was another change to their routine. On 15 August the Japanese POW administration took over the camps bringing in Korean guards. This ushered in a new era and also brutality which was to last for the remainder of the war.

Korea had been colonised by Japan thirty-five years earlier and the Koreans had been subjected to years of oppression. Japanese was taught in the schools and no Korean could hold any position of power or influence. When the Japanese recruited men for the Imperial Japanese Army they refused to give them a rank and treated them with contempt as inferiors. It is hardly surprising that given thirty-five years of brutal subjugation the Koreans took every chance to mete out brutality to the Allied prisoners. They constantly heaped insults on the heads of the white prisoners who, the Japanese reminded them, had dominated Asiatic peoples for far too long. The catalogue of horrors stemming from the Korean guards begins with this change in the summer of 1942.

On 30 August 1942 the Imperial Japanese Army received an order from Tokyo that all prisoners were to sign a declaration undertaking not to try to escape. This caused a major incident. The prisoners refused to sign the form as the declaration was in direct contravention of the Geneva Convention which states that it is the duty of a prisoner of war to attempt to escape. Where they might have escaped to was not the point, it was the principle. On 1 September the Japanese warned Lieutenant Colonel Holmes, the senior officer in charge of Changi camp, that they would take coercive measures if the prisoners continued to refuse to sign. They refused.

The following day all prisoners in the Changi area were given until 6 p.m. to pack up and march two miles to the square in front of Selerang barracks. They moved all the essentials they could including cooking equipment and utensils, rice and food reserves. The Japanese were surprised that the prisoners had taken such a stand but were clearly prepared to take action. 'Sikh guards and machine gun posts surrounded the six barrack blocks which surrounded the square,' Captain Robinson wrote. 'Into this accommodation nearly 15,000 British troops were packed. Not an inch of floor space was to be seen when beds were down. The centre of the square was rapidly opened up for latrines and the scanty water points were controlled and scheduled.'[27]

The density, one prisoner worked out, was the equivalent of

a million people per square mile: 'Viewed from the top of one of the barracks, Selerang was an incredible sight. Troops were packed everywhere like sardines on every floor, on the roof, in every nook and cranny, but still it was hardly possible to lie down; if you did lie down your body was immediately sandwiched between the sweating bodies of your two neighbours.'[28]

The heat and the smell from sweating men and the latrines attracted flies – harbingers of disease. By the second day the medical officers reported an increase in the number of cases of dysentery and diphtheria. They became increasingly concerned about an epidemic and told Lieutenant Colonel Holmes so. Meanwhile he was sent for every day and made attempts to negotiate with the Japanese a compromise on the wording of the document. On 5 September the Allied doctors told Holmes that the latrines would only be sufficient for a few more days and that sickness was rapidly increasing to the point of an epidemic. The Japanese then threatened to empty the hospital on to the square if they did not sign by 3 p.m. Holmes consulted the senior medical officer and then, taking full responsibility himself, signed the necessary order that officers and men 'would now sign as "duress" had been established'.[29]

News of this reached Bukit Timah on the evening of 5 September and Toosey ordered all the men in his camp to sign as well. The declaration read: 'I, the undersigned, hereby solemnly swear on my honour that I will not, under any circumstances, attempt escape.' The Selerang incident was the largest of its kind, but in other prison camps and in Pudu Jail in Kuala Lumpur prisoners stood out against the non-escape order from Tokyo. As at Selerang the Japanese were unmoved and threatened to shoot those who refused. In the end they all agreed to sign.

By late September the Shinto shrine, named Shonan Jinjya, was almost complete and the Japanese organised an unveiling ceremony. Two further shrines were erected including one to fallen British soldiers. The respect the Japanese showed for the dead was in marked contrast, many felt, to their attitude to the living.

During September the rumours in Bukit Timah became increasingly fanciful. Charles Steel wrote a list in his next letter to his wife (October 1942):

(a) Hitler is dead.

(b) The European war is over.

(c) The Italian Fleet in Singapore.

(d) The Japanese can't feed us (Don't we know it!) and are sending us all to a neutral country.

(e) The Japanese are sending half of us home with the rising sun tattooed on our foreheads. The other half will be killed if the former are taken in battle.

(f) We are to build a railway from Thailand to Burma – over mountains and through swamps, a feat attempted by Great Britain but given up owing to high death rate of coolies.

(g) We are going to march to Thailand (800 miles).

(h) Germans at Alexandria.

(i) Japanese in Australia.[30]

One of these rumours soon proved to have more than a grain of truth: just a few days later Toosey was ordered to organise the camp into battalions of 650 men in preparation for a journey to Thailand where they would be required to labour on a railway from Thailand to Burma. This would be through some of the most inhospitable, disease-ridden jungle in the world. The Japanese told them they were going to a beautiful country where there was plenty of food and where they would be required to do light work.

On 22 October 1942 Toosey left Bukit Timah with 650 men made up of 400 men of his own regiment and completed by 250 from the Norfolks, Suffolks and RASC. 'We were handed a good supply of Red Cross clothing by the Japanese, which served to equip 90 per cent of the party with one of each essential article, including boots. We were also fortunate enough to be able to take with us a good supply of Red Cross medicines and some food.'[31] This was the last Red Cross handout they would receive for two years.

They were marched through the streets of Singapore, carrying all their bags and belongings. When they arrived at Singapore station Toosey was appalled at the spectacle that confronted him. A train with twenty-odd goods trucks. These were closed steel trucks used to transport rice and rubber and did not look as though they had been cleaned out since they were last used. 'Good God! They can't do this to British officers!'[32] one major exclaimed. He was wrong. This was the transport to Thailand, a journey of 1440 kilometres. It would take four long days and nights.

Toosey's men were paraded on the platform and after a tedious wait they were addressed by a Japanese officer. The train was in the charge of a Japanese sergeant and four other ranks. A tiny guard for 650 men. The Japanese officer barked instructions: 'Obey all the commander's orders and those of the Imperial Japanese Army; disobedience will be punished on the spot (commanders in the trucks are responsible); take great care with the natives and neither buy from them nor change money.' One officer noted in his diary, 'they are thieves and will take us down, even to stealing our boots off our feet!'[33]

'The guards are not here to watch you,' the Japanese officer continued, 'because you are gentlemen. They are on the train to take care of natives!'[34] They were cautioned about the danger of fire, allowing their arms and legs to hang out of the carriage

Train to Siam, May 1943 *by Ronald Searle.*

doors because the bridges were narrow, and about leaving the trucks without permission.

This was the first journey Toosey and his men had made under Japanese organisation and although they were later to suffer much harsher conditions, it came as a severe shock. He was ordered to get all the men and equipment into the trucks, although he could not see how this could be achieved. Eventually after much pushing and shoving they succeeded.

There was no room for the rice boilers and ovens they had brought from Bukit Timah. The Japanese officer offered to send these on later. They never saw the boilers and ovens again. In retrospect the discomfort of travelling with cooking kit would have been a price worth paying for the future convenience in their jungle camps.

Finally, after a long delay, the train shuddered out of the station and began the long, slow journey to Thailand. As they crossed the causeway they saw how little it had taken to repair the damage. All the way up the peninsula they saw shored-up bridges. The Japanese engineers, Toosey said later, were extremely efficient and had repaired the bridges down Malaya five times as fast as anyone had estimated they could.

There are many accounts of the train journeys to Thailand and the horrible discomforts. Toosey's description of his experience in his camp report was briefer than most: 'The journey by rail took four days and nights and was most uncomfortable. We were packed 31 to a metal truck, including all our baggage. The food arrangements for the journey were sufficient to keep us alive but were very badly organised.'[35]

By day, as the sun rose, the steel walls of the trucks became too hot to touch. Conditions inside were insufferable. There was so little room that the men were forced to stand or crouch, clutching their bags and trying to keep their balance in claustrophobic conditions. 'The situation precisely,' Toosey recalled later, 'was that nobody could lie down, some could sit down but we had to take it in turns. During the day time the steel doors were pulled together and so we got no air at all. These trucks were like an oven, it was really dreadful.' They sat in pools of perspiration and prayed for evening. Night, however, brought no sleep. A fitful semi-consciousness was the best they could hope for. One officer wrote of this journey:

A short halt and we were off again . . . trying to sleep on a night to be remembered. Filthy-dirty and smelly humanity massed approximately thirty to a box about 3 m x 6.5 m with all equipment. No room for everyone to lie down, so we must try to sleep in a squatting position with a horrible aching in the bent knees. As people get uncontrollably sleepy, their legs and arms tumble onto other forms. To add to the trouble, the floor of wood and metal has no springs to speak of, and there is continually the most diabolical stopping and starting with a ringing, crashing of trucks, and finally a most teeth-shattering crash of your own truck.[36]

At night the doors of the carriages were opened. 'We got fresh air,' Toosey recalled, 'but in that part of the world, especially when we were going over what are known as the Highlands in Malaya, it became bitterly cold.'[37] On the second morning they were allowed to disembark at a small station. They were all black with soot and staggering on unsteady feet, limbs aching after hours in the same, cramped position. The lavatories were insufficient for the number of men who needed to answer the calls of nature so they had to use the side of the track in full view of the native population.

Toosey oversaw the distribution of food to the men. The train stopped three times in every twenty-four hours, and the guards produced buckets of rice and stew which were very welcome. Water was always in short supply and the men had to run the gauntlet of the guards to get their water-bottles filled up from the engine. It tasted oily but it was at least boiled and therefore safe to drink.

'But it was a very unhappy journey', Toosey said, 'because at least two of the men in the truck I happened to be in got dysentery during the journey and there was nothing the poor devils could do about it but just make a mess where they were.'[38] This, added to their thirst, discomfort and claustrophobia, made the journey one they never forgot.

Around them the countryside was changing. After the rubber plantations and jungle of Malaya they passed through vast, watery paddy-fields punctuated by jagged outcrops of limestone rock and little bamboo huts with thatched roofs. Toosey could see the workers in the fields – almost all Chinese – wearing great straw hats with a peak in the centre like a pagoda. They looked like mushrooms above the rice in the fields. Closer to the Thai border the country became more rugged with sparse jungle and there were fewer huts. The train stopped at Hat Yai Junction and the men disembarked for another meal of rice and vegetable stew.

At Hat Yai Junction Toosey had his first proper sight of the Thai. He saw that their dress was more European than in Malaya: the men wore trousers rather than sarongs. The women, wearing sarongs and blouses, were voluptuous with raven-black hair and good teeth. They had lovely smiles. The children were running around in ragged Western dress and many were naked. The stench from the train should have been reason enough for Thais to keep their distance but they were keen to barter for anything – fountain pens, watches and even woolly clothes.

The final leg of the journey was made in darkness, but by the light of a bright, full moon they could see water everywhere. 'Our first impression of Thailand was one of wetness everywhere,' Captain Robinson wrote, 'a vast paddy land with hundreds of rivers big and small. Drab wooden houses, often on piles, introduced us to the unlovely Thai dwelling.'[39] Thai cattle with spreading horns were startled from their sleep by the train as it rattled by. Occasionally they saw an elephant chained to a tree close to a few bamboo huts. The roads had gone and in their place wide rivers appeared.

At 4 a.m. the train halted at Ban Pong station. The market town of Ban Pong is thirty miles from Bangkok and is a junction on the Singapore to Bangkok line. In 1942 the town had a few stone buildings and a busy main street with shops and stalls selling all manner of produce. The prisoners were ordered to disembark. Toosey oversaw the unloading of the exhausted, hungry men and their filthy possessions. As they were collecting their belongings he was told that the local Japanese commander, Colonel Ishi, wished to inspect the new arrivals. They paraded outside the station, stood smartly to attention despite their exhaustion and listened to a speech from the large, fat, elderly Japanese colonel. The prisoners had already experienced the tendency of the Japanese to make speeches. Now they were being welcomed to Thailand and told they would be well treated if they worked hard.

Colonel Ishi left the station and Toosey was told to march to the local staging camp on the other side of the town. It was a distance of a mile or so, past a Catholic church and down a lane between fields to a low-lying area. Only the very sickest of his men, about six, who were incapable of marching, were taken by truck.

Ban Pong staging camp brought a new and very unpleasant surprise. It was on the site of a former paddy-field and the whole area was flooded after the monsoon rains. The ground beneath their feet had degenerated into a sea of sticky, smelly mud. Toosey was disgusted. 'It was the most filthy mess I have ever seen in my life. There was nobody really in charge and therefore nobody to exert discipline to see that the place was kept reasonably clean. It was in a very low swampy area and certainly in a quarter of the huts, the bamboo slats on which we lay, had the water lapping just underneath them, and in that water was excreta from the latrines which hadn't been properly dug and had overflowed into the camp. It was perfectly horrible.'[40] Another prisoner described it as being knee-deep in water and looking like a cross between an abandoned fairground and a gypsy encampment in a very wet summer at home.

When Toosey met the British major in charge of the camp he

berated him for the filthy state it was in. The officer began to make excuses about it only being a transit camp and did he not know how difficult the Japanese could be? Toosey pulled himself up to his full height and said that, in his opinion, the camp was a disgrace and 'the British P.O.W. staff in the camp had lost grip and given up hope'. The only way to get anything done, he told the officer, was to stand up to the Japanese. The major tried to reason with him but Toosey just lost his temper and stamped his foot, intolerant of what he saw as a defeatist attitude. However, the poor major did indeed have an impossible task on his hands.

Toosey knew that hunger and lack of sleep combined with the horrors of their current camp was having a marked effect on morale. He had to deal with the men's immediate needs as best he could, and then see what improvements could be made for the dysentery sufferers, a handful of whom were stretcher cases. He told the men they would be moving on the following day and urged them to get as much rest as possible. They struggled through the heavy, stinking mud and sought bed-space in the bamboo huts. 'The conditions on the bamboo shelves along each side of the hut were extremely cramped but at least the men could stretch out full and in their tired state they were able to ignore the many different types of bug and fly that pestered them.'[41] On waking, later in the afternoon, they explored the camp. There was little to reassure them. The latrines were the worst they had encountered so far: 'basically a morass, covered with flies and maggots and totally open to general view'.[42]

That evening they walked out of camp to a well where they filled their water-bottles and had a perfunctory wash. Toosey even managed to shave, which made him feel better. The track to the well was firm underfoot and the evening air was cool and fresh. En route they encountered local people who were friendly and seemed anxious to buy valuables from them. In turn they received bananas and hard-boiled eggs. Earlier in the afternoon Toosey had negotiated with the camp guards and had got some extra rice for his men from the camp canteen. It was always a battle to get food for men in transit. The Japanese issued food to the prison camps based on the usual camp strength and made no concessions for transit parties who could swell the size of a camp by 100 per cent. However, that night Toosey's men settled for the night on full stomachs.

'Fortunately we only stayed one night,' he wrote, 'I left behind me a supply of medicines and Red Cross food to help this camp.'[43]

As dawn broke the camp bugler called the reveille and a meal of rice and thin stew was served. The Japanese maintained Tokyo time in Thailand, even though there was a two-hour time difference. At nine o'clock, or rather seven o'clock Thai time, the men were called out on parade and there began an interminable wait. Although the men were allowed to stand easy and, eventually, to sit down, no one was allowed to leave the parade ground. In the growing tropical heat, with mud underfoot, this was exhausting. Toosey and his fellow officers had by now begun to understand how unpredictable and apparently inefficient their captors could be but they also realised that the Japanese had 'begun to learn the lesson that was, if you wanted work out of these men, you didn't want them to die en route. It was a better thing to truck them as far as the road was capable of carrying them.'[44]

A convey of open trucks arrived at the end of the morning. The prisoners were loaded into the trucks for the fifty kilometre journey to the next camp. For their gear there were little river barges they nicknamed pom poms, from the noise of the engines. Their belongings were piled into these and taken by river.

The convoy of lorries left Ban Pong and sped through the

paddy-fields along bumpy roads towards the provincial town of Kanchanaburi that gave its name to the province between Bangkok and Burma. The road to Kanchanaburi was in good repair, although the monsoon rains had washed it away here and there. Toosey learned later that it had been improved by a group of prisoners from Ban Pong. All along the roadside there were signs of local Thai life. Long-horned cattle, tethered by the neck, nosed around in the grass lazily while naked children with pot bellies and dirty faces ran in and out of the bamboo and attap thatched dwellings. Frequently there were street vendors at the roadside chopping and cooking delicious-smelling snacks while others pulled hand carts piled high with bananas or papaya. It was at once bewildering and charming.

The scenery to the north-west began to change. Behind the endless vista of paddy-fields emerged a hazy spine of jagged lime-stone hills, rocky, craggy, with vegetation up to their summits on all but the steepest cliffs. The red-brown earth, the expanses of blue-brown water and the bright, bright green of the vegetation made a picture of great natural bounty.

After an hour they reached Kanchanaburi, a small, prosperous market town on the banks of the Mae Khlong river. The Thai name, pronounced 'Garn-cha-na-boori', means town of gold. In 1942 it had a population of about 5000 and its main trade, apart from the river, was the local paper factory that employed several hundred local people. There was a magnificent temple not far from the factory and the main street was a hive of activity. The convoy drove past the town gate, an impressive white monument, and down the main street. Thronging the street, a smooth dirt surface, were traders on foot, on bicycle, and men walking slowly behind buffalo carts. Some were carrying huge, ungainly bundles. On either side of the road the wooden houses were overflowing with produce. The shops on the ground floor sold food of all kinds and in every other store, it seemed, someone was cooking. Wandering barefoot out of town were gentle-featured saffron clad monks on their way to their monastery at Tha Maa Kham.

At the far end of the high street the convoy stopped. The lorries could go no further. Toosey was told the men would have to march the last few kilometres to the camp. No sooner had they unloaded their kit than the lorries sped off. Thais flocked around the prisoners intent on trading food for anything they could get. The guards tried to chase them away, brandishing their bayonets, but the Thais were insistent. It was good business.

Eventually the guards ordered Toosey to march the men out of town towards the hills. It was hot and they were thirsty, tired and very dirty. The march was about five kilometres through low jungle scrub. They could see a great river over to their left, thronged with all manner of river craft, and beyond the river green jungle towards the limestone hills and beyond. Way, way beyond was Burma.

5

BUILDING BRIDGES ON
THE KHWAE MAE KHLONG

They had disappeared off the face of the planet into a land
which most of them had never heard of, held at the mercy
of unintelligible, cruel and alien guards. They were trapped
in a place of strange landscapes, strange food, strange
vegetation and very strange noises. All they had was each
other, and after food, mateship was the most valued
commodity. Where could they turn? Who would be there
for them? In some cases, the answers were deeply
disturbing.

Patricia Mark

Colonel Toosey and his men marched to the sound of the regi-
mental band into Tamarkan camp. Their new home was situated
on the River Mae Khlong just above the confluence with the
Khwae Noi, the river that flowed from the Burma border. The
Thai word for river is *khwae* and *noi* means little, so that the
Khwae Noi is the little river and the Mae Khlong, sometimes

called the Khwae Yai, is the big river. It was the word Khwae, or Kwai, that registered with the prisoners.

Toosey was relieved that they had not found themselves in a place as squalid as Ban Pong. The camp was bounded by a bamboo fence but this was more a demarcation than a prison wall. On one side there was the river they had followed from Kanchanaburi, on the other the area where the Japanese engineers were housed. The site was good. It was above the flood level of the river and had a natural spring that ran with beautiful cold, clear water that needed no purifying. Beyond the camp on three sides were the limestone hills and the jungle.

They were greeted by Major John Roberts of the 80th Anti-Tank Regiment and Captain David Boyle of the Argyll and

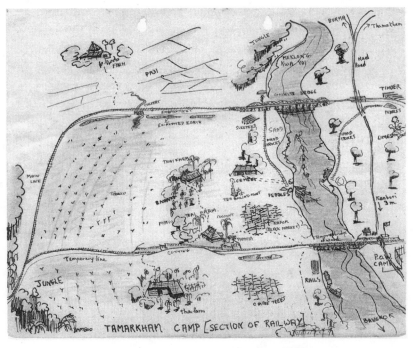

Sketch map of Tamarkan area by Stephen Alexander.

Sutherland Highlanders. Roberts had arrived at the beginning of October with a group of 200 men from Ban Pong. The Japanese operated on the basis of giving as little information as possible to the prisoners, so all Roberts had been told was that they would have to construct their own accommodation. He had learned that the locals called the area Tha Maa Kham meaning the place where horses cross the river – referring to the historical fact that this was where the Burmese crossed the river as they advanced towards the ancient Thai capital. The prisoners all referred to the camp as Tamarkan and this spelling has stuck.

First Roberts's men had to construct huts for the Japanese and then for themselves. Hut building was a new experience for the prisoners: not a nail was used in the construction and the huts were made entirely from local materials. Large bamboos up to five inches in diameter were delivered by barge to the camp. These had to be hauled up the steep river bank by hand. Some of them were one and a half times the length of a telegraph pole. The huts were twenty feet wide and 300 feet long. One former prisoner, Joseph Gordon Smith of the Argylls, explained the technique: 'Four stout bamboo poles were placed in a position on the ground to act as supports, one at each end, and the remaining two spaced out over the intervening span. More bamboos were then cut to length and positioned to complete the structure, and the whole was then bound together with lengths of vine. It is a peculiarity of Japanese saws', he added, 'that they cut when pulled, not when pushed, as in Europe.'[1]

As the framework of the huts was being erected by one gang of men, another was at work producing the attap thatch. The men took a piece of bamboo split in half, about four feet long, and 'folding palm leaves in the middle, they attached them to the bamboo so that they formed a sort of flag, each leaf overlapping its neighbour by about half its width'. The leaves were stitched or knitted into place using creeper and the attap was laid on the structure like enormous overlapping roof tiles. This thatch, if well kept up, was waterproof but all too often the prisoners were unable to maintain their attap roofs and they began to leak.

The walls of the huts were also covered with attap, which went from ground level to just under the eaves; there were door-ways at either end of the huts. Then they built the sleeping platforms. In some camps men slept directly on the mud floor but in Tamarkan and other more permanent camps in the base area around Kanchanaburi they built a sleeping platform along the full length of the hut and about two feet off the ground. According to Smith: 'This was done by lashing more bamboos between the poles and covering them with a layer of split bamboo, again held by creeper ties. The same was done at the other side of the hut, so that we finished up with a three hundred foot long platform down each side, and a gangway with an earth floor down the middle.'[2] In Tamarkan the men had about 18 inches by 6 feet of space, just enough to lie in but not enough to turn over without disturbing their neighbours. The agony of sleeping on iron-hard, slippery bamboo was an unwelcome real-ity which was to affect them for the next three years. Bamboo, in fact, dominated their lives. They had bamboo beds, bamboo water-bottles, bamboo wash-basins, bamboo latrine seats, bamboo stretchers. Toosey smoked a bamboo pipe. This hard, versatile grass that grows up to four feet a day in the jungle became their friend and enemy simultaneously.

By the time Toosey and his men marched into Tamarkan there were five completed huts for the prisoners and a set of superior-looking constructions for the Japanese accommodation.

Captain David Boyle had arrived at Tamarkan a fortnight after Major Roberts with 110 men and officers on 20 October 1942. He remembered Toosey's arrival: 'One was very much on one's own in those days and it was very pleasant to see a well organised party as they still were, still very much running their own show, and I can't remember any question but that Toosey was going to assume command of the camp straight away and one was very glad to see it happen.'[3]

Roberts handed over to Toosey on the day after his arrival. That day he was involved in an altercation with the Japanese and Toosey had to intervene. 'On 27 October a Japanese soldier came into the cookhouse and demanded men to work for him. Having been refused these men by Major Roberts he struck the latter across the face with a stick. Major Roberts promptly punched the soldier and knocked him down. The case was immediately taken up to the Japanese Camp Command and an apology was received for the soldier's conduct.'[4] This was the first in a long series of altercations with the guards at Tamarkan that ended in violence. Although they became used to the Japanese method of disciplining men, the hard physical nature of the beatings was always a shock.

As in Singapore, the Japanese in Thailand expected the camps to be run by Allied officers. This was almost unheard of for a prisoner-of-war camp where the idea of imprisoned officers having any authority was anathema. It was born of necessity as the Japanese had nearly 90,000 Allied prisoners in over a thousand camps in their newly captured territories. For those prisoners who ended up in camps where their senior officers were prepared to take charge and organise the camps efficiently this was a great benefit.

However, some senior commanders, trained and willing to take responsibility for their men in battle, found the new situation beyond their capabilities. 'The rules of the game not only changed, but had been, by and large, discarded,' Patricia Mark, daughter of Dr Jim Mark, explained. 'Too many regressed into petty personality conflicts and administrative minutiae. A very few adapted their training and their understanding of what it was to be a senior officer in His Majesty's forces and became innovators and true leaders, adept at negotiations which put the lives of their men ahead of blind obedience to the King's Regulations.' For the Territorial Army officers with their civilian careers and experiences it was easier to make this transition than for many of the older, Indian Army regulars who had spent a lifetime in the army.

Toosey saw the need to adapt to the new situation facing him. The crushed morale and all that that implied had shocked him in Ban Pong. As the senior officer at Tamarkan he assumed control and he set about doing it in a way that had more echoes of his civilian life than his military one. He was faced not with a military problem but with a combination of administrative, engineering and labour issues. It was clear the prisoners were merely to be used as slaves. The Japanese, he knew, despised them for having capitulated and they intended not only to work them like slaves but to remind them constantly of their ignominy. Toosey, as the senior British officer, was simply the chief slave.

The first thing Toosey did was to select a team of twelve officers and NCOs to work with him in the camp administration. He had 1500 men from several different regiments including two Scottish regiments, the Argyll and Sutherland Highlanders and the Gordon Highlanders. From his own 135th he appointed Malcolm Northcote to be on the staff as well as his own regimental sergeant major, RSM Coles, who would be responsible for discipline. All the rest he picked from other regiments.

Toosey chose carefully and his choices were not uncontroversial. Roberts remained on the staff as a hut commander but the man he had used as his translator, Captain Gordon Skinner, who had worked in business in Japan before the war and spoke fluent Japanese, was overlooked. Instead, Toosey chose the young captain from the Argylls, David Boyle, who spoke rudimentary, pidgin Japanese that he had taught himself while imprisoned in Pudu Jail in Kuala Lumpur. Boyle became his adjutant and translator and remained with Toosey throughout the whole of the three and a half years in captivity. The job of interpreter was one of the most delicate and difficult in a situation where yawning cultural caverns existed. Boyle would always translate Toosey's commands verbatim – as best he could – whereas a more experienced Japanese speaker with knowledge of the culture might have demurred from translating commands that he knew might offend. As Toosey said, 'We were not trying to philosophise with them.' Another interpreter, Bill Drower, explained in his memoirs: 'Interpreting was a precarious undertaking; if one had to report something intensely displeasing to one's captors, the odds were high that a beating would ensue.'

Toosey later described David Boyle as one of the most impressive young men he had ever met in his life. Boyle was just twenty-three. He was born in Scotland but educated in Guildford where his father moved to work for the Air Ministry. He followed his father into the Argyll and Sutherland Highlanders, having attended the Royal Military Academy at Sandhurst. In 1940 he was posted to Malaya to join his regular battalion and there he came under the command of the energetic and widely respected Lieutenant Colonel Ian Stewart. Boyle commanded D Company of the 2nd Argylls and fought in Malaya where he was captured at Slim River. He and ten others spent their first night of captivity in a Japanese brothel before they were sent to Pudu Jail in Kuala Lumpur. There he shared a cell with an Australian called Russell Braddon and watched, in anguish, the death of around forty Argylls in Pudu. They died of their battle injuries, of malaria and dysentery. There was almost nothing the doctors in the jail could do for them as they had little medicine and barely any equipment. It was heartbreaking. When the time came for working parties to be sent to Thailand Boyle volunteered immediately, along with Russell Braddon and an American journalist, Eugene Pomeroy, from the *Christian Science Monitor* who had joined the Indian Army.

Other members of Boyle's party from Pudu Jail included Captain Jim Mark, a doctor with the 198th Ambulance Corps, Second Lieutenant Gordon Smith of the Argylls, who had been in the middle of his medical studies when war broke out, and Regimental Sergeant Major Alexander 'Sandy' McTavish.

Toosey chose as his second-in-command Major Reggie Lees. He had arrived the day after Toosey at Tamarkan, in charge of a group that comprised his own men from the 2nd Gordon Highlanders, plus members of British infantry battalions. By the time his men had been welcomed into the camp the number of prisoners in Tamarkan was 1500. The camp strength was further increased to 1650 in November and was to remain at that strength until 1000 Dutchmen arrived in February of the following year.

Reggie Lees became Phil Toosey's closest friend in captivity. He was the only man who called him by his Christian name in three and a half years. Born April 1899, Lees was five years older than Toosey and had a breadth of experience that few others in the administration had. He was a professional soldier and, although an Englishman by birth, had spent his army career with the Gordon Highlanders. Commissioned in December 1917, he was sent to the First Battalion of the Gordons where he fought in Belgium and France. He was wounded but not seriously and after the war he continued to serve with the Gordons. His army career took him to Turkey, Malta, Ireland, India and, on two occasions, to Aberdeen.

At six feet one Reggie Lees was slim built and still very fit. He played cricket with passion and had been appointed Boxing Officer to the Gordons prior to the war. As devoted to his men as Toosey, the two of them hit it off as soon as they met. He inspired people with his warm and generous personality and was admired and loved in the camps; years later men's eyes would fill with tears at the mention of his name. When Toosey was separated from him in May 1943 it was a crushing personal blow.

The Japanese despised ill health considering it a sign of weakness. The doctors received no support from them and often had to make desperate decisions, when faced with impossible demands for fit men for working parties, about whether a man could or could not go to work. All this was to come but Toosey understood that the doctors had a different role in the prison camps. They were no longer fighting a rearguard action with wounded men while the soldiers fought the enemy. The doctors became front-line soldiers in the war against inhumanity, indifference and neglect. They were not fighting the Japanese; they were fighting the attitude of the Japanese.

Historically, at times the relationship between the medical corps and the fighting troops had been an uncomfortable one. Toosey needed his senior medical officer to be a man who was prepared to work within his team, not a doctor who would insist on independence and refuse to accept his authority. He chose Dr Jim Mark from Northern Ireland. At twenty-eight Mark was newly qualified. He had been captured in Malaya and he was in Pudu Jail where he and Robbie Welsh, also a doctor, battled in desperate conditions to treat men suffering from dysentery, beri beri and pellagra as well as from their wounds. It had been a stark induction and when volunteers were called for to go to Thailand Jim Mark had been among the first to step forward.

The relationship and understanding between the colonel and

his doctors was very important. Jim Mark's daughter, Paddy, wrote, 'I think one of the reasons that Phil Toosey was so important to Jim Mark was that in him, Jim saw a reflection of values that he himself espoused and tried to practice. So for him to find himself working with a man of Phil Toosey's stature was not only very reassuring but also encouraged him to build on those values for they were shown to be so worthwhile.'[5] Toosey attached enormous importance to his staff and they were individually and collectively a great strength to him and to the prisoners in Tamarkan. He did his best to defend them against the Japanese, often at the risk of personal injury. In turn they were intensely loyal.

There was only ever a handful of Japanese at Tamarkan, the majority of the guards being Koreans and of them there were only a dozen or so. How was it that fifteen guards could keep 2500 men under control and prevent them from escaping? The answer was depressingly simple. Fear and lack of opportunity. The distance escapees would have to cover in order to get to safety was vast and the jungle environment inhospitable, full of the threat of disease and danger. The Japanese had made it clear in Singapore, even before they forced the prisoners to sign the non-escape paper in September 1942, that they would treat men who attempted to escape with extreme force and, if necessary, would execute them. Even if the prisoners could escape and get to the caves in the hills they could see above Kanchanaburi there was little prospect of them getting help from the local Thais who, at this stage in the war, were inclined to be anti-British. European features were highly recognisable and the Japanese let it be known they would pay a sum of money to anyone who captured and handed over an escaped prisoner, albeit if often a paltry amount. Escape by river was not possible as it flowed towards the Gulf of Siam and away from the Allied forces in Burma and India. Despite dreams and plans of escape the reality was that only a handful of men who even attempted to escape succeeded. The remainder died in the attempt or were executed on recapture.

The Japanese commandant of the camp, for the first two months, was Lieutenant Kosakata: 'a stupid man', Toosey wrote, 'who made himself awkward whenever possible, and although very unhelpful he was not dangerous'. Kosakata refused to be interviewed by Toosey. He summoned him to give orders but otherwise Toosey had to deal with his second in command, the Sergeant Major Teruo Saito. He too was strict and gave few concessions but in Toosey's opinion he was honest and fair.

Saito was unusual in that he was a regular warrant officer from the Imperial Japanese Army. He was thirty-two and had served in the cavalry in China during the 1930s. It was not clear to anyone in the camp why Saito had been sidelined to become a prison guard, a role that carried with it only marginally less stigma than that of being a prisoner of war. The advantage to the prisoners was that Saito knew and understood the military mind. Toosey recognised this, and worked on the premise that there was no problem between two soldiers that need remain unsolved. He also understood that Saito simply wished to do his job and get home. Saito was not as vindictive as some but nor was he a compassionate man. When Toosey explained to him in the summer of 1943 that the duties for one hospital chaplain in a camp for 3000 British, Dutch and Australian servicemen, where deaths were occurring up to four times a day, were too onerous, Saito replied that there was nothing more to be said at a burial than 'Paradise – Amen'. Others did not share Toosey's assessment of Saito; they found him too strict and unbending. One of his Japanese colleagues, Sergeant Ginzo Sahano, who was at Tamarkan from 1943–5 explained: 'Mr Saito believed in military discipline. Certain things could be permitted while others simply could not. He believed that black was black and white was white.'[6]

Another Japanese guard at Tamarkan, Sergeant Murakami, had come from the big prison camp at the base workshops at the Bangkok end of the railway, Nong Pladuk. Murakami had already established for himself a reputation at Nong Pladuk for being kind and generous and at Tamarkan he tried to get the best available facilities and rations for the cookhouse and for the camp canteen. He was hampered by Kosakata and Saito but nevertheless the small amount of help he could give to the prisoners was appreciated.

The remaining guards were Koreans, with whom they had the most trouble. The Koreans on the whole, as almost every prisoner experienced, were very much worse than the Japanese. The simple reason for this, Toosey explained, was that, 'the Japanese had sat on their heads for a very long time and when they got the opportunity of sitting on some white men's heads they took it with both hands'.[7] These men were often peasants with no education and only a few weeks' training by the Japanese Army. The Japanese treated them badly and the Koreans were only too happy to take out their anger on the prisoners. Some were extremely violent and the prisoners soon gave them descriptive nicknames – Mad Mongrel, Dr Death, and at Tamarkan, the Undertaker. The majority of the men in camp had little or no contact with Kosakata or Saito but they did come into contact – and initially conflict – with the Koreans.

Lieutenant Kosakata sent for Toosey the day after he had arrived in camp. He delivered a succinct message through David Boyle which, translated, was an order to provide the labour to build two bridges over the Mae Khlong river. Kosakata saluted and Toosey walked out of his office to deliver this message to the men.

Using prisoners to build a railway to aid the Japanese war effort contravened all international laws governing prisoners of war. The Japanese showed no regard for such niceties and whenever an Allied officer brought up the question of prisoner-of-war conventions they simply dismissed it. The 'disgraced' army had no status in the eyes of the captors. The question Toosey faced was not whether the prisoners should work but how best he could control the situation so that the men were protected, as far as possible, from the Japanese and negotiate the least worst working conditions.

Their job was to build a wooden service bridge and, a hundred metres or so further upstream, a concrete and steel bridge. The monsoon in southern Thailand caused the rivers to rise dramatically. Rainfall in Kanchanaburi in September and October was on average 112 inches out of the total annual rainfall of 280 inches. This meant that the Mae Khlong swelled to over 300 metres wide and the Japanese engineers knew from the outset that this would have to be spanned by a permanent structure rather than a wooden bridge that might be swept away when the river was in spate. Futamatsu, the civilian chief engineer, had been asked to design both the wooden bridge and the concrete and steel one that would replace the wooden bridge as soon as it was ready. The prisoners also had to construct two kilometres of railway embankment either side of the river.

In the film *The Bridge on the River Kwai* British prisoners of war designed and built a large wooden bridge over a fictitious river. It has led people to believe that there was just one bridge constructed on the Thailand–Burma railway. In fact there were in total 688 bridges built along its 415km length and not one of them crossed the Khwae Noi. This number included dozens of little bridges that spanned creaks and gulleys in the mountainous terrain north-west of Kanchanaburi. Of the 688 all but 7 were built of locally grown timber to an American design for wooden structures. This had been developed during the First World War by Merriman and Wiggin and illustrated in a handbook of the same name. A photograph of a Japanese engineer of the 9th Railway Regiment taken in 1942 shows him studying this handbook. Of the seven steel and concrete bridges, six were in Burma and only one in Thailand, designed to span the mighty Khwae Mae Khlong.

The wooden bridge was to be built entirely by hand. The tools used were axes, handsaws and adzes, hand-trucks and man-powered pile-drivers. The men building the embankments leading to this bridge used chunkels and shovels for digging and cane baskets or rice-sack stretchers for carrying the soil away. All the wooden bridges built on the Thai–Burma railway were built to the same pattern. They were described by the Japanese as 'lyonhyakkora' or 'columns of pillars'. Piles were driven down into the river bed then timber crown- and cross-beams were loaded on top and finally, the girders.

Timbers for the wooden bridge were floated down the river where they were manhandled into position by the work parties and then hammered into the silt using an old-fashioned pulley system. Pile-driving was tedious work and went on for several weeks. The pile-driver was a primitive affair, a steel-capped wooden block slung from a pulley and operated by twenty or so prisoners standing on barges anchored mid-stream. The prisoners assigned to this job provided the muscle to pull on the plumb-bob tow-rope. 'The yo-heave-ho work on the site was construction work which in pre-war Japan would have seemed very ordinary but conjectures might be made in consideration of its large scale nature,' wrote Kazuya Tsukamoto in an article in Japanese about the railway. The prisoners found it anything but ordinary. It was desperately hard work for starving men working under a blistering tropical sun with no shirts and often no hats to protect them: 'the monotony of it', wrote Stephen Alexander, 'and the primitive nature of the tools and the sheer numbers of men slaving away – some digging, some in long snaking queues carrying baskets of earth, some chaining sand and stones from the river bed – made for a positively biblical scene'.[8]

Once the piles had been driven into the river bed the cross-beams were heaved into place and the trestle was then ready for the rails. All the material for the railway that could not be cut down from the jungle was brought to Tamarkan by barge. These barges had to be unloaded by the men and the job they all hated most was unloading the rails. It was back-breaking, dangerous work. 'First we would have to heave up the rails into our bent

Pile driving by Stephen Alexander.

arms and then manipulate them from the horizontal up the river bank,' Alexander explained. 'This at once shifted the balance and pairs at the back might suddenly find themselves collapsing and the rail lashing about viciously.'[9] Men were frequently injured doing this work and Dr Jim Mark and his medical team had to deal with fractures, cuts and grazes, the latter turning septic all too quickly in the tropical heat.

'The bridge building site seemed as if it were on fire with enthusiasm,' Futamatsu, the engineer, wrote. 'The construction of the wooden bridge, at a pinch, advanced quickly in this way and in mid-December it was nearly completed. Although made of wood, it showed majestic form, tall and stout, reflected on the surface of the Mae Khlong.' Just a few days later there was a tremendous storm and the wooden bridge was partially swept away. At first the prisoners were delighted but their joy was shortlived when they were ordered to rebuild it in double-quick time.

By February trains loaded with trucks and wagons carrying Japanese troops were crossing the wooden bridge. The prisoners stared in amazement as the first train went over without the bridge collapsing. Few of them had believed that the bridge would stand up to the weight of a loaded train. 'A wooden bridge if well constructed takes the same weight as a steel one', a Dutch railway expert explained, 'but it is far easier to fit and will be far quicker repaired after having been hit, provided one has ready-made piles and logs between any two bridges and sufficient labour.'[10]

At the same time as the wooden bridge was under construction work started on the steel bridge. This was altogether a more serious engineering exercise and here the Japanese were forced to employ heavy machinery as well as the prisoners' labour. The piers for this bridge were built not of wood but of concrete. A temporary wooden coffer dam was erected and filled with earth. Then concrete rings, that had been fabricated by the prisoners on the side of the river using a concrete mixer, were placed into the dam and the earth removed from the centre. As the weight of the concrete rings increased they sank into the river bed. The next task was to remove the silt from under the rings so that they would sink deeper. Futamatsu wanted the foundations to be sunk to 8 metres. Normally such work would be carried out mechanically but the Japanese had been unable to find the necessary specialist equipment in the area. So to begin with this dangerous work had to be undertaken by the prisoners. One of the men who did this was Private Robert Hislop who described his experiences:

> About four of us used to do this work. We used to wear a very old-fashioned diving helmet which was fitted with an air pipe which in turn was fitted to an old-time air pump. We used to have to get inside these concrete pillars and go down to the bed of the river and keep removing the river-bed from under the concrete so that the pillars would sink. This was quite unpleasant as it was quite dark and we had to keep our bodies upright because if you bent over water was liable to get inside the helmet. I cannot remember how long we used to be under water before we came up for a spell, but it certainly seemed like a hell of a long time.[11]

The Japanese allowed Hislop and the other divers extra rations. They continued with this until December when Futamatsu, who had been searching for the right piece of equipment, received a telegram that a Gatmel dredging machine had been located in an industrial area south of Bangkok. This was brought to Tamarkan and work on the concrete pillars for the steel bridge accelerated. Once the excavation had been completed, sand and pebbles, carried by lines of prisoners using baskets and stretchers, were poured into the moulds to make the foundations. On top of the foundations shaped wooden moulds were erected which were to be filled with concrete. Bamboo scaffolding was put up around the moulds on the top of which were platforms for the concrete mixers. 'Up long ramps queues of men chained baskets and sacks of sand, pebbles and cement to feed them and fill the moulds. It was even more Cecil B. De Mille than the building of the wooden bridge because the scale was so much greater, with hundreds of cursing men and excited Nips milling around, barges pom-pomming up the river, tipper trucks squeaking along narrow-gauge supply lines, and over all – in this dry season – the blinding glare of the sun above and the white sand below.'[12]

The pillars were completed by January and the steel work, imported from Java Railways, was hoisted into position over the next few weeks. 'Comb-shaped steel trusses for the girders of the steel bridge called curved-chord Warren-type half-through (Pony-type, Curved Chord Half-through) trusses, make a span of 20.8 metres between piers,' Futamatsu wrote. 'The cross beams were loaded one after another onto the bridge, whose concrete legs had previously been finished and the Mae Khlong bridge was nearing completion.'[13]

Did you help the Japanese to build the bridge? Toosey was once asked in an interview. 'No, we did not help the Japs build their bridge,' he replied. 'We did as little as we could and were as bloody-minded as possible – for which we got severely beaten up. We collected huge numbers of white ants for the wooden bridge and stationed them in various parts and they really did their job properly. And of course we had to mix the concrete. Well, you can perfectly easily make a proper Charlie of mixing concrete if you want to.'[14]

Photograph of the almost completed steel bridge taken by a Thai in the spring of 1943 and given after the war to Arthur Osborne, Toosey's batman.

Despite this robust claim wholesale sabotage was not possible. The prisoners were closely supervised by the engineers who would mete out bashings to anyone who they thought might be slacking, let alone sabotaging the work. As the guards were afraid of the engineers they too would be on the prisoners' backs. Misunderstandings led to as many confrontations as anything else in the early days.

The job of the guards at Tamarkan was to keep the prisoners under control in the camp and to supply a work-force for the Japanese engineers, who were part of the railway engineering unit, for labour on the railway. The Japanese engineers who were responsible for building the railway were quite separate from the guards and they lived in separate camps. The relationship between the railway engineering unit and the camp guards was at best tense and at times dreadful. The camp guards were often failed soldiers, drunks or rice farmers and the engineers had little more regard for them than they did for the prisoners. So the stage was set from the outset for confrontation between any two of the three parties. The engineers demanded a certain number of men made up into working parties and this, initially, was organised by the guards. The men would be called out on to parade, or *tenko*, and then divided up into work groups. It was frequently chaotic. The guards also had to hand out tools to the prisoners each morning and collect them again each evening. They also insisted on counting the men on parade morning and night. This was a lengthy and tedious process for the tired, hungry men because the guards would get confused and the counting had to start again. Tenkos could last over an hour.

Toosey saw that by careful manoeuvring, some of the areas of confrontation could be directly avoided. This was where the relationship with Saito proved to be so useful. Over the first few weeks Toosey went out to work with the men on the bridge as did the other officers at his insistence. At this stage the Japanese did not require officers to work. Toosey was thus able to watch the guards and the engineers and to intervene on behalf of the men if incidents arose, which they did regularly, often as a result of misunderstanding instructions. This had a dual benefit for the men: they knew there was someone prepared to stand up for them and the Japanese were kept in check by his presence.

He always took care to dress smartly and even when he discarded his shirt, in order to preserve some degree of neatness, he ensured that his shorts were clean, his socks pulled up and his shoes, if he was wearing them, polished. He was easily recognised by his webbing belt that he kept whitened. Around the camp he walked more often than not in bare feet or in a pair of clompers, wooden clogs with a strap over the ball of the foot, but out on the bridge he wore shoes. He would also carry a swagger stick. This gave him a certain authority with the guards and even the engineers. He never let his standards slip.

George 'Dutch' Holland remembered being marched back into camp from working on the bridge: 'We'd come back from work so tired and hungry but Toosey would be standing there and he'd shout "Right, lads, bags of swank" and we'd put our shovels over our shoulders and straighten our backs and march into camp. He'd salute the Japanese with a half smile on his face and the men would shout "you bastards".'

Toosey began to negotiate with Saito to try to take control of as many aspects of camp and working life as he could so that he could minimise the amount of contact the prisoners had with the guards. He did this by reassuring Saito and Kosakata that if he had more control the men would behave better. The first thing he cleared was the question of discipline. 'The discipline of the camp was controlled on normal military lines; through a Camp Orderly Room. The men were punished by us for breaches of discipline which affected the well being of the community, such as theft, dirtiness, disobedience of our orders, and on only one occasion can I remember any objection being made to this discipline.'[15]

There was a small hut built beside the camp office that became known as the 'no-good hut' and Toosey used this as a punishment cell. He was clear that if discipline were allowed to break down there would be trouble among the men. Anarchy would reign and the morale in camp would collapse.

This is what happened at the outset at Chungkai camp, just 5 kilometres further up the railway. It was documented in a book by Ernest Gordon called *Miracle on the Kwai*. 'We lived by the law of the jungle, "red in tooth and claw"', he wrote, '– the law of the survival of the fittest. It was a case of "I look out for myself and to hell with everyone else." This attitude became our norm. The weak were trampled underfoot, the sick ignored or resented, the dead forgotten . . . Everyone was his own keeper. It was free enterprise at its worst, with all restraints of morality gone. The officers, as much as the other ranks, became subject to the same decay of morale.'[16] The situation at Chungkai was redeemed by the appointment of Lieutenant Colonel Cary Owtram, another TA officer, who took over command of Chungkai in the summer of 1943. He introduced a police force and imposed order on the camp.

Toosey had no intention of letting morale and discipline sink for even the shortest time. He was strict with the men but not unkind. He had a great sense of community and he held that up as the model of civilised behaviour. Each man in his camp had a duty towards his fellow men and in order to hold on to that he had to be tough on discipline.

Although he ran Tamarkan on military lines Toosey was prepared to dispense with those areas of military tradition that he found anomalous in the prison camp situation. In a most unusual and, for some, controversial move he insisted that officers should sleep in the same huts as their men. 'The officer had the section by the door so that he could oversee the whole hut and if anything went wrong he could attend to it,' he explained. 'Under those conditions one simply had to share the same conditions as the men. I insisted that officers received precisely the same food as the men; we didn't have an officers' mess or anything like that because it would immediately have caused a rift.' [17] The food was distributed as evenly as possible between every member of the camp, officer or man, ill or working. In order to enforce this he regularly oversaw the distribution of food by the cookhouse. He knew full well that some officers in other camps were not fair and got themselves a bad reputation.

On one occasion he heard that one of his men had stolen a blanket from a dying man and sold it to the Thais in exchange for food. Toosey was furious and sent for him. He recognised him immediately as a man he had had up in front of him for running away in the battle for Singapore. He had a good memory for names and faces. 'I know you,' he said to the man. 'No, sir, I've never seen you in my life,' the man replied. But Toosey stood his ground. 'I have you know. I'm just going to tell you this. If you ever dare to step out of line I'll starve you to death and you know I have the power to do it because I've got control of the food. Now, you are going to be beaten up by two regimental sergeant majors behind this hut and if you dare to do anything about it or report me after the war, all I can tell you is that you will suffer more than I will.'[18] From that moment, Toosey recalled, the man never put a foot wrong.

Toosey's outburst was deliberately shocking. He had a clear message for the men in his camp: he was prepared to do anything he could to stand up for them, feed them and get the best conditions from their captors. In return he expected a certain loyalty and a level of discipline. If this were to break down he would have a rabble on his hands and that would undermine all his efforts. When he found men wanting he made an example of them.

He insisted that the officers should go out on to the railway to supervise work so that they could intervene on behalf of their men if it became necessary. Some officers resented this and complained that they could not be seen to be working but he was unimpressed. Their role, Toosey told them, was supervisory but some lent a hand as they found they could not stand back and watch the men lifting impossibly heavy weights or struggling with unwieldy loads.

However, in November the Japanese announced that all officers should join their men in labouring on the railway and if

necessary form officer working parties. This was in direct contravention of the Hague Convention which states that officer
prisoners should not be expected to work. The officers at
Chungkai took a stand against the Japanese and refused.
Eventually the Japanese forced them at gunpoint in a scene very
reminiscent of the film *The Bridge on the River Kwai* when the fictitious Colonel Saito orders a jeep with machine guns to bring the
officers to their senses. One officer at Chungkai in November
1942 recalled: 'Machine guns were posted around us. When the
order to load was given, our commanding officer yielded and
work resumed.'[19]

The same order was received at Tamarkan. It happened on
the day of another incident. The officers, as usual, were on the
bridge looking out for their men. Toosey wrote:

> Kosakata ordered Lieutenant Bridge to get into the cutting and
> work with the men. The officer flatly refused and when
> Lieutenant Kosakata tried to push him, Lieutenant Bridge resis-
> ted. A short tussle ensued and eventually two Japanese guards
> were called over and Lieutenant Bridge was taken back to
> camp, where he was confined in the guardroom. I complained
> immediately and was told that the Camp Commandant had the
> power to execute Lieutenant Bridge if he considered it neces-
> sary. At the same time I was given the order that – in future –
> all officers would work. I replied that this was contrary to the
> Hague Convention which Japan had signed, but at this period
> of the war, the Japanese, believing they were winning, were not
> interested in any International Law.[20]

Toosey called the officers together. David Boyle remembered
the conversation well: 'He told the officers that in his opinion
they would have to work for the Japanese but that he was pre-

pared to insist that they should work with their men rather than in officer-only work parties. In other words they should remain as a buffer between the Japanese and the men; that they would go out with their own particular platoon, their own unit and the Japanese would tell them what to do, they would do it and would also work alongside the men.'[21]

Toosey made it clear that this decision was to be taken by the officers themselves and that he would not insist upon it nor would he order them to work. He said, 'You've got to understand the Japanese mentality. It is no use saying we are doing this under duress and then giving in, because they will only look down on us. What you've got to do is decide: either you are going to work and we will try and get the best terms we can or you are not going to work and you are going to stand there if necessary until they shoot you.'[22] He then said to the officers, 'If you refuse I will stand and get shot with you.' The officers agreed to work and to be seen to be doing so willingly.

Toosey believed that one objective of the Japanese in demanding that the officers work was to humiliate them further in front of the men. That the officers agreed to work willingly and to work alongside their men had exactly the opposite effect. The men became more, and not less, loyal. After a short time Kosakata stopped insisting the officers do manual work but they continued to go out and oversee their men. 'The officer's lot was not a happy one,' Stephen Alexander wrote. 'In the first place he suffered long periods of solitary boredom . . . And then he had to decide how far to brave the Nip's fury by standing up for the men – "they were sick", "had been working too long", "needed a tea break" – and how far to risk the men's scorn as a "Jap-Happy Bastard" by shouting orders to them.'[23]

Toosey was always happy to do manual work in camp and one of the tasks he most enjoyed was chopping wood for the cookhouse. He also helped to dig latrines and malarial drains with his customary energy and enthusiasm. The Japanese could never understand why he was prepared to work like a labourer. For him it provided a welcome respite from camp administration.

During the first weeks at Tamarkan the food was dismal and the combination of inadequate rations and hard manual work had a progressive impact on the health of the men in the camp. They were given broken rice, meagre amounts of meat and a vegetable they called Chinese radish which Toosey complained was like eating small bits of wood. The cooks did their best but thirty-five men cooking for 1650 could turn out little more than what was known as jungle stew. In time they became more proficient at cooking rice in a variety of ways but at the outset it was uniformly dull and tasteless. The starvation rations for those doing heavy manual work were inadequate. Jim Mark reported a steady rise in deficiency diseases and dysentery became a problem once again. He told Toosey that this last was a serious problem that could only be overcome by strict camp hygiene and rigorous self-discipline. On 15 November 1942 they had their first death – a thirty-five-year-old married man from the East Surrey Regiment. He was buried in a graveyard close to the Buddhist temple of Tha Maa Kham, about a kilometre from the camp. Toosey attended the funeral service. It was the first of over two hundred for him at Tamarkan. He attended every one and if necessary took services himself in the absence of the padre.

As the camp settled into a routine Toosey began to see what he could do to improve the lot of the men. Having negotiated with Saito and Kosakata that discipline would be run by his own administration, he then set about taking over other tasks that the guards carried out. He got Saito to agree to one tenko parade a day and for the counting to be done in English, not Japanese. For his part he would get each officer in charge of a hut to count the men in the evening and he would submit the result of that count to the Japanese guardroom. It was a concession and made a difference to the men who, on returning from work on the bridge, could eat as soon as they got back to camp rather than standing around on parade. They might also have time to bathe in the river.

The next concession was to get agreement from Kosakata that British officers rather than the Koreans could hand out the work tools to the men. This removed another point of conflict. Kosakata agreed that Toosey's officers could supply the men for work. The Japanese engineers were persuaded to give the administration a note the night before of the number of men required for work the following day. 'We were able to get the parties ready and there was no mucking about for the troops. All you had to do was to say "Alright thirty men pile driving and two officers and off they went." Again it lessened the strain on the troops themselves,'[24] explained David Boyle.

Then Toosey argued with Saito that if the men were to work hard for the Japanese they needed one rest day a week. By the end of November the men were given one 'yasume' or rest day off per week or ten days. It was not necessarily on Sunday but that did not matter. This was a day when they could do things for themselves: wash clothes, repair kit, make their living spaces in the huts a little more bearable, de-louse their beds and so on. Toosey got permission for sports to take place on yasume days. There was a football league, and if they had the energy they could play basketball, baseball and volley-ball. The officers joined in and there are records in prisoners' diaries of the fiercely fought competitions.

However, all of these concessions counted as naught in comparison to the question of food. Saito was frustrated by the number of sick men in camp and harangued Toosey and Lees for not being able to supply enough men for work. He accused the sick of a lack of moral fibre. In return, Toosey and Lees badgered Saito about the rations. Toosey wrote:

> In conjunction with Major Lees I had many interviews with the Japanese, telling them if they wished the work to be completed according to the schedule they must:
>
> (a)   increase the rations.
> (b)   give the Troops regular working hours.
> (c)   allow one holiday per week.
>
> With the assistance of Sergeant Major Saito, who had obviously handled troops before, (b) and (c) above soon came into force and the rations improved slightly. These measures caused an immediate drop in the sick figures.[25]

Toosey decided that he would object to every random beating up inflicted on the men by the Japanese and the Koreans. He let this be known among the men and they knew they could come to him for support. Occasionally, if a man had done something that he regarded as foolish he would dismiss him, but by and large he defended everyone who came to him with a legitimate complaint. The result for him and David Boyle was often painful as the guards were unpredictable and would take a swipe at one or both of them. Toosey admitted, 'I didn't particularly like being kicked up the arse, for one thing, nor having my head split open with a bamboo cane, and so forth.'[26] Occasionally he thought he could not face another beating up for complaining but the men relied on him and he continued to defend them: 'If you took responsibility as I did there was no question about it, it increased your suffering very considerably. I reached the stage when I said, "I really cannot go into that hut again and get beaten up." I reached the limit, almost, of endurance but then I thought: "They rely on you, you must go."'[27]

One of the more amusing incidents stuck in his mind:

When a Jock from the Gordon Highlanders came to see me and said, in the language of the day, that he had classified, which meant he had been beaten up, I asked him, 'Why?'

He replied, 'Well, I was very bloody minded, so perhaps you had better not complain.'

His head was as thick as two planks and he stood there scratching it.

Finally he said, 'Well, sir, on second thoughts perhaps you'd better, because I don't mind being hit over the head with an iron crowbar but I do object to being knocked into the river, because I can't swim.'[28]

Toosey saw to it that those men and officers who stayed in camp to run it had jobs that kept them occupied beyond the working hours of the men out at work. Even the light sick could contribute to camp life. He tried to ensure that the men returning from the bridge had a hot meal and that things were laid out for them just as they would have been had they been in action. This could be late into the night when, on occasion, the engineers wanted to get a certain piece of work finished. Sometimes, towards the end of the bridge-building time in April 1943, the men did not return until two in the morning. At any one time there were never more than a handful of men in camp and it was a battle to keep the cookhouse stocked with firewood, the latrines dug, attap roofs maintained against decay and the camp clean and hygienic.

In August 1942 the Japanese had announced they would pay officers at the equivalent rate of their IJA counterparts in local currency. 'This unexpected provision clearly reflects Article 23 of the Geneva Convention,' explains Sibylla Jane Flower, 'which directed that "officers who are prisoners of war shall receive from the detaining power the same pay as officers of corresponding rank in the armed forces of that power." By the end of 1942 all officers were paid, at least in theory, on a sliding scale ranging down from the equivalent of 220 Straits dollars for lieutenant colonels down to eighty-five for lieutenants.' [29]

However, the officers received only a very small proportion of this money in practice, the majority being held back for the so-called 'rent, rice and rags' as well as the amount that was deposited in a Japanese bank 'for repayment after the war'. Nevertheless a guaranteed income, however small, was a great advantage to them. The men received money only if they worked and their pay was a mere pittance: 30 cents a day for NCOs and 25 cents for privates by February 1943. With this the men could afford twenty to twenty-five cigarettes and a few duck eggs a week. In Thailand they were paid in the local currency, as Charles Steel explained to his wife Louise in a letter in November 1942:

> The Thai currency system is centred on the TICAL (or BAHT), worth 1/10 pre-war. It is composed of 100 STERANGS. A five cent piece (we call sterangs cents and Ticals dollars) is a small white metal coin with a hole in it. The 10-cent piece is the same, only larger. Notes start at 50c and are issued for 1 Tical, 5, 10, 20, 50, 100, 1000 Ticals. All notes before the war were printed by De la Rue of London, but already the Thai and Japanese are printing their own – and very badly too. [30]

The money for the workforce and officers was given to Toosey at the end of each week and he and his officers would distribute it. At Tamarkan the men received their pay in full; from the officers' pay Toosey deducted thirty per cent. This tax went towards the hospital fund and towards food for the sick men, who the Japanese put on to half rations and no pay.

By early December, Toosey had persuaded Kosakata that it would be better to allow the men to have a canteen in camp rather than letting them deal with the Thais outside the fence. It was another minor triumph. The canteen proved to be one of the saving graces of Tamarkan and the ability to purchase little extra quantities of food made a big difference. The canteen was run by Malcolm Northcote with the cooperation and, at times, assistance, of the Japanese guard Murakami. Northcote was allowed to go with the rations lorry into Kanchanaburi to stock up on food and articles for the canteen. On occasion he was able to exchange news or pick up gossip but this was dangerous and he had to be careful so as not to draw attention to himself.

The single most useful item for sale in the camp canteen was the duck egg. A Thai duck egg was about the same size as a European chicken's egg and had a fishy flavour. The duck egg, Jim Mark told his daughter, saved more lives than the medicine that was available and combined with hygiene, made the most dramatic contribution to health in the prison camps. Duck eggs were sold to camps up and down the railway in their thousands. At a cost of 5 cents each at the end of 1942 the men could afford to buy three or four a week to supplement their diet.

Despite the canteen, men were still hungry and desperate for food. One of the camp rules at Tamarkan was no racketeering. Toosey was firm on this. However, there were men who braved the guards and were prepared to go outside at night to negotiate with the Thais. He struck a deal with these men. They would give him 10 per cent of their profits, for the hospital fund, and in return he would stand up for them if they were caught. It was a good arrangement for both sides as the hospital benefited. The canteen made a profit on average of 4000 Ticals a month and this too was handed over to camp welfare funds.

Toosey asked the administration to save up funds so that a special lunch could be prepared for Christmas 1942. Although they were short of all the traditional ingredients the cooks prepared a meal that included rice rissoles and a sort of plum pudding. In keeping with army tradition the men were served on Christmas Day by the officers. The evening before they had sung carols and had a church service at which one of the guards had solemnly presented Toosey with a note enclosing 30 Japanese dollars for the hospital to mark the birth of his first daughter.

Doctors at Tamarkan still had a quantity of medicine that they had brought with them from Singapore, which came from the Red Cross supplies of September 1942. However, Jim Mark and

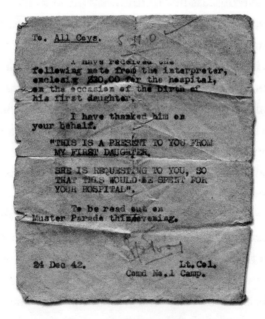

*Photograph of original note given to Jim Mark by Toosey,
to be read out on parade, 24 December 1942.*

his team were frustrated in their attempts to cure the men by lack of the appropriate medicines to treat tropical diseases. Although the Japanese had secured the majority of the world's supply of quinine they restricted the supply to the prisoners. Few of the men had mosquito nets and malaria was with them from the outset. Jim Mark noticed that there were certain men who appeared to be immune to malaria even if they were bitten by the mosquitoes. He was one of these fortunates. Toosey was another.

The scourge in the camp was dysentery. Without emetine it was difficult to treat and Mark told Toosey that the best possible way of keeping the disease at bay was to step up the camp's hygiene. At Tamarkan this was an easier task than in other camps because of the supply of clean water. Nevertheless, it was an important one. Toosey ordered the latrines to be dug deeper than before. The carpenters fashioned wooden covers to keep the flies and maggots in the latrines. Malarial drains were dug, refuse was carefully disposed of, both from the cookhouse and from the canteen, and incinerated; fly-swatting parties brought him evidence of their catches. He insisted on good personal hygiene and would not allow beards on the grounds that they harboured lice and lowered morale. He organised for the bamboo slats on which the men lay to be disinfested on a regular basis. The bamboo was drawn through fire and this killed the bedbugs.

All these measures added together, including Toosey's weekly camp inspection, reduced the disease rate in Tamarkan so that by the end of April 1943, when the bridges were finished, only 9 men had died out of the 2600 who had lived in the camp. That was a death rate, Jim Mark noted with justifiable pride, of less than 0.4 per cent. However, all those who died had succumbed to disease as a result of overwork and undernourishment.

Tamarkan became renowned up and down the railway as the best prison camp in Thailand. With its low death rate and high morale, it was seen as an example of how a camp should be run. Toosey was proud of its reputation although he readily admitted he had been fortunate that the site had access to clean water and the supplies at Kanchanaburi. Its reputation for discipline he put down to the tireless work of his officers on behalf of the men. Some men and officers were critical of Toosey's inner circle. They saw it as a privilege that was denied to others. In fact it was not easy working for Toosey. He led by example and his officers understood that, in his determination to achieve his aims in running the camp to the best of his ability, there would necessarily be confrontation with the Japanese. That would include them too. He wrote of his trials and errors: 'Different methods were necessary to meet the peculiarities of Japanese personnel in charge. Generally speaking, a combination of diplomacy, combined with firmness and good discipline was the most successful, but, in some cases, where one had to handle sadistic semi-civilised and stupid individuals, no methods produced much result.'[31]

Toosey had his critics about other aspects of his leadership too. There were some junior officers and men, particularly among the Argylls, who thought Toosey was too military and that the spit and polish approach was over the top in the prison camps. Some of them did not like the fact that he was prepared to punish his own men while others accused him of being 'Jap happy'. 'He gladly accepted responsibilities,' Stephen Alexander wrote, 'and put many of his fellow colonels to shame by his confidence and vitality; and he saw to it that his reputation impressed the Nips to our advantage, if also to his own. To what extent Phil Toosey was the "fucking gentleman" of the Aussies or the "Jap-happy bastard" of some others was much discussed.' None of this bothered Toosey. His only concern was to look after the physical and emotional well being of his men. 'His methods and military panache impressed the Japanese and they thought him an honourable man.'[32] Ian Watt concluded: 'Looked at from outside, Toosey's remarkable success obviously involved an increase in the degree of our collaboration with the enemy. It is on the interpretation of this fact that the main divergences later occurred in the novel *Bridge on the River Kwai* and the movie.'[33]

In spite of Tamarkan's good reputation and all attempts by Toosey and his team to bring some semblance of order and to sustain morale, there was nevertheless a handful of individuals for whom the greatest challenge was to make a bid for freedom, regardless of the overwhelming odds against success.

6

ESCAPE TO THE JUNGLE

The Japanese refuted the statement that slave labour is not necessarily efficient. It is very efficient if the owners of the slaves have power over life and death and if they have no regard whatsoever for the lives of their slaves.

Warmenhoven Report p. 6

Kosakata was replaced at the end of December by Lieutenant Tagasaki, an officer the men quickly nicknamed 'The Frog'. 'As his name would suggest', Stephen Alexander wrote, 'he was not one of the really vicious Japs but mild and studious in appearance, looking more like a bank manager than an army officer. Though strict he was on the whole fair.'[1] When asked if he had managed to establish any form of relationship with the senior Japanese command at Tamarkan, Toosey responded with a hollow laugh. 'Tagasaki treated me like dirt. He never interviewed me except with his drawn sword on the table. There was no question of any sort of relationship.'[2]

On only the second day of Tagasaki's rule there was an incident. The Scottish regiments had succeeded in smuggling some Thai whisky into the camp in order to celebrate Hogmanay: 'On the night of 31 December 1942 to the swirl of the pipers Argylls ran and reeled through the camp even entering the guardroom. Unfortunately a guard was assaulted and punched by three returning Jock revellers.'³ Toosey was awoken at 3 a.m. by a furious Tagasaki who demanded to know who was to blame. Toosey escorted him on a tour of the huts asking for the men responsible to come forward. By five o'clock no one had owned up so at eight: 'Tagasaki ordered that the whole camp should stand to attention until the culprits came forward.' Toosey recalled, 'I, together with all members of the Highland regiments, asked that we be allowed to do the punishment for the offenders but this was not permitted. Eventually, four men came forward and said that they had been responsible.'⁴ Toosey felt certain that these were not the culprits and thought them very brave for taking the punishment. They were forced to stand outside the guardroom the following day for twelve hours. It was an ugly situation and difficult for Toosey as Tagasaki had only been in command of Tamarkan for twenty-four hours. Their relationship had got off to a bad start.

Tagasaki was strict and he was determined to keep order. Although there were no sentries posted outside Toosey's camp office, the situation in camp was unpleasant as the guards had free access to wander through the camp at will. They would walk into any hut they liked day or night. Such access was against all international laws but protest was useless. The Japanese were paranoid about spying and if they thought the prisoners had any sort of radio they assumed it would be used to broadcast rather than receive news. Therefore the Koreans were ordered to snoop and to be on the lookout for any illicit activities such as writing a diary, listening to a forbidden radio and, later, for much less serious offences, such as not having water in the ashtrays. This made for a nerve-racking atmosphere with the result that the prisoners always had to have a sentry of their own posted at the door of the hut in order to warn of an approach by a guard. When not wandering into the huts the Korean guards would sit on a little bench near the guardroom. One of their number would be on duty on the gate and the other four or five would often sit quite still, but awake, for their entire watch.

The thing that angered Toosey more than anything else about the Koreans, more even than their brutality towards the prisoners, was the way they fed themselves. Their hut had its own kitchen and, in his words, they ate like fighting cocks. Toosey knew of this from personal experience; when the Japanese corporal, who had responsibility for the Koreans, was changed Toosey was ordered to have a meal with him. It was a marvellous spread and he learned from the men who worked in the Korean quarters that they were getting this sort of food all the time. It sickened him. Not only did the Koreans receive better rations anyway but they also stole from the prisoners' rations.

The Koreans and the Japanese had prisoners working for them doing menial tasks such as cleaning their huts, washing their clothes and working in their cookhouse. There were usually four or five prisoners working in this way and they were easily recognised in the camp as they were the only well fed men. 'Those jobs were very highly prized,' Toosey said, 'but on the other hand they were very decent about it because they would take considerable risks. If a man was dangerously ill I would ask them if they could get a bit of extra food and they nearly always got it for me from the Japanese cookhouse. They smuggled what they could, but only for a single individual.'[5] It would have been impossible for the men working for the guards to do more than this and anything they could steal would have been a mere drop in the ocean for 2500 hungry men.

Flare-ups and arguments between the Koreans and the prisoners were regular occurrences, particularly at the beginning. On one occasion David Boyle lost his temper with a guard. 'We were counting off working parties and there was a particularly thick Korean guard who said he wanted twenty-eight men in one party. I pointed out to him that there were twenty-eight men there. He started arguing and one thing led to another. I called him a stupid so and so and then he hit me and then I let go in the vernacular.' The guard, who by this time was used to hearing the men swearing, started laying into Boyle with his rifle butt. By the time Toosey managed to intervene physically and stop the fight the guard had broken Boyle's arm and several ribs. Toosey helped him to his hut where he ordered him to go to bed and asked the doctors to make him as comfortable as possible. The working parties went out that day but when they returned they found Toosey standing guard in front of the hut where Boyle was lying.

He determined to make an example of this case and show the Japanese that they could not just hit people, particularly key people, and get away with it. When the Japanese called for Boyle that evening Toosey sent them a message to say that he was ill and that as no one else could speak Japanese there would be no working parties the following day. 'There was quite a scene but he just stood firmly at the hut door and said, "No, I don't understand Japanese." And eventually, the Korean guard who had come knew that it was more than his life was worth to strike Toosey so he retired and there was no work for about two days.'[6] The strike was finally resolved when Saito punished the guard who had beaten up Boyle and the camp went back to work.

In late January 1943 six men planned an escape attempt from Tamarkan. In the film *The Bridge on the River Kwai* Colonel

Nicholson tells Commander Shears that there will be no escape plan: 'Of course, it's normally the duty of a captured soldier to attempt escape', he says, 'but my men and I are involved in a curious legal point of which you are unaware. In Singapore, we were ordered to surrender by Command Headquarters, ordered, mind you. Therefore, in our case, escape might well be an infraction of military law. I suggest that we drop the subject of escape.'[7] Toosey's attitude was very different from Nicholson's. In Singapore Toosey had obeyed General Percival's order following the surrender that officers should stay with their men rather than attempt to escape, but he paid no attention at all to the Japanese order signed under duress by Lieutenant Colonel Holmes following the Selerang incident in September 1942. Not only did he make no attempt to stop the escape, he in fact offered to help the men who were brave enough to try. Stephen Alexander recalled Lieutenant Stuart Simmonds, who went out on working parties with the drivers, reporting back to Toosey on possible escape routes. The local farmers warned Simmonds that 'escape was hopeless, not merely because of the jungle but because prisoners would be instantly recognisable'.[8]

Toosey was privy to the secret at the outset. The preparations were thorough and the men involved all felt they had a good chance of making it back to British lines. 'They came to see me, Captain Eugene C. Pomeroy of the 2/12 F.F. Rifles of the Indian Army and Lieutenant Eric Howard of the 80th Anti Tank Regiment,' Toosey recalled. 'Pomeroy was an American journalist, Howard was the son of Lord Howard, a very splendid young man . . . Four privates, all from the East Surrey Regiment, formed the other part of the group, Privates Cleaver, Dorval, Richardson and Croker. I said I would like to go with them and they responded that I must not, for if I did the morale of the troops would break.' Pomeroy pointed out, too, that it was

Toosey's duty to stay with the men. '"Well", I said, "it's entirely up to you, if you wish to have a go. I will hide your disappearance for as long as I can."' Toosey in fact managed, by means of moving men around on the parade ground during tenko, to cover their disappearance for three days. 'He had to report them missing,' Private Fred Eva explained in an interview in 1999, 'because we never knew when the Japs would call a snap search. He himself reported they were missing. It was a clever ploy really because it looked as though he was on the guards' side.'[9]

The men were at this stage still relatively fit and had saved up a little money for the escape. Pomeroy had made himself cards with questions written in English on one side and in Thai on the other. The preparations were, however, inadequate and although Toosey had given them a month's worth of hard rations they would always be short of medicine. Soon after they escaped they split up into two parties, Pomeroy and Howard making their own way into the jungle. There was a real sense of excitement in camp for the first few days but this soon came to an end.

The four soldiers from the East Surrey Regiment were captured after ten days on the run. They were brought back through the camp, where they spent an hour during which Toosey was able to talk briefly to them and hear their story as well as getting some idea of what had become of the other two men. Then they were taken off into the jungle towards Chungkai where they were forced to dig their own graves. The prisoners in Tamarkan heard shots and knew they had been executed.

It was a full fortnight after this that the two officers were recaptured. They had been spotted by local Thais and sold to the Japanese. They were brought back into camp on the back of a lorry and interrogated for three days by the Kempei Tai, the Japanese secret police. 'The power behind the whole Japanese discipline,' Toosey explained later, 'lay with the Kempei Tai. They were a body comparable to the Gestapo in Germany and trained in the most extreme forms of sadism. When any prisoners were handed over to them for examination before trial they were always beaten up and subjected to any form of torture the Kempeis thought fit to use.'[10] Fred Eva remembered seeing Pomeroy and Howard coming into camp: 'It wasn't so much the fact that they were dishevelled. It was the look in their eyes, the hopelessness in their eyes. They knew they were finished.' Toosey knew they were being horribly tortured and he made endless requests to Tagasaki to intervene but he was always turned down.

Three days later Pomeroy and Howard were put on the back of a truck and driven out of camp. No one had been allowed to speak to them but they did succeed in stealing from the Japanese the diary Eugene Pomeroy had kept. It was a heart-breaking document. The diary spoke first of their euphoria at being free, of hearing the cock crow in the morning, of their hopes and plans. They had had to keep close to the river as they needed access to water but gradually they became ill, their progress shortened each day and then they got malaria. Their early joy was replaced in the diary by despair and finally recognition that they would not succeed in escaping. Toosey said later that they had gone the wrong way. 'Instinctively', he said, 'you go towards your friends and away from your enemies. In fact they should have gone towards Bangkok and not away from it. I will always have that on my conscience that I didn't advise them to go towards Bangkok.' The fact was the two men were instantly recognisable as Europeans even in multi-cultural Bangkok and it was most unlikely they would ever have managed to get away from Thailand at that stage in the war. They had a price on their heads and sooner or later somebody would hand them over to the Japanese.

The two officers were taken out in a truck with an escort of six guards. 'The truck travelled two miles, as checked later in the reading on the speedometer, and returned without them,' Toosey wrote. 'The local Thais and, subsequently, the Koreans, told us that they had been bayoneted.' Later research showed that they were probably driven to the vicinity of Tamarkan graveyard where they had to dig their own graves before being bayoneted, the customary form of execution for a Japanese officer.

'When the Japs did discover their absence,' Toosey wrote in his report at the end of the war, 'The Kempei Tai were sent into the Camp and these questioned very closely all men who had been sleeping in close proximity to the absentees.' Toosey could see that this situation would lead to unnecessary suffering so he told Saito that he alone had known of their intention to escape and that he should therefore shoulder the responsibility. Saito was furious and roundly condemned Toosey. He was forced to stand to attention outside the guardhouse for a day in the full tropical sun. It was a public punishment, meant to set an example to the men and to humiliate Toosey. More significantly, however, it was for the benefit of the much-feared Kempei Tai. It was, in effect, a punishment to save Saito from loss of face but it also unques-tionably saved Toosey from being interrogated by them on that occasion. This strengthened the bond of understanding between Toosey and Saito. It was never a friendship but a degree of respect that each had accepted the other's role. 'After that', Toosey said, 'Saito did what little he could to help us.'[11]

Other prisoners were sceptical. Remembering the same event, Stephen Alexander wrote fifty years later:

They [Pomeroy and Howard] were betrayed by Thai police, brought back roped together – I remember the sickening silence in the camp as they passed through – and thrown into the guardroom. Of course there was hell to pay. Toosey had covered for them all for three days, and then on a morning roll call a discrepancy was spotted. He confessed that six men had escaped and the Nips laughed heartily – until they realised he was serious. Thereafter a man only needed to drop his shaving brush through the fence and fish for it to be savagely beaten for attempting to escape. As for Toosey, he was made to stand to attention all day in front of the guardroom; he had betrayed the trust in him, and favours were no longer to be granted. The scene was darkening everywhere.[12]

The mood in Tamarkan had changed for ever. This had as much to do with the arrival of 1000 Dutch prisoners from Java in February 1943 as it did with the execution of Pomeroy and Howard. When the Dutch first marched into Tamarkan the Allied prisoners were surprised by them. The Netherlands East Indies Army comprised an eclectic mixture of men from Holland, colonials and ex-pats from Java, Sumatra and other islands of the East Indies and a large proportion of Javanese Dutch. They ranged in age from fifteen to sixty-nine and some of the older men had been in the equivalent of the Home Guard. 'There was an inherent problem in the Dutch army of which the other Allies were initially unaware and this was the question of the Eurasian Dutch soldiers. Joining the Army in the Dutch East Indies conferred on the natives of Sumatra, Java and so on a certain social standing that the native Dutch found unacceptable.'[13]

Initially, there was some jealousy and jostling for position. The Dutch had better equipment than the British prisoners and that gave rise to a round of stealing that had to be brought quickly under control. After a few weeks things evened out and they found a way of getting along together without acrimony. Five extra huts had been constructed to accommodate the newcomers and a Dutch cookhouse was erected which prompted a healthy rivalry between it and the British counterpart. The British doctors were concerned by the attitude of the Dutch to hygiene, particularly when preparing food. Jim Mark voiced this concern and urged Toosey to keep up the standard of hygiene in the camp to control the spread of disease.

Dutch senior officers were not as inclusive towards their men as Toosey's. In the first round of discussions about camp administration Toosey made it clear that there was no question of shared leadership in the camp. 'I always insisted on being in complete command, since dual command is unsatisfactory, but other nationalities always had their own commanders and staff who promulgated my orders to their own people. This method was completely satisfactory, provided scrupulous fairness was observed. Our relations with the Dutch troops in particular have been very satisfactory.' He proposed to Lieutenant Colonel Scheurer that he should continue as the officer in charge of the Dutch troops and that he should report directly to Toosey. Scheurer would have his own adjutant, Lieutenant de Grijs, and the rest of the camp administration would remain unchanged. Toosey and Scheurer quickly established a good working relationship.

For their part the Dutch, and particularly the Javanese, brought with them a wide and useful knowledge of jungle food and medicine. While out on working parties they were able to identify roots, shoots and leaves that could be added to the cooking pot, bringing additional vital nutrition and vitamins to their poor diet. They were also better versed than the British doctors in tropical medicine and once again their knowledge of native plants was helpful.

Some of the Dutchmen spoke good English and others were anxious to improve theirs, so that there was communication between the groups of prisoners, despite their separate huts and cookhouse. One Dutch prisoner, Dick Van Zoonen, was keen to practise his schoolboy English and made good use of conversations with the British. He had an excellent visual memory so at the beginning he would ask the English how this or that word was spelled. He was sometimes nonplussed when they told him they did not know how to spell it, just how to pronounce it.

By the time Van Zoonen arrived the river was low and the work on the bridge was not threatened by the monsoon rains or winter storms. One of the most unpleasant and back-breaking tasks he recalled was to carry drinking water to the Japanese anti-aircraft position above Tamarkan. The position was sixty metres above the river and the water was carried in forty-litre barrels hung between two bamboo poles on the thin, bare shoulders of two prisoners. The Japanese were already anxious that the RAF would attack the bridge in due course.

By the end of April 1943 work on the steel bridge was almost complete. Unlike the film there was no elaborate unveiling ceremony, nor was the bridge sabotaged. The first to cross the steel bridge was an infantry regiment, on foot. The prisoners were handed a copy of a letter from the Japanese that read:

TO ALL ENGLISH AND DUTCH

Since coming here for the construction of the MEKURON BRIDGE, all men have worked very hard, day or night, rain or fine, through scorching heat, mastering every difficulty and have obeyed Japanese orders.

I am very satisfied with the result achieved. I now give a letter of thanks to all men for their work.

Take good care of yourselves and keep your chins up. And I hope you will return to our camp safe and in good spirits.

And I pray to God for the sake of all men.[14]

With that the prisoners were organised in groups to go further up the railway. Toosey made repeated appeals to be allowed to go with his men but he was refused. The Japanese told him he was to remain behind in Tamarkan and to run it as a hospital camp. He was to be left only David Boyle, H.S. Woods his quartermaster, and Dr Jim Mark from his original close-knit team. Reggie Lees, to Toosey's great sadness, was sent off with a plate-laying party. The two men were not to meet again in camp until September 1944. Groups from the English and Scottish regiments went up to the Kinsayok region and the Dutch to Lin Tin.

Those men were to witness first-hand the desperate conditions of the camps in the jungle. The monsoon, overwork, malnourishment and cholera thundered down on them. They were subjected to the worst conditions imaginable. As Toosey's staff officer in a later camp commented: 'Up-jungle nothing held the beast in check.'[15]

What was the Thailand–Burma railway for? The Japanese needed to get troops and stores to Burma in order to protect the westernmost land of their new empire and to launch their planned invasion of India. The route they had been using was by sea but their ships were vulnerable to torpedo attack and they realised they would have to find a more secure and reliable route overland. By 1942 this need had become more urgent and it was decided to begin work on the railway that summer.

The route the Japanese chose ran from Nong Pladuk, west of Bangkok, to Thanbyuzayat in Burma where it joined up with an existing railway that ran to Rangoon. The distance was 415 kilometres, roughly the same distance as London to Paris, and for all but 60 kilometres the railway was to cut through jungle, hills, rocky outcrops and curve around steep hillsides in some of the most inhospitable and disease-ridden country on the planet. The Japanese carried out a feasibility study in 1939–40 which concluded that this railway could be built by two railway regiments in approximately twelve months.

After the war some Japanese, and indeed a few prisoners, claimed that the Thailand–Burma railway was built without a survey of the area having been done first. A historian of the railway, Colonel Warmenhoven, wrote in 1947: 'The achievement to build a railway right through the jungle with hundreds of technical problems of the first order is so great in itself that the Japanese hardly need to add to it by boasting they did it without any previous survey and only using the existing very approximate maps.'[16]

In fact far more prisoners of war agreed that the Japanese built the railway to a more or less complete survey plan. They found evidence of the survey at various points along the route, including torn

Ren-ichi Sugano, 1942, one of the Japanese engineers and Company Commander of the 9th Railway Regiment. He kept a secret photographic record of the construction of the railway.

flags on trees, distinct traces of former paths to the river and 'some prisoners even claimed to have seen German survey maps with Japanese translations on them in the hands of Japanese officers'.[17] Warmenhoven wrote, 'Another indication was that when a mistake was made near Kinsayok where the track was dug out too deep in the rock and for [a] kilometre's length a raised track had to be built, the Japanese inspecting officer referred repeatedly in his excited harangue to a map which gave the accurate heights of the terrain, which map the local Jap seemed to have badly interpreted.'[18]

What had prevented anybody from considering the possibility of building a railway between Thailand and Burma prior to the war was the question of labour. There was insufficient labour in the local area around Kanchanaburi and to import labour from other parts of Thailand would have meant the same problems with accommodation, food and communication as the Japanese found. What the Japanese now had in plenty, however, was slave labour.

On 5 June 1942 a zero kilometre signpost was hammered into the ground at Nong Pladuk, 5 kilometres east of Ban Pong where a staging camp was built to deal with prisoners coming from Singapore to work on the railway. The first stretch of track from Nong Pladuk to Kanchanaburi, at the 57-kilometre mark, crossed easy, flat terrain and presented no major obstacles. The first big engineering problem was crossing the Mae Khlong at Tamarkan. From Tamarkan to Chungkai the railway ran more or less straight for some 5 kilometres to where the next significant problem was encountered. Close to the riverbank the prisoners had to hack a cutting through a 100-metre-long and 15-metre-deep rock crag. The prisoners used crowbars, hammers and explosives to remove 10,000 cubic metres of rock. There were many serious injuries during the construction of this cutting. After 50 kilometres beyond Chungkai came one of the largest structures on the railway: three viaducts linking narrow ledges blasted out of the rockface over 30 metres above the river. The trestle-bridge construction clung to the steep hillside and snaked around its rocky profile in an S-bend for 300 metres. It was known as the Wang Pho Viaduct. It took six months and 2000 men to build it. From Wang Pho the railway track led up into the jungle towards a place called Hin Tok Mountain and from there to Kinsayok, Lin Tin, Tha Khanun and Songkurai, 288 kilometres from Nong Pladuk, near the Three Pagodas Pass and one of the remotest regions on the railway.

Work had started on the Burma end of the railway at the same time and the initial programme was for the work to be completed by December 1943. However, by February 1943 the Japanese became worried. Ports in Burma, including Rangoon

Will Wilder sketch of Wang Pho viaduct.

and Moulmein, were being mined from the air and this was creating additional hazards to the sea traffic and thus to their vital supplies. They already had 40,000 Allied prisoners working in Thailand and Burma but the Japanese realised this was not enough, so they began to bring in prisoners from the Dutch East Indies, which is where the consignment of 1000 Dutch at Tamarkan came from. Then they began to bring up more prisoners from Singapore and to recruit Tamils, Burmese and Javanese. Most of the labourers who worked on the Thailand stretch of the railway were Tamils who came from the British rubber plantations in Malaya. There they had enjoyed good care and medical treatment, and the move up to Thailand, where they were left entirely to their own devices, was a devastating blow. They came in their thousands, bringing their wives and children, as the Japanese had told them they would receive good food and light work. 'Most of them had already suffered considerably in the period between the loss of Malaya and their transfer to Siam,' Warmenhoven wrote. 'Many of them were accompanied by their families. Nothing could be worse than their fate.'[19] By the summer of 1943 there were 60,000 Allied prisoners of war and over 150,000 Asian labourers working on the railway.

All these extra men put a great strain on the Japanese infrastructure in Thailand and in particular on the woefully inadequate medical stores. As the railway progressed and it moved further away from the base at Kanchanaburi and into the jungle, so the problems increased. Camps were often temporary and the huts, if such existed, were shabbily made and poorly maintained. Often men were sleeping in grossly overcrowded, leaky tents. Some had to put up with no cover at all. Up country the food supply was less reliable than in the base camps. The Khwae Noi river, which was the main supply route for food, was low in the dry season and the area towards the Three Pagodas Pass was always difficult to service. Supplies, which often lay in the open in sacks or baskets for days on end as they were towed in barges upstream, frequently arrived rotten. And, of course, further away from the base camps the guards were more arbitrary in their rough treatment of the prisoners.

Three things happened in May 1943 to make the plight of the men further up the line ghastly beyond anyone's nightmares. First, the Japanese decreed that the railway should be completed by August and not December 1943, as first planned. This decision ushered in the so-called 'Speedo' period, when men were forced to work harder and faster, during the night and in shifts so that sometimes they were working for eighteen or more hours at a stretch. They barely had time to eat when they got back to the camps and were often too exhausted to do anything other than sleep. The Japanese drove them like slaves. As the days turned into weeks the situation deteriorated. Warmenhoven wrote:

> Sick and half sick people were whipped out of their huts and forced to work. The work started early in the morning and lasted until late at night. In many camps people died by the hundreds from ill treatment, lack of food, overwork and diseases. The speed in which the line was built was miraculous. Bridges, viaducts, deep cuttings in hard rock, embankments, everything seemed to get into existence by magic, in reality however by the work of desperate men.[20]

Secondly, the monsoon broke towards the end of May and this added to their discomfort. Rain fell incessantly and the men were always soaked. So were their belongings in their makeshift huts or tents. The camps turned into filthy quagmires and men slithered and slipped in bare feet, broken boots or clompers. The sun seldom penetrated the jungle canopy. Latrines overflowed. Food supplies were interrupted, sometimes for days, while the traders battled with the now swollen river and the inaccessibility of many of the camps. When one part of the railway was finished the men were told to pack up and march through the jungle to the next working site. Australian journalist and prisoner Russell Braddon wrote: 'The jungle, though invisible, made its presence felt with vines that tripped and bamboo spikes that pierced, but most of all by a faint, all pervading stink of leaf mould, bugs in the bark of giant trees, fungus and stagnant water. No place that smelt like that could be meant by God to be inhabited by man.'[21]

There was no time to organise the camps, to improve the facilities. Lieutenant Louis Baume kept a diary throughout his three and a half years in captivity. Originally in a camp at Nong Pladuk, he was moved up to the jungle in spring 1943: 'Everything in the camp is of the same drab colour: the bamboo and attap huts, grey with age and decay; the mud, a uniform dirty brown; even the sky and the trees are grey and dripping, for the sun rarely breaks through. And in the camp, grey skeletons clothed in filthy rags, with dirty matted hair and eyes, dull and lifeless, staring out of cadaverous faces; rarely a smile, never the sound of laughter or song; and the air, heavy with gloom and hopelessness.'[22]

Thirdly, and most destructively of all, a cholera epidemic raged through the jungle. This most deadly and feared of diseases appeared in the camps in May 1943, cutting a swathe through the starving, exhausted men, moving inexorably through the water and the flies to the next camp. The Japanese were terrified of cholera, they ordered the doctors to isolate the patients in tented areas away from the main camp and they themselves would take precautions such as wearing masks or spreading lime around their compounds. The disease spread. Few of the Allied doctors had ever been confronted with it before but they recognised it all right when it appeared among the men. 'Cholera is a disease that makes chronic diarrhoea look like constipation,' Dr Rowley Richards of the AIF warned the men in his camp. 'Never drink unboiled water – it's really not worth the risk.'[23]

'I had never seen a case', Dr Stanley Pavillard wrote, 'but I was almost obsessed by the fear of it. The section of my textbook on tropical diseases which dealt with cholera was the only part of that book which escaped being used as cigarette paper. Now this terrifying thing was at work and near us; I gave further and more urgent lectures, and insisted that full precautions were to be rigorously observed.'[24]

The onset of the disease is sudden and the signs are unmistakable. 'Cholera broke out and every day more men suddenly vomited a greenish fluid, their bowels melted, their flesh withered off their bones and – looking like strips of potato that had been baked to a crisp in the oven and allowed to go cold – they died.'[25]

It was not only the Allied prisoners who were dying of cholera but also the Asian labourers. There was no hierarchy in the Tamil camps and no organisation. The men were driven out to work and had no time to make the camp habitable, to dig latrines or even to build themselves proper shelter. As a result, disease spread like wildfire and the death toll in their camps shook even the Japanese. When cholera struck things went from bad to disastrous in an instant. Without any sort of administration and no doctors to help them the Tamils died in their thousands. In one camp alone, next to a British camp, 240 men died in one twenty-four-hour period. The Japanese ordered the prisoners to bury the labourers' dead along with their own. It was a desperate business. Dr Pavillard described the scene: 'The cholera compound was hellish in every way. The stench from the burial pit was everywhere. When one approached the pit to use it one saw bubbling millions of maggots. The cholera victims from the

Sick and Dying: Cholera, Thailand, 1943 *by Ronald Searle.*

Asian camp had no doctors or orderlies to look after them, and the Japanese made no provision at all for them to have food or water. They were just dumped in our camp to lie on the ground in the open until they died or were taken by us into a tent.'[26]

The doctors did everything they could and were endlessly inventive. Dr Pavillard fashioned a distillation apparatus out of an army food container, some old stethoscopes and the ubiquitous bamboo. It was primitive but it worked, so he built a second one, and with this he was able to rehydrate intravenously some of the victims and thus give them a chance of surviving. 'I managed to save many lives in this way,' he wrote, 'pouring anything up to eight or ten pints of my saline solution into the patients' veins every twenty four hours'. Dr Rowley Richards had a similar arrangement in his camp and out of six hundred men he lost only thirty-four to cholera, a remarkable achievement attained only by sheer hard work and a grim determination not to let it wipe out his men. He and others instituted the strictest hygiene rules: every drop of water had to be boiled, swimming in the river was forbidden and the cholera patients were isolated from the main camps. The cholera compounds became places of fear and death.

Terrible though cholera was, it was only one of the diseases in the jungle that was claiming lives. The deficiency diseases that had first appeared in Changi and the Thailand base camps began to spread out of control: beri beri, dysentery and pellagra. Then there was malaria. Without mosquito nets and quinine there was nothing the doctors could do to prevent or cure it. Even the Japanese had to acknowledge that men who were suffering from one or more of these conditions could not be treated in the jungle camps.

By mid-April 1943 the Japanese had become sufficiently concerned about the health of the prisoners working on the railway, and the threat that this posed to their timetable, that they began to make arrangements for the very sick to be evacuated to dedicated hospital camps in Burma and Thailand. They had a plentiful supply of prisoners in Singapore so they made arrangements for these men to be brought up to Thailand in order to replace the sick.

The camp commandants of the jungle camps learned about these plans on 16 April but it was only announced at the very last minute that medical officers from the jungle camps would be required in the base area. It must have seemed a very bitter loss in the terrible circumstances of Hintok, about 100 kilometres north-west of Tamarkan. An Australian doctor who became a legend on the Thailand–Burma railway, Lieutenant Colonel Edward 'Weary' Dunlop, was about to lose one of his senior medical officers, Dr Arthur A. Moon. He had the highest opinion of Arthur Moon and would feel his loss keenly. He wrote in his diary on 28 April 1943: 'We were told that one MO must go to K'buri base hospital, so after a brief discussion Major Moon started to pack immediately. This is a serious loss as Arthur has done magnificent work with the sick and is one of the most thorough, loyal and capable souls living.'[27]

As Dr Moon packed his bags and made his journey towards Tamarkan, Toosey received instructions that Tamarkan was to become a hospital camp. As a work camp it had had its problems of organisation, and he had come up against the brutality of the Japanese and Koreans, but he knew the attitude of the Japanese towards the sick would bring new problems. This situation was going to be a further test of Toosey's ability to manage the Japanese. Up to now, he and his administration had tried to prevent the worst excesses of the guards and engineers and successes had been small but significant – rest days, regular working hours and slightly improved rations. Now Toosey had to run a hospital and he had to establish an administration that would work with a completely different focus and with medical officers, a subgroup of men with their own agenda.

By and large, the doctors in Thailand found themselves in an unimaginable and appalling situation for which none of their training had prepared them. This was particularly true in the camps up jungle where they were so far from supplies of food and medicine. Here they were ruled by irrational despots with whom there was no reasoning. Their values and principles were trampled underfoot. It was as though, stripped of all diagnostic aids and therapeutic agents, they had been flung back into the darkest of dark ages when famine and pestilence stalked the land, decimating populations and destroying all community and social life. Their job was all but impossible yet they had, somehow, to adjust to circumstance and press forward with their best efforts.[28]

'To the outsider our quick, matter-of-fact manner of handling mangled humanity might have appeared callous', wrote Dr Pavillard, 'but inwardly we suffered and felt ourselves ageing as the war progressed. For reward we had our patients' trust and gratitude.'[29]

At the base camps, such as Tamarkan, the doctors at least had some chance of creating order. Toosey and Dr Jim Mark had already seen to basic hygiene so when Moon walked into the camp his first impression was positive. 'I arrived at Tamarkan in the evening of 1 May 1943. We were warmly welcomed by Colonel Toosey and his staff, were fed, had time for a quick look round the empty camp and then bedded down in one of the large huts. My immediate reaction was a feeling of relief on having arrived at a clean, well established camp, under the command of a friendly and energetic British officer.'[30] Arthur Moon was a well-respected gynaecologist from Sydney. He was in his early forties, of slight build and had a quiet, polite authority that belied an iron will and a warm sense of humour. His nephew, Peter Jones, described his brows 'furrowed in eager concern and his twinkling attentive eyes'.[31] The moment he and Toosey met there was a mutual understanding and respect. This turned into a warm, lifelong friendship.

Moon had been captured on Java with Lieutenant Colonel Weary Dunlop. From Java, via Singapore to Hintok in Thailand, he had witnessed the devastating effect of a poor diet and terrible working conditions on the men in his camp. He was a stern and outspoken critic of the Japanese attitude towards rations and he had already submitted a long report on A-Vitaminosis to the Japanese command before the end of 1942, warning of the dire consequences of this on the health of the prisoners. While in Java he had also experimented with yeast and protein as a help in the battle against vitamin-deficiency diseases and this knowledge he brought to Tamarkan.

He had seen in the jungle the effect of loss of morale. At one camp near the river at Konyu, a group of British officers had suffered particularly badly. They were bearded, long haired and walked around in pyjamas and sarongs. It had given Moon and Dunlop pause for thought and they renewed with increased vigour their lectures to the men on the importance of hygiene, discipline and morale.

It was obvious to Toosey that he had in Moon not only a doctor of great experience and knowledge but a man he could trust. Moon had an exceptionally sympathetic bedside manner which made a lasting impression on his patients: 'I don't remember his face now at all,' Kevin Fagan wrote fifty years later, 'but I do remember the kindness, the compassion and most of all that he believed in me, something that brings its own comfort in a degraded life.'[32]

Toosey appointed Major Moon above Captain Jim Mark, and being a thoughtful and modest man Moon asked politely whether Mark had any objection to his taking over as Senior Medical Officer. Mark was relieved and delighted to work alongside him. It was a great reassurance to have a surgeon in the camp, especially one with the experience and authority of one of Sydney's most respected surgeons, albeit a specialist in gynaecology. Before the first sick men arrived in camp the medical team had grown to nine doctors – four Dutch, four British and one Australian – plus forty-five medical orderlies.

Tamarkan was a hospital only in name; the Japanese allowed no additional building. The layout of the huts made examination of patients cumbersome and difficult. Ideally there should have been individual beds but at first this was not possible given the restrictions of space. The doctors found themselves having to clamber onto the bamboo platforms to examine their patients in the semi-darkness. 'Hospitals suggest hygiene and a beautiful clean environment,' George 'Dutch' Holland, a medical orderly at Tamarkan, said, 'here it was a compound for desperately sick people.'

The orderlies were unsung heroes of the hospital huts in all the camps. At Tamarkan most were qualified and attached to a medical team but in the jungle camps they were principally volunteers. 'The only qualification', Russell Braddon, one such orderly, wrote, 'was how to empty a bed pan.'[33] These men worked in a strange world; they stayed awake at night and watched while others slept and died. They were tireless and unselfish. Often they knew they could not help the sick but their attention and kindness brought hope into the degrading hospital huts. 'The gratitude of men for a drag upwards as they tried to rise, or a restraining arm as they fell back too quickly. The supreme pathos of 200 dying men who, relaxed and unselfconscious in their sleep, looked like children . . .'[34] Sometimes they had to bully the patients for their own good, force them to take a mouthful of food or move to prevent sores when every bone in their bodies ached.

The first distribution of medicines for the hospital at Tamarkan was woeful: 'Our supply of drugs, brought up from Singapore, was practically exhausted and issues from the Japanese were negligible. The first I received for a hospital of 3,000 patients was a small bottle of iodine crystals, three bandages and four aspirin tablets,'[35] Toosey wrote. On the other hand he knew he had to give Dr Moon the administrative and moral support he required. One of the most useful roles Toosey could perform was in isolating the doctors and medical orderlies from the Japanese and Korean guards so that they could concentrate on their medical work rather than having to run the gauntlet of camp organisation. Toosey set up a command structure whereby all the camp and hut administration was done by non-medical officers who reported directly to him. They dealt with discipline, food, welfare, camp maintenance and amenities such as sport and entertainment. Each hut had three officers and an NCO to take responsibility for the individual concerns of their group of men. Moon had charge of all matters medical and reported to Toosey. This meant that the doctors need only concern themselves with medical matters, which was not the case in other camps. When the senior command failed to create a culture which protected not only the sick, but also the medical staff, doctors up and down the line were rendered impotent to protect their patients. The smooth running, efficiency and, above all, morale at Tamarkan made a big difference to the success of the hospital. Moon summed this up in his camp report: 'The success of this dual control depended on the harmonious relations and co-operation between the medical and non-medical staff. This scheme was entirely successful and continued for the duration of the hospital.'[36]

7

TAMARKAN BASE HOSPITAL

I watched the doctor in my camp – a certain A.A. Moon, an Australian gynaecologist – cut off a leg underneath a mosquito net with a local anaesthetic, his main tool was the cook-house saw, admittedly sterilised and sharpened up for the occasion.

Phil Toosey Camp Report

On 3 May 1943 the first party of sick men arrived at Tamarkan by barge. Toosey went down to the river to meet them smartly dressed as usual and accompanied by Dr Moon and Captain Boyle. What they saw shocked them to the core. Here before them stood and lay streaks of misery, travesties of human beings, who only eighteen months before had been strong young men in the prime of life. Victims of the Japanese and the jungle.

The first thing Toosey did was to reassure them that they were safe. 'The C.O. spoke kindly to me, assured me that I was out of danger and would soon be on my feet again,' one young officer wrote. 'It was probably a formality, for the doctor had yet to examine me: but it was tremendously encouraging.'[1] Toosey had already made up his mind that he would personally greet every party of sick men that arrived at Tamarkan. 'We always managed to give newly arrived parties a meal, whatever time of day or night it was,' he wrote. 'This normally consisted of a cake and a cup of hot sweet tea. Many men burst into tears on receiving any food or help at all after the brutally inhuman treatment they had received on the journey from the Japanese.'[2]

From then on parties of sick arrived at Tamarkan averaging about a hundred a day. They often arrived at night and were dumped in the paddy-fields far from camp so that search parties had to be sent out to find them and bring them to Tamarkan. 'The sick were in an appalling condition,' Toosey wrote. 'Approximately seventy-five per cent of the parties were stretcher cases and men frequently arrived dead. They were brought in cattle trucks, the load being thirty or forty men per truck. No arrangements had been made by the Japanese for feeding or medical treatment on the journey. During this period we saw scenes of misery that will live for ever in the memories of all of us.'[3]

'A point to be emphasised,' wrote Captain Blackater, an early sick arrival at Tamarkan, 'is that all those evacuated to base camps were patients whom the doctors in the jungle considered had a chance of recovery and whom they considered able to stand the journey; the hopeless cases remained.'[4]

Night after night Toosey would be informed that another truckload had been dumped and he would have to arrange for a search party to go out and find the men and bring them into camp. 'It is impossible to describe adequately the condition of these men. I remember one man who was so thin that he could be lifted easily on one arm. His hair was growing down his back and was full of maggots. His clothing consisted of a ragged pair

Unloading Prisoners on the Banks of the River *by Jack Chalker.*

of shorts soaked with dysentery excreta; he was lousy, and covered with flies all the time, which he was too weak to brush away from his face and his eyes and the sore places on his body.'[5]

In his fury, Toosey demanded that the Japanese see these parties as they came in. But with the exception of the commandant, Sergeant Hosomi, they were wholly unmoved and sometimes even laughed. 'He [Hosomi] did his best to help, but on account of his inferior rank he was powerless to do any good,' Toosey wrote. 'The Japanese doctor visited the camp approximately once a month, but only on one occasion did he enter the wards, this occasion being when a Thai Mission visited the camp with a Japanese major. I managed to manoeuvre them into the Ulcer Ward, but the stink was so frightful and the sights so grim that they left at once, one of the officers retching outside.'[6] The only reaction of the Japanese doctor was that the prisoners should swat more flies.

Once the incoming patients had had their first meal the men were stripped of all their clothes and belongings, which were taken away to be deloused and disinfected. The boots and clothes of those who had been in the cholera camps were burned. They were all washed and shaved and given clean 'Jap-happys', a piece of fabric with ties, worn as a loin cloth – the universal dress on the railway – and put into a hospital hut where they were isolated from the convalescents so that their conditions could be monitored. The fear of cholera was ever present but it never appeared in Tamarkan, although there was an outbreak just up river at Chungkai and in the big hospital in Kanchanaburi.

The morning after their arrival Toosey would give the newly arrived sick men a pep talk. He would explain to them the camp rules and read out a list of dos and don'ts which, he emphasised, were for the good of everyone in the camp and concentrated principally on hygiene and discipline. Len Baynes arrived in camp on 11 May 1943:

> Colonel Toosey told us to sit on our kits while he spoke to us. 'This is Tamarkan camp', he told us, 'and it's about the cleanest in Thailand. I'm going to rely on you to help me keep it this way.' This was the first and only time that I was welcomed to a camp, but then Toosey was a quite exceptional officer . . . After our pep talk we were allocated a space each in a nice clean hut, and at five o'clock given our first meal. As soon as we had eaten we were called out again and taken down to the river to wash. The Colonel had no intention of letting us remain in our dirt any longer than was necessary.[7]

'I was not cured', another incoming patient wrote, 'but the feeling of freedom from the jungle was a relief; we all had that feeling. We could look to the distant hills across open country, we could see sunset and dawn, we could breathe. Only one fear haunted – would we have to go back?'[8]

Despite all the care and help the doctors and orderlies could offer, some men found it was not enough. Alec Young, who had been too ill to go up jungle after working on the bridge, wrote in his diary in May 1943: 'Daily comes to me a tremendous yearning for human intimacy – companionship. I think this longing is taking root in me. I miss the motherly care and gentle influence of women. I never realised how essentially men are made for women and vice versa until I had to endure so long isolation from the other sex.'[9]

Toosey made sure that he was visible in the camp as much as possible. He visited the hospital huts daily chatting to the patients, enquiring as to how their conditions were progressing, asking if there was anything they wanted. He had a gift for remembering names and faces, often recognising men he had seen months or even a year before in Singapore. His presence provided great reassurance and the men looked to him as an example. 'His organisational flair was first class,' Jack Caplan wrote in 1960. 'New latrines were built *before* the old ones overflowed. He made war on mosquitoes and flies alike. He instilled in the men the necessity for hygiene . . . and discipline was essential if we were to remain intact, and stay alive to see freedom. He was the man who gave us renewed strength when things appeared at their blackest.'[10]

The doctors told Toosey that the emotional wellbeing of the patients was of equal importance to their physical state. He organised parties of officers to make visits to the sick on a regular basis. Some of the huts housed gruesome sights but the officers undertook this work cheerfully and Toosey joined in the ward visits. 'I well recall your cheery voice as you walked through the huts speaking to one and another,' a prisoner wrote to him twenty years later. '"And how's my skeleton today?" was a greeting I received on more than one occasion.'[11] While making visits to the huts he realised that the convalescent men needed things to keep them occupied. For those who were too ill to sit up and take part in the low-key camp life of a hospital he organised readings. Officers would be asked to go into a hut and read books out loud. These readings were very popular, though the choice of books was limited. A great favourite in Tamarkan, he remembered, was *Alice in Wonderland*.

'I shall ever remember the understanding kindness we received on arrival at Tamarkan from up country,' Australian Private Lionel McCosker wrote in a letter to Toosey after the war. 'Your boundless untiring enthusiasm in your work for the men, outstanding courage and remarkable administrative capacity together with the loyal cooperation and great skill of your doctors made the "way" easier for the boys gone "west" and a "path" possible for many to return.'[12] Some men had had such terrible experiences that they lost the will to live. The padre and others would try to pay special attention to these men but often there was nothing he could do for them. A few developed serious mental problems and these men were later moved to a large hospital camp at Nakhon Pathom, near Bangkok.

Once they were a little stronger, recovering men were invited to contribute to camp life. Fly swatting was a vital duty and made a difference to the camp hygiene. Fly swats were handed out to patients who were still bedridden but prepared to help. Some convalescents who were more mobile chose to make things with their hands – surgical instruments for the hospital, for example. Dr Moon made a request for a pair of surgical tongs which he required to carry out a certain operation. These were made for him by a Dutch naval rating and the operation was held up until the little masterpiece was finished. The patient's life was saved.

Another man, a Dutch torpedo maker, built a microscope using lenses taken from a camera and a pair of binoculars, as well as a sensitive pair of apothecary scales, which he fashioned out of a comb, a toothbrush and a fork. Other men put their skills to good use working on the crosses that were required on a daily basis for the cemetery. Often, close friends of the dead would ask if they could carve the epitaph on the cross. All this activity Toosey encouraged. Not only did it keep the men busy but it gave them a purpose and a reason to look forward.

When he was asked years later what it was that made some men survive in the camps and others give up, he replied:

> The fact is a very large number of the younger men died. There were two reasons for it. One was the lack of food, which was worse for them than the older men because they were growing bone as well as living. But the other, which was vital in a very large number of cases, was they had no code of behaviour. They were utterly lost. I still believe that a man is at his toughest between the ages of twenty-eight and thirty-five. He's got the background, he's got some stability and he's got his full physical powers. Those men withstood it extremely well, that middle group, so to speak.[13]

There were some exceptions. The Dutch padre, Johan Carel Hamel, who arrived in Tamarkan on 5 May with a group of 640 sick Dutchmen from Lin Tin, 120 kilometres from Tamarkan, was in his late forties. He and the Dutch had been transported by lorry along dirt roads and tracks and the padre had hurt his back during the journey so that he spent the first few days lying on a bamboo platform. 'The space around me – there was even room for my luggage – meant an unknown luxury,'[14] he wrote later. Once he began to feel better he became more interested in his surroundings. He was impressed by the efficiency of Tamarkan and noticed that there were no long tenko parades but rather one count in the morning and thereafter only those in charge of huts or with other camp responsibilities had to appear, the rest were counted in their huts. 'The sick were indeed treated as patients. I took a few days' rest until I could presume that none of my vertebrae were damaged. Pain I did not have anymore, I could move freely.'[15]

Johan Carel Hamel was a grandfather. Born in 1897 in Amsterdam, he moved to the USA where he studied at the Drew Theological Seminar of the Methodist Episcopal Church in Madison, New Jersey. In 1932 he moved with his wife and three young children to Sumatra. In 1941 Hamel volunteered for a position as an army chaplain and was given the rank of Captain.

When the Japanese invaded the Dutch East Indies, Hamel was offered freedom. He refused. He chose to stay with his men. He would have ended up in a civilian internee camp anyway, he explained later. From Java he was sent to Singapore and from there transported by train to Ban Pong and then up the railway. He went first to Kinsayok and then on to Lin Tin. What he saw in the jungle camps appalled him. Men were starving, disease ridden, demoralised and yet worse was to come. When he and the 640 sick Dutchmen were brought down to Tamarkan by lorry the monsoon had not yet broken.

Soon after Hamel arrived the British padre was moved up country with a group of healthy men. Hamel took over the pastoral care of the British as well as the Dutch and his workload more than doubled. 'Visiting patients was a never ending job. But where I came, I did not have to come empty handed. Both the Dutch captain commander and Colonel Toosey gave me some money to spend for purchases for the serious patients. Also my own small fund kept growing and enabled me to relieve the worst suffering. I never had much, certainly never too much, but always sufficient to bring the sick some joy.'[16] He had a number of young men who came to him for Bible readings and confirmation classes. 'The celebration of the Lord's Supper was a great problem', he wrote, 'but we counted it lightly. In the months past we had learned to see that the temporary is the given. Was there no wine, why not use cold tea? The Lord's Supper under such perilous circumstances said more to many than the high ceremony in earlier times had ever done.'[17]

One of Hamel's duties was to take the funeral services. He took the majority of them at Tamarkan. The cemetery lay a kilometre from the camp along a sandy track and next to the large, brightly coloured Buddhist temple of Tha Maa Kham. The Japanese respected the dead and had negotiated with the Thai authorities about land for the cemeteries near the town of Kanchanaburi. In most cases the cemeteries were attached to or an extension of already existing burial grounds. The war graves cemetery in the centre of Kanchanaburi, already in use during the war, was next door to the Chinese burial ground. At Tamarkan the Japanese acquired a piece of land to the north-west of the temple, on a rise above the flood plain. There the British and Dutch organised a tidy little cemetery with an entrance gate, flowerbeds and paths between the graves. By the end of the war 373 men had been buried there, 172 of them British, 99 Australians, 97 Dutch and 5 Americans.

The Japanese demanded that the dead were buried immediately. From time to time they would make a burial party wait if they thought another man was about to die, so that two could be buried together. Often, however, Hamel had to trudge up and down the dusty, sandy road two or three times a day to conduct the funeral of a young man. No matter how many times he did this, it moved him deeply. He decided to adopt the English burial ritual, which he translated into Dutch for those funerals of his fellow countrymen. 'At the entrance of the cemetery we started singing De Profundis, psalm 130. Who will forget the simple soldier's burial, which was every time closed with the moving trumpet signals of the Last Post and Reveille? The Englishman has truly understood well, that the last mile covered is not the last one, and the Reveille reminds the living of the promise of resurrection and life eternal . . .'[18]

Toosey attended every funeral service. Occasionally, when the padre was exhausted or ill, he had to take the service himself. He would walk behind the burial party, watching them carry the body of one of their friends, wrapped in a rice sack on a bamboo stretcher. 'About this business of death,' Toosey said years later, 'if you'd seen death as I have seen it when I was burying anything up to six men a day for months on end, well death itself is a pure incident and nothing else. One thing I discovered was that those men who had had the benefit of a religious background, even though they may not have been actively practising Christians, curiously enough survived much better than those who were atheists, who had no belief or faith in anything.'

Hamel was as moved as Moon and Toosey by the state of the men who arrived in the hospital: 'due to lack of medicines, dressings and the right kind of nursing the patients arrived in this pitiful condition, dirty, covered with unsightly wounds and rife with vermin. With tender care they were received and their treatment started immediately.'[19] Those who needed isolation were put in quarantine while others were admitted to the relevant hospital ward. The serious cases were put into a hut with individual beds so that the medical orderlies could approach them from all sides and this made it easier to administer help and treatment. Many were so exhausted from their journey that they died a few hours after arrival. On one occasion a man was carried into a hut, he could not speak. He looked around with a mask-like expression; nobody knew who this man was. The padre was called for as they realised there was little time left. On his way to the hut an Englishman handed him a small sheaf of paper with the words: 'These papers belong to a serious patient who arrived with the last transport.'

Hamel looked through the bundle and recognised the sick man from the photograph in his military passport. On the last page he had written his will, leaving everything to his sister, with her address. The padre remembered that the dying man's brother-in-law was in camp. 'Without delay I went to the person in question and asked him if there was indeed a family relationship between him and the dying man. He confirmed this whereupon I told him the sad news. Together we walked to the sick hut. And on seeing him a joyful sign of recognition appeared on the face of the dying man and a great rest came over him. Nobody has ever heard what he wanted to say, but he understood us. In peace did he die.'[20]

Another young man staggered into Tamarkan, weighed down by two heavy bags but he would not let them go. He was suffering from cerebral malaria and collapsed and died only a few hours afterwards. The orderlies who sorted through his possessions were astonished to find the bags full of door locks and knobs, nails of every size and all kinds of household utensils. These would have been useless in the jungle but the man had never had the heart to leave anything behind. He had picked up everything he could just in case in might come in useful later.

Within the daily routine of Tamarkan recovering patients were encouraged to play cards, chess and checkers. Board games were manufactured in many camps and some chess sets came to be much admired and prized. One group of men in Chungkai became so good at chess that they set themselves the challenge of playing chess without a board and chess men. The old boy scouts in Tamarkan formed a tight knit group, holding meetings and readings at least once a week. They also did what they could to help out those in the hospital huts less fortunate than they were.

'Those who were not tied to their beds found work in a primitive cigarettes factory, where innumerable cigarettes for the inhabitants of Tamarkan were made. They also started with the manufacture of yeast.'[21] The yeast was made from human urine and was used to make bread, a very welcome change from rice cakes, even though, as Toosey explained, it was made with rice flour. The doctors assured the prisoners it was safe and very healthy because urine was rich in vitamin B. From time to time, Dick Van Zoonen recalled, they would find two empty drums near the urinals with a sign saying: 'These two to be filled tonight, otherwise no yeast tomorrow.'[22]

Other men found an outlet for their artistic skills. Many mess tins were beautifully engraved with the words 'Give us our daily bread' and with scenes from life in the camps. On 9 September Toosey organised an art and crafts exhibition. The Dutch, acknowledged as the most artistic group in Tamarkan, won most of the prizes. They would make works of art out of anything they could find – pieces of wood, nuts, bone, glass. One Dutch archaeologist formed a beautiful collection of pre-historic stone tools that he found when working on the railway embankment and digging graves in the cemetery at Tamarkan.

In addition to hand crafts there were also countless manuscripts, diaries and stories that were carefully hidden from the Japanese and Korean guards. This was dangerous as the Japanese were fanatical in their searches. Anyone found to have a map or manuscript in his possession was likely to be sent before the Kempei Tai and tortured, imprisoned and possibly even executed. In view of this, it is remarkable how many men remained determined to record their experiences for posterity.

Despite the good atmosphere in Tamarkan sick men were dying from diseases which, in a normal hospital, were easily treatable. Dr Moon was troubled. He and Toosey had many discussions but they could not see how the hospital could be improved without more money and medicine. There were nearly 3000 men in camp and of those only 400 were working and thus receiving pay. Toosey had already levied a tax of 30 per cent on the officers during the bridge-building days in order to pay for food for the sick but this was just a drop in the ocean for the 2500 hospital patients in need of more than the half rations the Japanese issued. He increased the levy on the officers to 60 per cent but still it was not enough. By early June 1943 things in Tamarkan, while immeasurably better than conditions up in the jungle, were desperate.

Almost the only thing the doctors and orderlies had in their medical armoury was kindness and a willingness to pay attention, to listen, to reassure and to comfort, which was very demanding emotionally. Blackater remembered the doctor in the dysentery ward: 'Captain Ralston had no drugs, but endless patience. Daily he listened to everything the men had to tell him. He knew, and they knew, just how little he could do for them, but that morning talk – the MO had listened – was a tonic in itself. Men pinned their faith on him and many were cured.'[23] The medical teams gave so much of themselves but what they really needed, Arthur Moon complained, was medicine:

The Japanese medical orderly [Odshare] responsible for the administration of 3,000 sick admitted having been a 'rice labourer' in civilian life. He lacked intelligence and was utterly inefficient and afraid to issue the meagre medical supplies he received. I think his inefficiency annoyed even Saito and it was a great relief when he left Tamarkan on the 16th June. His successor, Asma, was a different type and his effort to do all in his power to help is recorded. He rarely went near the wards and interfered as little as possible with our organisation. Unfortunately both he and the Gunso lacked rank and influence at I.J.A. H.Q. and all their efforts could not achieve much against an inefficient higher authority disinterested in the welfare of sick prisoners.[24]

Then, out of the blue at the beginning of June 1943, a team of Japanese officials made a visit to Tamarkan from Chungkai. They were accompanied by an interpreter who took Toosey to one side. He explained that the nearby hospital camp at Chungkai was receiving outside help, from sympathetic Thais, who were supplying medicine and money to the prisoners. He said that he would be willing to put Toosey in touch with the organisers of the scheme and explained that what he needed was his number, rank and name, which he would pass on to the relevant people.

This put Toosey in an extremely difficult position. He was aware that the Japanese would try any tricks to catch the officers out, particularly the camp commanders, and he was anxious this might be a Japanese trap. To him the young Anglo-Thai looked suspiciously Japanese and he shared this concern with Arthur Moon. The doctor was unequivocal. He saw here a real possibility to help the men in his care and he was determined not to let it slip away. He told Toosey bluntly that if it was a risk, then it was nevertheless a risk worth taking: 'We are in such desperate need of more medicine and more money, Colonel, that it's worth taking the risk, come what may.' So Toosey wrote down his number, rank and name on a small piece of paper and handed it over to the young officer, who turned out to be Corporal R.C.H.

'Johnny' Johnson, an Anglo-Thai soldier from the Malay Volunteers. Johnson took the note and told Toosey that he should go out with the ration lorry when it next went into Kanchanaburi and there he should acquaint himself with the grocer supplying the camps, a Mr Boon Pong.

With this was ushered in the second period of life at Tamarkan hospital camp. It coincided with a change in the Japanese command. Saito was replaced by Sergeant Hosomi who was more sympathetic and helpful towards the sick. A few days after his conversation with Corporal Johnson, Toosey got permission from the guards to go with the ration lorry, as planned. He was accompanied by two Japanese who were easily persuaded to visit Boon Pong's premises as there was a Japanese restaurant next door. Once the guards were out of the way, Toosey identified himself to Boon Pong. 'The way it started was like this,' explained Toosey. 'I went down with the ration lorry driven by the Japs into Kanchanaburi where we loaded up with vegetables and rice, no meat, for the camp. Boon Pong managed to get me on one side and he said, "I've had your number, rank and name, I'll do what I can to help you. The way I will do it is this: in the basket of vegetables you will find packages of medicine so please go through the vegetables very carefully" . . . As far as the money is concerned this was handed over and . . . carried into camp in the driver's Jap happy.'[25] The scheme to get money and medicine into the camp was necessarily completely secret and only four or five men knew about it including Moon, Toosey and David Boyle. Two drivers helped them out when it became obvious that Toosey would draw attention to himself and put the scheme in jeopardy if he continued to go into Kanchanaburi with the ration lorry.

Boon Pong was a provision merchant who was contracted by the Japanese to supply the prison canteens right up the river, as far as Tha Khanun, around the 218 kilometre mark, some 150 kilometres from Kanchanaburi. Born in 1906 in the town, Boon Pong had had no contact with Europeans prior to the outbreak of the war. He was the eldest son of a local doctor and the family was held in high regard in the town. His mother owned land on the other side of the river and the family occupied a fine three-storey house on the old high street. The upper floors of the house provided living accommodation and the ground floor was a shop. Boon Pong had ten siblings, of whom six survived into adulthood, the youngest being born in 1934. Boon Pong's parents lived in the house, as did one of his brothers. Boon Pong did not follow his father into medicine but set himself up as a grocer. The business ran well and by the mid-1930s he decided he should expand and set up a buying agency in Bangkok. He married a headmistress and they had one daughter, Panee. Boon Pong's enterprise proved to be unprofitable and he soon returned to Kanchanaburi, where he continued to work at his store, expanding the wholesale activities and setting the whole business on a sound financial footing. His wife and daughter remained in Bangkok until shortly before the outbreak of the war. In Kanchanaburi Boon Pong played a role in the political life of the town, serving more than one term as mayor in the 1930s.

He was a strong personality. He neither drank nor smoked and he disapproved of both habits. He was devoted to his family and his energies were directed, pre-war, to assuring the business ran profitably. When the Japanese began to negotiate the purchase of land for a cemetery at Chungkai, land which happened to belong to his mother, it was Boon Pong who dealt with them and it was through this contact that he was contracted to supply the prison camp canteens with food.

During his time in Bangkok, Boon Pong had made what turned out to be useful contacts in the Anglo-Siam Corporation, one of these being Corporal Johnson, who had worked for the corporation prior to the war. In early 1943 Boon Pong met Johnson on a visit to deliver food to Chungkai. He recognised him immediately and Johnson asked him whether he could get medicine for men dying of diphtheria. Boon Pong replied that he would see what he could do. On his next visit to Bangkok he approached a Chinese doctor and purchased a small quantity of the requisite drugs with his own personal money. When he next made a delivery to Chungkai he passed the drugs over to Johnson who then asked him if he could arrange to cash personal cheques for the prisoners so that they could buy more food for the sick men, who were receiving no pay from the Japanese. Boon Pong realised that he would need additional support from other businessmen in order to cash the personal cheques as suggested by Johnson. He attempted to persuade other Thais and Chinese merchants in Bangkok to assist. It was risky and many of the people he approached were afraid. It was through these enquiries that he made contact with other people who were also trying to help the prisoners.

The most significant assistance came from members of the ex-pat community in Bangkok and for Toosey there was one man in particular who was the lynchpin. Peter Heath was an employee of the Borneo Company and had been working in Bangkok since 1934. When the Japanese entered the city in December 1941 Heath was imprisoned in a civilian internment camp under the command of the Thai Army. The camp was in the centre of Bangkok and did not have the strict regime of civilian camps run by the Japanese. In June 1942 news started to filter through that 'European prisoners of war had been transferred from Malaya for work on a railway line between Ban Pong and Moulmein . . . and it was not long before some contact was established and small sums of money were collected discreetly from the internees.'[26]

The initial contact was with prisoners in the camp at Nong

The three eldest Toosey children, Patsey, Arthur and Phil, Birkenhead, 1909.

Tennis party at Alan Tod's house, Maryton Grange, Liverpool, mid-1930s. Back row: Phil Toosey and Alan Tod. Front row, left to right: Arthur Goffey, William Roberts, Helen Long, Robert Campbell, Cyril Faulkner, Edmund Philip Anderton.

3

59th West Lancashire officers. Front row seated, left to right: Major Phil Toosey, Major Douglas Crawford, General Sir Hugh Jeudwine, Lieutenant Colonel Cotton, Colonel Alan Tod, Major Hubert Servaes, Major H.K. Dimoline.

4

Toosey receiving congratulations from Alderman F. T. Richardson, Lord Mayor of Liverpool, on winning the King's Cup, 3 October 1935. Lieutenant Colonel Cotton is in the centre.

Alex Toosey with Patrick (10), Gillian (9) and Nicholas (4) on holiday in Wales, summer 1944.

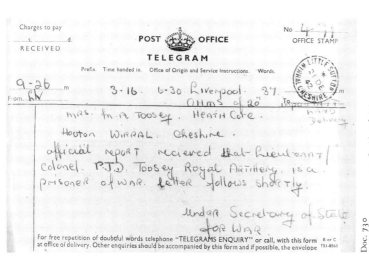

First official notice of Toosey's imprisonment received by Alex three days before Christmas 1942.

Doc. 730

The Selerang Incident, September 1942. The Japanese herded 17,000 men into Selerang square at a density of 1 million men per square mile.

Hu. 92335

Train Journey to Thailand by Jack Chalker, October 1942. Thirty-one men crammed into steel rice trucks for a journey that took four days and nights.

Aerial view of Tamarkan camp taken by the RAF in 1945 showing two bridges across the Khwae Mae Khlong. The camp is sited to the south east of the wooden bridge and about 100m from the steel bridge (top).

Hu. 92331

View of Tamarkan camp with the theatre hut on the right and the living huts in a row on the left.

Prisoners thatching a hut using attap palm leaves.

Bathing in the river was one of the great benefits of Tamarkan until the cholera outbreak in 1943. The man in the foreground is wearing the ubiquitous Jap-happy or loin cloth.

David Boyle, Toosey's adjutant and translator. Described by Toosey as one of the bravest young men he had ever met, Boyle was awarded an MBE after the war on Toosey's recommendation.

Stephen Alexander was a second lieutenant in Toosey's regiment.

Lieutenant Colonel Philip Toosey, c. 1942

Sergeant Major Teruo Saito, 1934.

Yoshihiko Futamatsu, the Japanese engineer in charge of the wooden and steel bridges at Tamarkan.

Korean guards at Nong Pladuk. One of the six guards on duty would be on the gate and the other five would sit all day long on the wooden bench. This was the guard for 3,000 men at the gates of Nong Pladuk.

The wooden bridge nearing completion, January 1943.

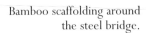

Bamboo scaffolding around the steel bridge.

Lifting comb steel trusses on to the steel bridge, April 1943. Here the Japanese had to use heavy machinery and large cranes. All the other bridges in Thailand were built by hand.

A post-war photograph of a train on the wooden bridge with the steel bridge in the background.

Dutch prisoners inside a typical hut. These men had wooden sleeping platforms, an improvement on split bamboo, but no bedding or mosquito nets.

Kanyu Riverside Camp: Dysentery Ward, 1943 by Stanley Gimson. Dysentery killed more men on the railway than any other disease. Emetine was the only effective medicine to treat it and was in short supply even on the black market.

A Prisoner Sick with Beri Beri, Changi Gaol, 1944 by Ronald Searle. This was one of the vitamin deficiency diseases suffered by the prisoners.

Major Arthur Moon, 1940. Moon was the senior medical officer at Tamarkan from May to December 1943. He was endlessly kind to the patients in his care and had a gentle bedside manner.

Captain Jim Mark, 198th Field Ambulance corps. Like Moon he worked tirelessly and with patience and good humour in terrible circumstances.

Boon Pong, the Thai provision merchant in Kanchanaburi who smuggled money and medicine for the secret V-scheme into Tamarkan and other camps.

Tamarkan graveyard. Despite the great efforts of the medical teams, 401 men died at Tamarkan between 15 November 1942 and 15 August 1945. After the war the bodies were moved to the Commonwealth war cemeteries at Kanchanaburi and Chungkai.

Inside cover of a programme by Norman Pritchard for a concert called 'Any More for Sailing?' performed in Nong Pladuk in July 1944. Pritchard created the spray effect background by shaving colour pigment off his toothbrush on to the paper.

David Lean's bridge is blown high into the sky by saboteurs from Pierre Boulle's fictional Force 316.

The real bridges built by the prisoners at Tamarkan were bombed by the RAF and the USAAF and finally put beyond repair in June 1945.

The steel bridge during a bombing raid. The reflection of a falling bomb can be seen in the water to the north of the bridge.

Queuing for food at the officers' camp, 1945. In this camp they were so short of space and amenities that they had to queue for everything. On one occasion a Dutch officer spotted a queue forming, grabbed his mess tin and joined the end of the line only to discover he was queuing for confession.

Hu. 4547

35

An officer examining his kit in a hut at the officers' camp, 1945.

Hu. 4548

36

Retrieving buried papers and secret diaries after the war.

Hu. 4549

37

Captain W. M. 'Bill' Drower, 1941.
Interpreter in the officers' camp, he
incurred the wrath of Captain Noguchi
who condemned him to solitary
confinement 'forever'.

Bill Drower sketched by Fred Ransome
Smith two days after his release from his
prison hut on 16 August 1945.

39

Noguchi was the Japanese guard in charge of the officers' camp. Toosey described him as a sadist of
the worst type. He was tried and hanged after the war for the attempted murder of Bill Drower.

40

Taken at the end of August 1945 by Lieutenant Colonel David Smiley of the liberating Force 136, this photograph shows Toosey, centre, surrounded by friendly Thai officers who had been operating behind the scenes in the vicinity of Ubon camp where Toosey rejoined his men. Regimental Sergeant Major Sandy McTavish is on the right in his kilt next to Dr Smyth from Nong Pladuk.

BUCKINGHAM PALACE

The Queen and I bid you a very warm welcome home.

Through all the great trials and sufferings which you have undergone at the hands of the Japanese, you and your comrades have been constantly in our thoughts. We know from the accounts we have already received how heavy those sufferings have been. We know also that these have been endured by you with the highest courage.

We mourn with you the deaths of so many of your gallant comrades.

With all our hearts, we hope that your return from captivity will bring you and your families a full measure of happiness, which you may long enjoy together.

George R.I

September 1945.

The King's message to the returning men.

42

Toosey (right) with his son Patrick and Doug Mather in North Wales, 1946.

Toosey with Alex, Gillian and Arthur Osborne, 1954. Toosey gave Osborne one of Dinah's puppies on this visit.

44

Alex, 1946.

45

Toosey, 1959. He did not like having his photograph taken but here he is looking proud at Patrick's wedding.

Pierre Boulle, author of
*The Bridge on the River
Kwai*.

47

Alec Guinness and
Sam Spiegel on the
film set of *The Bridge
on the River Kwai*, Sri
Lanka, 1957.

Toosey on a cruise to Norway with Douglas Crawford in the 1950s.

Toosey on a family holiday in France with Alex, Nicholas and Patrick, 1957. Patrick is holding Gillian's glass of beer while she takes the photograph.

50

Toosey at the Blackpool FEPOW reunion with Prince Philip, 1973.

51

Saito at Phil Toosey's grave, 12 August 1984, which would have been Toosey's eightieth birthday. Saito had come to pay his respects to the man who had changed the philosophy of his life.

Pladuk at the Bangkok end of the railway line. A driver, Corporal Paton, was approached in September 1942 with a note given to him by a Mr Hong, the Chinese servant of a civilian internee, Ken Gairdner. Paton took the note straight to his senior officer, Major Paddy Sykes, who was concerned it might be a plot by the Japanese, but in the end he decided they were in such need of medicines and food that it was worth taking the risk. Sykes would supply information about Japanese troop movements and news of the prison camps, which was passed on to the Allies and in return Ken Gairdner supplied funds to help the camp to buy extra supplies. Gairdner recruited Peter Heath to help him raise funds: 'At first Heath co-operated', wrote Sibylla Jane Flower in 2003, 'but he soon disengaged himself on the grounds that Gairdner's lack of discretion among the other internees posed an unnecessary threat to an extremely hazardous undertaking.'[27] This fear proved to be groundless and the contact between Gairdner and the prison camp at Nong Pladuk ran successfully. Meanwhile, Peter Heath determined to continue to help the prisoners but in a way that he felt would ensure greater secrecy. He encouraged Dick Hempson from the Anglo-Thai Corporation to help him and together they 'set up their own aid organisation involving French, Danish and Swiss nationals in Bangkok'.[28] As Heath and Hempson had spread their net wider than Gairdner they were able to raise more substantial sums of money. Confusingly both schemes used the letter 'V' as their sobriquet. The funds were spent mainly on medicines and these were smuggled, along with money, by a variety of means into the prison camps around the Kanchanaburi area.

The aim of the scheme, as far as Peter Heath was concerned, was to reach as many camps and prisoners of war as possible. He was motivated by his deep Christian belief and was, by coincidence, a member of the same sect – the Catholic Apostolic

Church — as Toosey's father, Charlie. Heath made efforts to get in touch with the senior camp commander or the senior medical officer and he always asked for acknowledgement of every gift of money or medicine so that he could be sure it was not intercepted by the Japanese and that the whole amount was getting through. He always asked about the number of deaths in the camps and this, presumably, was intended to get back to the British Government.

It was the great good fortune of Toosey to become part of this network and through the so-called V-scheme he was able to obtain money and medicines for Tamarkan that saved many lives. 'Messages and money had to be smuggled in and out of the camp, and there was the ever present danger that if the organisation were ever traced to the camp, it would involve many friends who had lent their money and help,'[29] Peter Heath wrote. In the internment camp he had to be as careful as the prisoners in their camps. Prior to any inspection by the Japanese he insisted that all unnecessary papers were burned and that the essential receipts and letters were buried within the compound. When asked years later why he had kept records, which would have been so incriminating if he had been caught, he said: 'We wanted a record, we were rather proud of it actually. You've got to put yourself in the position of a young man who had been interned and felt he ought to be fighting and wasn't. At one time I thought of offering to the Japanese to go up to the camps and act as a male nurse.'[30]

Toosey, having established contact through Boon Pong, sent Peter Heath the following short note on 11 June 1943:

There are 1,730 sick men in this camp; 28 have died during the last month. We have no money and the men do not receive pay. We are urgently in need of money for food and medicines.[31]

In his first communication to Toosey, Peter Heath replied:

30.6.43

Lt. Col. P.J.D. Toosey
Tamarkan Camp

Yours 11/6 recd. 28/6. Herewith Tcs [Ticals] 5,000/–.
Medicines will follow in the course of a week or two. We shall
endeavour to make regular monthly payments to arrive at yours
within the first week of the month. The amount will depend on
funds available.

Please acknowledge the safe arrival of the cash, as soon as
possible. If you prefer it use a nom-de-plume in future, now
that we know who you are. It would not serve as much protection if the contact was caught red-handed, but it is a definite
safeguard in case the note should be lost accidentally or fall into
wrong hands.

Drugs are getting very scarce and are controlled. The prices
are terrific and buying has to be done in the 'black market'.

We need hardly warn you to keep the matter as quiet as possible. We are doing everything possible to raise funds without
causing suspicion but people are very frightened – and not
without reason.

Please continue to give your sick and death figures.

Your note in Thai has been passed on to the right quarter but
they won't be able to do anything.

Good luck,[32]

There followed a monthly correspondence between the two
men until November 1943 when Tamarkan was dispersed. In
each note, Toosey, who signed himself 'V', acknowledged receipt
of the money and medicines, gave notice of the number of sick

and dead, 'sick now 2205, will shortly be 3000, deaths 66', and then asked for a particular drug – 'Emetine badly needed'. On every note Toosey thanked Heath 'your help is wonderful but we still need Emetine badly' . . . 'it is impossible now fully to express my gratitude, you are saving many lives'. With one note, in August 1943, at the camp's maximum capacity, Toosey included a report written by Dr Moon.

By October Moon had succeeded in improving the conditions in his hospital by means of imaginative and at times brilliant improvisation, greatly aided by medicine from the V-scheme. There was now a small pathology lab with two microscopes. Blood transfusions were made using blood that had had the clotting agent removed by bamboo whisk and facilities in the basic

Group photograph taken 13 October 1943. The only photograph of Toosey taken during captivity. Back row: Japanese guard, Major Arthur Moon, Sergeant Major Saito. Front row: David Boyle, Japanese guard, Toosey.

operating theatre were improved. When Toosey witnessed the first amputation in Tamarkan it was carried out by Arthur Moon using the cookhouse saw, sharpened and sterilised for the occasion. Now they had better tools thanks to careful purchasing with V-scheme money and the instrument makers among the Dutch. As the hospital became a little more sophisticated, so the need for more medical supplies grew. On 15 October 1943, Toosey wrote to Peter Heath:

> Total deaths 197, amputations for ulcers 10, results of operations satisfactory. Probably 12 more amputations. Beri-Beri and chronic Diarrhoea causing most deaths at present. Urgent Needs:
>
> Ampoules Vit.B. or Metaolin (Takeda)
> Further supplies M&B and Sulphanilamide
> Large ampoules Sterile Sodium Citrate for blood transfusion
> Tubes of plain cat gut surgical sutures.
> Silk worm Gut surgical suture
> Nicotinic Acid or Appellagrin (takeda)
> Evipan or Sodium pentothal for anaesthetic
> Further supplies Yatren or Stovarsol.[33]

Remarkably Peter Heath was able to supply many of the items on Moon's list and Toosey took delivery of seven parcels of medicines in early November 1943. The effect of the V-scheme money was immediate and dramatic. No one quite knew how the improvements had come about but the patients felt the benefit of them from the moment the first medicines were received.

'I was now in the dysentery ward,' Blackater wrote, 'and the officers were in a section by themselves.' Patients with chronic dysentery often had to relieve themselves twice an hour, if not more frequently. 'I was holding my own with a daily score of seven which just would not reduce, but it looked as if both Pearson and Hirsch would go. I watched them lose ground with alarming rapidity and then emetine arrived. It was miraculous! After the first injection they slept, after the second their score fell rapidly, their pains ceased, and, as the abbreviated course continued, they lived.'[34]

The money and medicines had to be smuggled into Tamarkan under the noses of the Korean guards. It was carefully arranged that Dr Moon would have his room next to the quartermaster's store. The carpenter cut a small hatch in the wall through which the precious goods were passed as the QM checked the stores. Often the medicines were hidden in wads of tobacco. One day a hypodermic syringe fell out of a packet and on to the ground at the feet of the Korean guard. In a split second a man bent down, picked it up and put it in his pocket. 'The Korean failed to register, and everyone breathed again.'[35] On another occasion Captain Hannah, who was charged with disguising the extra money coming into the camp accounts, stood on parade with 30,000 Ticals in notes stuffed in his pockets, socks, hat lining and shoes.

When Blackater had recovered sufficiently he moved into the officers' hut. It was a different world from the dysentery hut where the atmosphere was one of disease and death. He immediately felt better and wanted to take an active part in camp life. He went to see Toosey. Blackater wrote:

> I became a farmer. It was the happiest phase of my whole existence as a prisoner. Colonel Toosey decided to start a duck and pig farm, and when it became known that I had once been a poultry farmer, my fate was sealed. I was given a piece of waste ground away from the huts. The duck-pens

were fenced with split bamboo, and we made little gates of old matting and bamboo fastened with wire. It was amazing how much useful rubbish could be picked up. The ducks arrived – baskets of them – and life for Gathercole and me became difficult. Everywhere we went in that camp a murmur of quacking followed us; in our huts, as we walked about the camp, men quacked as we passed by. The pigs came too. That was a rush job, as they arrived before the pens were built. The Japs lent us a lorry, and a big working party, including the Colonel and David Boyle, worked till dark making the run.[36]

There were ten pigs in all, two of which were tame, and Blackater named them Lucille and Algernon. The farm soon became the centre of attention in the camp and the doctors encouraged the sick men who could walk to go down to the farm. Rows of men would lean on the fence and gaze at the little creatures inside. 'Personally I know of no more restful occupation; the pig is undoubtedly fascinating,' Blackater concluded. The farm supplied eggs, ducks and pork to 'Simpsons', the canteen. 'I would take them to the canteen by way of the hospital, as it amused men who had not been off their backs for six, eight or ten months to see the colourful birds in my arms. They liked to touch them – something from a world they had almost forgotten existed.'[37]

The hospital had been divided up into nine separate wards catering for different conditions. The worst two were ward 7 for the chronic dysentery and diarrhoeas and ward 3 where those men suffering from tropical ulcers were housed.

'On August 23rd camp strength was 3073,' Dr Moon recorded, 'of these there were 2,217 hospital cases, 580 convalescents and 124 fit. Tropical Ulcers and Nutritional Disease were now the outstanding medical problems.' Four days earlier Toosey had watched him carry out the first amputation. Ulcers proved to be one of the biggest problems for the doctors on the railway. Small scratches from bamboo spikes or sharp stones would become infected and very soon ulcerated. In the filthy jungle conditions of the upper sections of the railway there was little hope of these ulcers healing. Malnourished men with vitamin deficiencies watched tiny scratches grow rapidly and become infected, the ulcers spread, eating up the tissues until in some cases the bone was exposed.

The basic treatment for the ulcer patients was washing out the wounds and applying a dressing. In the jungle there were even fewer dressings than at Tamarkan. In many camps medical orderlies were forced to clean out the wound using a sterilised spoon while men held on to the patient who would writhe in unspeakable agony. Worse than the grotesque spectacle of the ulcers was the smell. 'From far away', Padre Hamel wrote, 'flies converged on the ulcer hut, allured by the stench of rotting flesh.' Many men record their revulsion at walking into the ulcer hut for the first time. When an ulcer had spread too far the only treatment available was amputation. Moon would talk to the patient and explain, in his gentle and quiet manner, that despite their best efforts nothing could be done to save the leg or arm. Bill Morrison, an Australian amputee at Tamarkan, remembered the doctor saying to him: 'I had to choose between going home with one leg or staying in Thailand with two legs. He meant the little cemetery on the hill.'[38] One of the padre's jobs was to sit at the head of the operating table and talk to the man who was undergoing the operation. These were carried out in a small bamboo hut under a mosquito net. Most of the time the patients had a spinal anaesthetic and the operation was carried out with the man fully conscious.

Despite these primitive conditions, a high proportion of the amputees survived. It was wonderful to see the men free of pain and sitting up on their bamboo, sometimes only hours after surgery, tucking into a meal such as they had not been able to face in weeks, Hamel observed. One amputee, George Downes, was very ill after his operation. He was the second person to have his leg amputated by Dr Moon. Toosey used some of the V-scheme money to buy him a chicken from the canteen. 'It was a very scrawny fowl', he said later, 'but undoubtedly it saved this man's life.' Toosey made a daily visit to the ulcer ward and one day, not long after the operation, he asked Downes when he could get on his crutches. When he learned it was to be the following day he asked him to come to his hut for coffee at 5 p.m. However, Downes was struck down with an attack of malaria and 'told the Colonel's batman to let him know that I wouldn't be able to come. But at 5 p.m. along came the Colonel to the hut with a tin plate and a cup of coffee in his hands. He sat down on my bamboo-slatted, sack-covered bed and said: "As you couldn't come to me, I thought I would visit you." And I dined on the fried egg, sweet potatoes, ersatz coffee he had brought me, with a Nippon cigarette to follow.'[39]

In all Dr Moon carried out eighteen amputations at Tamarkan. For the leg amputees the carpenters made crutches and then, as the wound healed, prosthetic limbs from bamboo and gut. Some men, who later had artificial legs supplied for them by the NHS, complained that they far preferred their bamboo legs that were light and more comfortable.

On the night of 28 September the ulcer ward collapsed during a heavy storm. By some miracle no one was killed but the exposure to the storm caused a setback to many cases and a recent amputation case developed pneumonia and later died. One patient, Edwin Webster, wrote an article years later about that night. He was ill in Tamarkan with spinal malaria and described the night that number 3 hut blew down:

> The thunder cracked and rolled like countless guns in barrage, the lightning had to be seen to be believed. We could hear the thatched roof of our hut creaking, and it could be seen swaying like a drunken man when all at once it happened. There could be heard above the noise of the storm a distinct cracking and groaning of bamboo; we were startled to say the very least, and then could be heard above the noise of the storm well, just a horrible din, cracking bamboo, rumbling and staccato cracks of thunder and the unmistakable sound of anguished human ones, pitiful in the extreme. We sat up rigid and scared then the shouting started. Everyone took it up. 'No 3 hut is down; the roof has collapsed; for god's sake give a hand with the boys!'
>
> Everyone in the camp who could walk made for the hut and offered to help. To see men who in these times would be considered 'very ill' trying their hardest to help really was touching and pathetic, but the one great feature was, no thought for themselves, only their comrades whose fate up to now we did not know.
>
> In the midst of the storm we heard the Colonel's voice, soothing the injured, organising carrying parties, making provision in the other huts for these men to have somewhere to lay. He ordered the hurricane lamps to be lit and the evacuation was soon underway. We were all too pleased to share our sleeping space with our unfortunate comrades, and everyone was given a smoke, and he told us that the cookhouse had received orders to brew 'tea' (a concoction we called tea) for everyone. When the tea came he supervised the issue, making sure everyone received a fair share, though he would not have one himself. Next he lit his cigarette and by means of chain lighting, saw to

it that everyone had his smoke. And when someone remarked it was well past lights out, and that we all would probably get into serious trouble he said in no uncertain voice, 'To hell with the Japs; I am in charge here.'[40]

By October the death figures for Tamarkan were dropping and by the middle of the month they were less than one a day. Up country the railway was nearing completion. The Burmese and Thai sections met at Konkuita: 'On 17 October 1943 the two stretches of rail, one snaking down from Thanbyuzayat, the other up from Nong Pladuk, finally linked up at Konkuita, 262 kilometres north of the Thailand terminus and about 40 kilometres from the Burma border, amid deep forest.'[41] The Japanese held as elaborate a ceremony as the jungle would permit on 25th October when Lieutenant Colonels Sasaki and Imai, who commanded the 5th and 9th Railway Regiments respectively, completed the railway by driving gun metal dog spikes into an ebony sleeper.

The railway had been built at a rate of half a mile a day and in a little over a year rather than the five years estimated by the Allies. The prisoners and Asian labourers had moved 4 million cubic metres of earth and had constructed 8 miles of bridges. There had been loss of life of over 12,000 Allied prisoners approximate to a man for every sleeper laid along its 415 kilometre length. More shocking still is the death rate of the Asian labourers. Over 93,000 Malay, Burmese, Javanese and Tamils died during the construction of the Thailand–Burma railway.
In the base area the completion of the railway was marked by an order for the prisoners to build a memorial in Kanchanaburi, a short distance from the site of the bridges at Tamarkan, to commemorate all those who died during the construction of the railway. It was a monument of some considerable size with steps

leading up to the memorial and eight plaques commemorating the men of individual nations. Each country's inscription is in their own language – English, Dutch, Malay, Tamil, Chinese, Thai, Indian and Japanese. The unveiling ceremony was held on 13 March 1944 and was attended by 1123 prisoners and by Japanese and Koreans. The roll of deceased was called showing Tamarkan deaths to date as:

British	129
Dutch	57
Australian	15
U.S.A.	1
Total	202.

Deputations of all nationalities had to be present and the prisoners watched in bemusement as Japanese senior officers gave moving speeches, some barely able to restrain their tears.

In many of the accounts that appeared postwar, former prisoners claim that the Thailand–Burma railway did not fulfil the needs of the Japanese. This was explained by Colonel Warmenhoven in his report in 1947: 'Naturally to be forced to support the enemy by building for him a line which was meant to be the means for the continuous success of that enemy was in a way demoralising and asked for certain compensation. The mental compensation was to argue that the line was a complete failure.'[42] However, throughout the next eighteen months the Japanese succeeded in moving on average 1000 tons of stores a day along its length. Admittedly they had hoped to move 3000 tons per day but they were nevertheless successful in supplying their army in Burma. In 1945 the railway was used to help their army to complete an orderly withdrawal. The journey time from Nong Pladuk to Moulmein varied depending on derailments, running repairs and, later, bomb attacks and the need for the trains to run only at night during this latter period. The average time in 1943–4 was approximately fifty hours.

One day, in late 1943, the Japanese announced that payment had arrived for those who had worked 'up country' and who had been transferred in the meantime to hospital in Tamarkan. Many of the men for whom the money was intended, however, were not in Tamarkan but in Chungkai. Toosey suggested that he and the padre should deliver the money up to the neighbouring camp, some 4 kilometres walk from the steel bridge.

Early the next morning the two men left Tamarkan accompanied by an armed Japanese soldier. No sooner had they walked over the bridge and around the curve than they were out of sight of the camp. They walked along the railway for an hour. The sun beat down on them but the change of scene and the brief sense of partial freedom were delightful. The railway ran straight for almost the whole distance to Chungkai. They walked along the track, listening to the rails popping in the heat as the metal expanded, watching the insects scuttle out of their path. They marvelled at the paddy-fields to their left and right, below the level of the railway. There were men ploughing with water buffalo, the great beasts plodding slowly through the mud, their barefoot drivers walking behind, skilfully managing the ploughs. Women in the next-door field were bent over picking rice. Others were fishing by hand, landing their catches in tin buckets. The only other noise came from the crickets and the quiet *slip slop* of the buffalo in the mud. It was a scene of the utmost tranquillity.

The name Chungkai comes from Chong, which means cutting and Kai which means water buffalo. Chungkai is thus the place where the water buffalo were led down to the river. The land on which the prison camp at Chungkai was built had belonged to Boon Pong's family. It was an enormous camp housing 9000 prisoners of war at its maximum strength. Visitors from another camp were a rare event. Hamel remembered their reception clearly: 'When they saw us enter the camp, the men prepared us a great welcome. Toosey was immediately received by the English, I by the Dutch. It was a great reunion with many old acquaintances. A chair and a table were brought after the first stormy welcome and for four hours I sat there amid a large crowd of people. The Japanese did not disturb us even once.'[43]

The situation at Chungkai was similar to that in Tamarkan: considerably better than up country, but still inadequate. The camp was now well organised and being run by a British officer, Lieutenant Colonel Cary Owtram. Like Toosey, Owtram was not a regular soldier but a TA officer. Also, like Toosey, he came from the north-west of England, from Blackpool. Toosey made a tour of the hospital huts and then, with the padre, visited the cemetery.

Chungkai cemetery was extensive. Even by the end of 1943 it had more than a thousand graves. They were told that every day as many as ten men were buried and it was not unusual for there to be fifteen funerals in twenty-four hours. The cemetery was beautifully kept. Each nationality had its own priest or chaplain and the Dutch had a number of devoted laymen as spiritual leaders. Toosey and Hamel returned to Tamarkan that evening carrying dozens of letters and messages, all carefully hidden. They made a second trip to Chungkai a few weeks later, this time by barge. Toosey welcomed any opportunity to escape the confines and pressures of camp life, if only briefly.

Life at Tamarkan was wearing. Toosey lived in daily fear of the V-scheme being uncovered and with the threat of unpredictable behaviour by the guards. Although he succeeded in restraining them from their worst excesses and confrontation was less frequent than during bridge construction there were still ugly episodes in camp.

When the Japanese bridge engineers evacuated Tamarkan they left a flimsy store full of tools. Unbeknown to anyone, a small group of British prisoners had discovered the store and had been systematically selling the tools to the Thais, making a lot of money. One night the Japanese, who had been tipped off, laid a trap and the men were caught. Alec Young recorded in his diary the indignation he felt, not at the Japanese, but at the men: '. . . the outlook for us is black. It has been threatened that if all the chunkel heads are not returned we will have to pay for them; also rations will be reduced to half scale; also the theatre will be pulled down; all singing will be forbidden in huts after dark; probably games too. Oh the selfishness of some, running the risk of such punishments on themselves and on others too. A whole campful of 3 or 4 thousand sick men!!!'[44]

The first Toosey knew about it was when he was summoned to the guard room to be told that the ten men were going to be interrogated by the Kempei Tai. He was horrified and asked Hosomi if he could deal with the men himself. No amount of appeal had any effect. The men had been caught stealing and the matter was out of Hosomi's hands, there was nothing to be done. There then followed an extraordinary scene when the Kempei Tai interpreter, who spoke good English, called for Toosey, his staff and all the field officers in camp. Captain Blackater recorded the speech in his diary:

Good day to you, gentlemen. Come closer, I will not bite you. As you know, we have had a serious case to deal with. Some very bad men have stolen and sold our property to the Thais. Some of these men will go to the State penitentiary for up to five years, the rest will probably be freed. You must co-operate, gentlemen, and stop these bad men, use your power to punish if they do wrong. Some days ago we had to deal with a case at a certain camp . . . This, gentlemen, cannot be allowed to happen, you understand. They were punished and with them an officer over sixty, unfortunately. We had another case, and unfortunately had to shoot two men. One was unmarried, the other had two children aged three and six.[45]

The interpreter spoke of an episode in a camp in Kanchanaburi where two officers, Hawley and Armitage, were beaten to death for their part in concealing and using a radio. In a string of shocking cases, the beating to death of these two men and the beatings meted out to their companions, stands out as one of particular brutality.

Toosey was unmoved by the interpreter's speech and refused to acknowledge the warning. He simply asked when they would get more meat for the camp. 'That was the occasion when I was called a lousy bastard,' he recalled. 'The meat was destined for the men up river who were working, not sick men who showed no spirit,' he was told. 'When would they get more medicines?' 'They were getting plenty of medicine, more than the soldiers in the IJA,' the interpreter replied. When Toosey asked for Red Cross medical supplies he was told he could not have any but that there were 30,000 letters for the prisoners in Kanchanaburi. They could not have those either because the Japanese had only two men available to censor the letters. Toosey then demanded to see the men who had been interrogated by the Kempei Tai. At first the Japanese refused but he stood his ground and eventually they gave in. He was shown into the guardroom and was confronted with a sight that shocked him:

There was Lawson standing, stark bollock naked. From his neck to his heels he was a mass of wheals from a whip. It was the most terrible sight. The whole of his back, right down to his buttocks, and including his buttocks, was raw. His front was covered with angry, red patches where they had burnt him with cigarettes. He was a tremendously brave man. I went up to him and asked him what the trouble was. 'Well Sir, I've told the buggers the truth but they won't believe me.' So I said, 'Have you any idea what they want you to say?' and he said, 'Yes, but I'm not going to say it because it isn't true.' So I said, 'Lawson, listen to me, you say what they want you to say and I will take full responsibility for you after the war.'[46]

So Lawson told the Kempei Tai what they wanted to hear about the theft and sale of the tools and the beating stopped. He and the other five were then taken to Bangkok where they stood trial and were sentenced to imprisonment ranging from six to eighteen months.

'It was a lesson I learned in those camps,' Toosey said later, 'that torture does not always produce the truth because so often the people who are doing the torturing have a fixed idea in their mind of what they want to hear.'[47]

In the middle of November the Japanese began to move fit men out of Tamarkan. Some were sent north to work on repairs on the railway. As construction was complete and the number of working men required was less, the rest were sent to other camps in the base area, at Chungkai and Nong Pladuk, at the zero kilometre point near Ban Pong. The sick were to be evacuated to a large new hospital camp at Nakhon Phatom which eventually housed 10,000 sick and convalescent men. Toosey was told he would be sent to run another camp. He expected the next move to be to Nakhon Phatom.

Tamarkan was to be handed over to an incoming Australian party under the command of Lieutenant Colonel Anderson, one of the great commanders on the railway and one of only two men to be awarded the Victoria Cross in the Malayan campaign. These men had begun their journey in Moulmein and had worked in the jungle on the Burma section of the line. Toosey discussed with Doctors Moon and Mark what they should do with the remaining stores at Tamarkan. They decided to sell the farm animals and food stores to the incoming Australians, but the medicines and welfare fund they divided between them, sure that they would have need of them in the future.

Moon took over command of Tamarkan from Toosey until the Australians arrived on 18 December, when he handed it over to them. He was sent up to Chungkai, where he worked once again with Weary Dunlop, and then later to Tha Muang. Jim Mark was sent to be the senior medical officer at the Aerodrome Camp in Kanchanaburi, which became known as Sanbunkensho. Life in his camp was relatively comfortable until the arrival, in the autumn of 1944, of a Japanese guard called Captain Noguchi.

Colonel Toosey and David Boyle were ordered to move on 11 December 1943. They were put on a train and sent south, not to Nakhon Phatom as Toosey expected. Saito, now at Nong Pladuk, had put in a request for him.

BY THE LIGHT OF THE
BOMBER'S MOON

There are few things so testing of morale as being bombed in
a P.O.W. Camp.

Dr Stanley Pavillard

What Toosey would have liked more than anything else was a
rest. He was mentally and physically exhausted from the daily
battles with Japanese administration at Tamarkan. When he and
David Boyle arrived at Nong Pladuk it seemed at first as if they
would be left alone. The camp had been run since the autumn of
1942 by Major Eddie Gill with a large administration that
included a highly regarded officer from the 4th Gurkha Rifles,
Major R.A.N. Davidson, as camp adjutant and Major Paddy Sykes
as messing officer.

Nong Pladuk was divided into two camps, Nong Pladuk I and
Nong Pladuk II. The camps together housed up to a maximum of
8000 prisoners who had worked on the railway. Some had been

members of plate-laying parties and went a long way up into the jungle to where the sleepers were laid and the rails were needed. Others worked in the colossal Hashimoto base workshops and railway sidings at Nong Pladuk, loading and unloading trains, shunting trucks and piling stores of supplies and ammunition. With the railway now finished, men worked in the yards at Hashimoto.

Although the two camps were only a kilometre apart, contact between them was strictly forbidden so that when Toosey arrived at Nong Pladuk I and Padre Carel Hamel at Nong Pladuk II the men never saw each other again. The padre regretted the loss of leadership:

> Now that the firm hand of Colonel Toosey was missing, the administration of the Dutch commander became more and more tyrannical. His military police created fear among the camp inhabitants. Once we believed, that the arrival of some Dutch field officers, who would take over the administration of the camp, would improve the situation. However when a Dutch Lt. Col. became commander of the camp, he still kept the captain as his adjutant and in practice the last one could enforce his will. As an excuse one has to admit that there was hardly any discipline among the men. Most of them were very unwilling and tried to avoid all duties. Too much the good had to suffer with the bad.[1]

Nong Pladuk I was situated in the paddy-field area alongside the main Bangkok to Singapore line, close to the junction of the Thailand–Burma railway. 'The Camp was surrounded by military objectives such as marshalling yards, engineering workshops and a Bofors Troop run by renegade Indians. The nearest objective to the Camp was the marshalling yards which were as close as 10 yards.'[2]

One of the earliest in Thailand, the camp was built in July 1942 and had many similarities with Tamarkan in that its permanent state gave the prisoners an opportunity to make improvements to their lives. There were two canteens and a small theatre. The name, in Thai, means 'fish pond' but Nong Pladuk was far from the river and there was no bathing which had been such a benefit at Tamarkan. It was, however, close to the market town of Ban Pong and on the whole the food at Nong Pladuk was better than at Tamarkan. There was more of it because this was a working camp and the men were paid and they received full IJA rations. Or at least they were supposed to.

Nong Pladuk also had better accommodation than Tamarkan and Toosey had a space in a hut with a wooden floor rather than bamboo slats above a mud floor which he had been used to. Some of the huts were built on stilts as the camp was liable to flooding during the monsoon. As in all other camps, the men were squeezed into the huts with five to seven men per 12 feet. The officers had a little more space but they were still cramped in their quarters.

One thing that struck Toosey and Boyle about Nong Pladuk camp was its uniform colour. Brown. The huts were brown, the old attap leaves on their roofs had turned brown with age, the ground was panned, brown mud, the men were sunburned brown, even their clothes were of a brownish hue. All this brown was in marked contrast to the bright greens of the banana trees outside the camp, of the deep red and clean white flowers of the frangipani trees near the cemetery. It was as if the natural, colourful beauty of their environs had been barred at the gates of the camp. During the dry season the camp was a dustbowl, during the rainy season it frequently flooded and the brown-red mud stuck to everything, sucking the heels off boots, drying onto men's legs and making the latrine dash at night a slippery exercise.

Drawing by Will Wilder of the interior of a hut at Nong Pladuk.
This drawing was commissioned by Toosey in 1945.

Others who had been further up the line had noticed the uniform brown too. Only they had come from a terrible place where everything was grey, the colour washed out under the heavy, rain canopy of the jungle. When arriving in Nong Pladuk they had been struck, as had the sick men arriving at Tamarkan, by brown men smiling. Lieutenant Louis Baume returned to Nong Pladuk from the jungle in August 1943 and wrote in his diary: 'They were all at the gate to meet us, Fred, Bill, Alan, Shirley and the rest. But we could hardly believe our eyes for having seen only grey, dirty, long haired skeletons with a despairing look in their eyes and never a ghost of a smile on their lips, we were suddenly confronted with what appeared to us as fat, sunburnt and radiant prisoners; it was only then that we realised how much we had changed.'[3]

The Japanese bored a deep well at Nong Pladuk and supplied a petrol engine and pump which helped the men extract water for the cookhouse and for drinking. All drinking water at Nong Pladuk had to be chlorinated. A second open well for clothes washing and general ablutions was not as deep as the cookhouse well. As a result, washing water, during the rainy season, was often muddy.

The pump's motor finally gave out in October 1944 and the Dutch, who had proved to be ingenious at solving many other engineering problems, designed and built a bamboo pump: 'This pump was sunk about 4 metres and delivered, in a satisfactory fashion, clear water. These pumps largely replaced the open well for washing water,'[4] the medical officer wrote in his camp report. So successful was this pump that when the men arrived at their next camp they immediately constructed another 'Dutch Pump' and had clear drinking and washing water right up to the end of the war.

On 16 January 1944, the Japanese administration at Nong Pladuk, encouraged by Saito, announced that Toosey was to take over command. The effort of running the camp for over a year had taken its toll on Major Gill's health and he was only too pleased to be relieved of the responsibility, although he continued to support the new administration. It was not a responsibility Toosey had looked for but he took it on energetically as usual:

My assumption of command of Nong Pladuk POW Camp coincided with the arrival of a new Japanese Group Commander in Thailand – Major Ebiko. He was the most sincere and tolerant Group Commander in Thailand. His chief asset was that he allowed me to interview him personally and thus enabled me to overcome the Red Tape, obstinacy and unwillingness to help, of all previous Japanese administrations. I frequently took advantage of this and obtained as a result the following improvements:

(a) An increase in the size of the Camp by about 1/3rd
(b) Sports facilities; instructional lectures and vocational training
(c) Subject to restrictions – Japanese Propaganda Newspapers
(d) Opportunities for buying drugs and medicines from Bangkok through the Japanese.[5]

Lieutenant Charles Wylie, who had been in Nong Pladuk for several months, was as surprised as many others that Toosey had demanded and been granted an interview with Ebiko: 'That was unusual in itself. Toosey told Ebiko that it was his personal responsibility to look after his men and Ebiko, in return, must agree to feed the prisoners and see they didn't escape. When cases came to beatings after that, the Japanese dealt with them more sympathetically. Toosey looked the part and they respected him.'[6]

While the improvements to the camp were felt by all men and the sports, in particular, became increasingly popular the continued corruption among the guards troubled everyone. Being close to the food market in Ban Pong meant the rations for this camp ought to have been good. There was an official ration scale issued by the IJA, which would have meant the same rations for the working prisoners as for their Army's soldiers. In reality, it was seldom what was received.

There were several issues, the first being bureaucracy. Ration scales for the camps were set a week in advance. This made it difficult for camps such as Nong Pladuk, which had varying strengths depending on whether they had an incoming party or not. It also had the unpleasant side-effect that the incoming parties were resented because all men in the camp went short. Sergeant Sherring, staff officer in Nong Pladuk for three years, wrote an extensive report for Toosey after the war in which he detailed all the problems he had encountered with rations:

> Between October 1942 and August 1944 thousands of men passed through Nong Pladuk Camp going to the jungle at first, and later coming down. At no time were we given the extra correct rations of fresh vegetables and meat, and never were we allowed extra 'general rations'. The I.J.A. excuse was always as follows: 'Our indent for your week's supply must be put in on Sunday and drawn on Monday – these parties were not expected and our stores will issue nothing until the next issue day.' As these men going up country were merely staying in our Camp for a few days they were never put on ration strength by the Japanese.[7]

The second problem was the quality of the food. All camps were supplied with the poorest quality rice which it took the cooks months to learn how to cook well. The vegetables supplied were sweet potato tops and Chinese radishes and they received very little meat. But the major problem at Nong Pladuk was swindling. Sergeant Sherring was constantly dismayed by the dishonesty of the Korean guards and the unwillingness of the Japanese administration to rein these men in. He wrote: 'The earliest instances of deliberate swindling were with oil. This was issued in 4 gallon cans and was Philippine Island Margarine. The cans bore a label which stated that the net contents in weight was 13.2 kg.' However, the Japanese quartermaster told Sherring that he was not to believe what was written on the tin but accept that they contained 19 kilogrammes of oil. Time and again he and Captain Moisson, one of the messing officers, took this up with the Japanese and were told: 'Our Quartermaster has certain deficiencies to make up. You must accept the cans as 19 kg.'[8]

The swindling fluctuated depending on the Japanese camp commander and the officer, often a Korean, in charge of the rations. A good camp commander could influence the handling of the rations and the benefit was quickly felt. An example of this was Sergeant Murakami. He was in charge of rations at Nong Pladuk in the summer of 1942 and moved to Tamarkan in the autumn. Toosey's gain was Major Gill's loss. Murakami's successor as the rations officer was Ezuma. Sherring wrote: 'He was to be with us for many a long day and was of the very worst type of sadist and racketeer. Ezuma began the swindles in real earnest. During the whole of this period, reputed weights were, on reweighing, found to be false. This can be laid at the Koreans' door. It was acknowledged by semi-friendly Koreans that their compatriot doing ration truck daily at any one period was a wealthy man.'[9] Certainly Ezuma and the other Koreans lived well and it was sickening for the hungry men to witness the heartless and deliberate cruelty of food swindles in a country that was rich in all natural foodstuffs.

The messing officers protested about the rackets frequently but to little avail. Often a strong protest would be met with an unpleasant rejoinder ending in a bout of face-slapping. If the Japanese camp commander was aware of what was going on he was either too weak to stop it or was himself profiting by it. In either case the swindling continued. They found that they were short on everything and the officers in charge of the rations for the prisoners reckoned they missed out on at least a quarter of what they should have got, and often more, and that what was supplied was of the lowest possible quality. 'I have been unable to ascertain how extensive was the swindle, but 25% at Xmas 1944 meant 500 kg of vegetables a day at an average of $1.20 per kgs. which meant $600 a day in someone's pocket,'[10] Sherring concluded.

The canteen proved, once again, to be a saving grace. On the whole supplies were regular and of fair quality. This made all the difference to the men who were able to purchase duck eggs, peanut buns or lentils from their wages to supplement their meals. The canteen was also useful for the hospital and the profits were used to buy extra food for the sick.

There was little Toosey found he could do about the swindling apart from complain, which he did. It had little effect as it had been going on for such a long time and was endemic. He turned his attention to things that could make a difference to the men's lives. 'We had a good concert party which usually played once a week, a football ground, and several basketball pitches,' he wrote. 'Normally we were allowed to play games after the day's work was finished and also all day on holidays. Sport reached a high level in this camp and helped greatly with maintaining morale. We ran football leagues and cup ties which provoked great enthusiasm. The men were also marched out to work every day to music played by the band.'

How could it happen that half-starved men could find the time and energy to entertain each other? The answer is the timescale. Three and a half years was long enough to make it necessary for the prisoners to create for themselves a form of society. They had rules and regulations, they formed groups and teams. Patricia Mark has looked into this aspect of the prisoners' lives for many years:

They played bridge and chess. They went to the improvised concerts and sang in choirs and acted in theatre performances.

The more artistically inclined sketched and painted. They gave and attended lectures on every topic under the sun. They became knowledgeable about the local flora and fauna. They found some spiritual comfort in the beauty of their surroundings. They brewed illicit beer and threw parties to celebrate birthdays or wedding anniversaries. And in their contact with this social fabric, which most of the time somehow remained intact, they managed to create a sort of civilisation in which they maintained their underlying personal integrity against the alien forces which always threatened to overwhelm them.[11]

Charles Wylie remembered talks given on every conceivable subject at Nong Pladuk. One favourite lecture was by an American mortician on embalming, another popular speaker was the cricket correspondent Jim Swanton. He could talk for hours about individual test matches and he always had a good audience. Wylie also recalled a man named Golly Mitchell who would appear on stage with his performing flea. However, one of the star turns was Fergus 'Gus' Anckorn, a magician who had become the youngest member of the Magic Circle in 1939. His stage name was Wizardus and his shows were so popular that the Japanese asked him to perform for them. Unfortunately things went awry as Anckorn explained to a friend, Norman Pritchard, in a letter sixty years later:

At Nong Pladuk I was sent to do a magic show to some Japanese officers including a general (with Toosey's permission). I did the show entirely in perfect Japanese, and they were delighted, lots of clapping and food. The general came and spoke to me and asked questions. And I said 'wakerimasen' [I don't know]. He then knocked me down and kicked my face and blackened my eyes. I think he thought I was being arrogant, having heard me speaking Japanese for three quarters of an hour and then saying 'wakerimasen'.

Toosey then got a card printed for me with words to the effect that I had learned the Japanese words for my show – but spoke none!

In any trouble after that I could flash the card and save a bashing! [12]

One of the more eccentric of the clubs and societies that were founded at Nong Pladuk was the cycle club. It had a strong membership of both Dutch and British prisoners and they held meetings where lectures would be given on everything from cycle maintenance to histories of the most famous races. The only thing lacking in the Nong Pladuk cycle club were the bicycles.

The Harboured Lights Concert Party was an impressive troupe, which included some talented artistes and directors. Toosey encouraged the party to put on as many performances as they could and he succeeded in persuading Ebiko to let the performers off work in order to rehearse. Norman Pritchard remembered being greeted by Toosey with enthusiasm when he learned that Pritchard was an artist with a special talent for calligraphy. He encouraged him to use this gift to produce the concert programmes, some of which were extremely detailed. Pritchard was a lance bombardier and was surprised that Toosey had taken notice of him, but Toosey dismissed this with a shrug: 'It's what you do when you're here that is important,' he told him, 'I am not concerned in the slightest in what rank you are. There are some in this camp who are highly ranked and are useless and some of you who are lowly ranked, or not ranked at all, who are the salt of the earth.' [13]

Pritchard had bought a box of paints with money he had

saved up by selling cigarettes (he was not a smoker), his pen and his signet ring. He gave the money to a driver who went out with the ration lorry and who had offered to buy the paints for him at the market in Ban Pong. The paintbox was his most treasured possession. In November 1944 Pritchard became friendly with a Dutch artist called Jan Van Holthe who lost all his worldly goods when his hut was destroyed in a bombing raid. Pritchard shared his paints with Van Holthe and the Dutchman said this simple act of camaraderie saved his sanity. In return he taught Pritchard perspective and other drawing techniques. Between them they produced a large number of concert programmes; Van Holthe sketched the figures and Pritchard did the backgrounds and calligraphy. Van Holthe made a series of cartoon sketches at the next camp sending up the Japanese and one of these was presented to Toosey by the Dutch at the very end of the war.

The Harboured Lights Concert Party put on a mixture of variety shows, revues and musical comedies as well as plays that they had written themselves. Titles such as 'When Day is Done'; 'Escapado Argentino', 'Invitation to Murder' and 'The Show Must Go On' were performed. The producer for most, if not all of the shows, was Lieutenant Allum. He had a team of men who worked with him including a musical director called Ace Connolly and a songwriter, Bob Gale, who also wrote scripts for some of the musicals. The men who played the female roles were particularly fêted and some gained a reputation that followed them from camp to camp. The main female impersonator was a man named Basil Ferron who also made costumes for the shows. However, the concert parties were not without their problems; directors and writers had to be careful with their scripts, particularly revues, because the Japanese were sensitive and feared being criticised or ridiculed in the performances. On one or two occasions the guards took exception to something in a play and there was trouble.

Toosey was called for when Sergeant Jim Pratt got into difficulty. He belonged to a different group called the Radioptimists Concert Party and had been holding a concert for the men in one of the huts. Pratt was stopped by a Japanese sentry who ordered him and two other men to report to the guardroom: '. . . there I was searched, kicked on both legs and beaten in the face at least a dozen times by a Guard Commander named Takamini. The interpreter was then sent for and I was told to relate what the concert was about. The Guard Commander accused me of insulting the Japanese Sergeant during the concert, which of course was not true.'[14] The beating continued and a further Japanese guard became involved. Finally, having been kicked in the stomach, bladder and privates, Pratt fell to his knees in pain. He told the guard commander that he would swear by anything he chose to produce that he had not insulted the sentry. An oath was taken and he was allowed to go back to his hut. His beating, however, left him with severe pains and he continued to pass mucus and pus in his stools, something which the medical staff were convinced had to do with his treatment in the guard room. He was still suffering from his injuries when Toosey saw him at the end of the war.

'The sing-songs and concerts always concluded with the National Anthem,' another prisoner recalled after the war. 'After a while, we were forbidden to sing the National Anthem, so we sang "Land of Hope and Glory" instead. The way in which we sang this wonderful song impressed the Japanese so much that it was not long before they stopped us singing this tune.'[15] So they adopted 'There'll Always Be An England' and the Australians added the extra words: 'And wherever there is England, Australia will be there too'.

Almost half the prison population in Nong Pladuk was Dutch and Toosey had three Dutch officers on his staff. Colonel Scheurer, who had been at Tamarkan, was in charge of the Dutch troops, Major Leemeyer was his adjutant, and Warrant Officer Slotboom was in charge of the Dutch office and administration. Relations between the two nationalities were on the whole harmonious. One Dutch doctor, C. H. den Hertog, wrote a speech which he planned to give at the end of the war and in it he described the Dutch characteristics:

> We Dutchmen are a rather difficult lot to deal with. Our love for freedom is so great that some of us fail to see the simple fact that also a democratic state and even a small community like a POW camp ought to have laws and regulations. Sometimes this side of our character is a liability, sometimes it is an asset. Bismarck knew it, when he said 'Of course you can eat the Dutchmen but you are bound to have stomach trouble' and the Germans in this war experienced it behind their lines. As an Englishman you did not know the simple trick that when you want a Dutchman to do something, just tell him not to do it and he will do it at once. But you had your own way of approaching us and you did not need much time to find the key to our hearts. From that moment we did many things because it was you who wanted them to be done and because you had our confidence. I think that is the secret of true leadership.[16]

Occasionally Toosey had to intervene when Dutch and English relations became strained but on the whole his method of encouraging friendly rivalry worked well. This was particularly successful in the cookhouses where the cooks tried to outdo each other in the preparation of the ubiquitous jungle stew. The Dutch were impressive improvisers and made use of their expertise to provide mechanical solutions such as the water pump, but they were also artistic. It was in the area of art and entertainment where the creative rivalry was most productive. Their concert parties were at least as good as the Harboured Lights and they were masters at stage design, even helping to rig some lighting in the theatre.

Despite concert parties, sports and the canteen, there were still men at Nong Pladuk who were suffering from chronic conditions as a result of what they had been through and witnessed on the railway. The doctors at Nong Pladuk had seen some appalling sights in 1943 and like the medics at Tamarkan, were frustrated by the lack of medicines and dressings. Also, like Tamarkan, the greatest assistance they received was from a branch of the V-scheme which managed to smuggle in medicines and food and had been operating successfully for eighteen months by the time Toosey arrived.

Run by Sykes and Davidson, the V-scheme at Nong Pladuk was the first of its kind between prisoner-of-war camps and the ex-pat civilians in Bangkok. The exchanges took place approximately once a month until the end of 1943 when the ration lorries were taken to a different buying point at the other end of Ban Pong. Gairdner supplied Sykes with small amounts of medicines, particularly emetine, and money with which to buy bulkier medicines and equipment in Ban Pong. This was about 250 to 400 Ticals a month. However, it was not enough and in July 1943, when the doctors and the medical team were desperate, Sykes arranged a 12,000 Tical loan with Gairdner. The loan was brought to Ban Pong by Mrs Gairdner, a Thai by birth, 'hidden in a bag of tapioca flour which she most gallantly and efficiently managed to pass, in front of the Japanese Guard, to Maj. Sykes on his weekly buying visit to Ban Pong'.[17]

The only other person aware of the V-scheme in Nong Pladuk

was Staff Sergeant Sherring. He had to deal with the money handed in by Corporal Paton. When Toosey and David Boyle were appointed to the administration, Sykes discussed with Davidson whether or not the two of them could be trusted. He had never informed Major Gill of the V-scheme as he felt it would put the camp commander in a difficult and dangerous position. Davidson believed he could trust Boyle, who was working as his deputy. Toosey was informed but took no part. He made it clear, however, that he was prepared to take responsibility for the scheme should it be uncovered and he undertook to give the drivers and others involved his protection.

The senior medical officer at Nong Pladuk was Major E.A. Smyth of the Royal Army Medical Corps. He was in this camp for the whole of his captivity with the exception of the last six months which he spent at Ubon. Dr Smyth and Colonel Toosey had a businesslike working relationship based on mutual respect. Toosey never interfered in the running of the hospital, the same policy he had adopted in Tamarkan. However, he took over responsibility for the hygiene in Nong Pladuk from the dental officer. This gave him an opportunity to step up the war on flies that the doctors were so concerned about. Dr Smyth noted in his report for Toosey that twenty men were able to kill 20,000 to 30,000 flies daily. He went on: '. . . when 100 men were employed, the daily kill was between 70,000 and 100,000. One of the most important facts about the prevention of fly borne disease that we have learned as POW has been the extreme value of fly swatting, which has enabled us to keep the flies at an extremely low figure in spite of the impossibility of dealing with all the fly breeding areas.'[18]

There were two different types of flies in the prison camps, Toosey explained in 1974. Bluebottles and their larvae were all around the latrines where they did useful work breaking down the faeces. The bluebottles seldom strayed into other areas of the camp and as such they were not considered dangerous harbingers of disease. The real nuisance was the house fly. These insects swarmed around the cookhouse, the huts and the hospital in vast numbers. They were particularly drawn to the ulcer ward, Dr Smyth noted. During the cholera outbreak in 1943 the doctors had to persuade desperately hungry men to throw away any food that had been contaminated by flies. When this was a plate of uneaten rice and stew it was particularly bitter to forgo it for fear of infection.

Swill also had to be carefully dealt with and, as at Tamarkan, as much of the small amount of waste as possible was incinerated, the rest buried in Otway pits. Nong Pladuk even had its own rat-catcher who was employed full time and kept busy. His average catch per month was between 150 and 200 rats.

The hospital at Nong Pladuk developed over time until it had an operating theatre, a ward master's office, a dental centre, a laboratory and separate wards, created by means of straw- or attap-matting partitions. Of necessity all the side areas of the hospital were very small. It still had a few Army stretchers on which the seriously ill patients slept. Others slept on the wooden floor. Some had fly sheets, others thin straw mats underneath them. Nevertheless the hospital was woefully short of equipment. For a 900-bed hospital there were only fifteen bedpans, which was a problem considering that many of the patients were suffering from conditions such as dysentery or chronic diarrhoea.

When Toosey was ordered to move to Nong Pladuk he took with him medical equipment and supplies, so cherished and expensively bought at such risk. The remaining money from the V-scheme and this medical equipment went to Dr Smyth. Thus the hospital at Nong Pladuk suddenly had an influx of valuable material that greatly boosted the stores and with this the morale

Hospital Hut at Nong Pladuk *by Jan Van Holthe.*

of the whole medical team. They now had a microscope, more bedpans, water sterilising powder, different types of ointment, chloroform, Dover's tablets, calomel, and quite a number of miscellaneous drugs. The most vital drug for Dr Smyth was emetine, the only really effective cure for amoebic dysentery. Although Toosey had brought a good quantity of emetine from Tamarkan, the Japanese kept over three-quarters of it.

'Throughout our three years in Thailand', Dr Smyth wrote, 'the success or failure of the Medical Department depended on the most scrupulous restrictions by whoever happened to be the

Senior Medical Officer on the use of all drugs and dressings. All essential drugs, such as Emetine, M&B 693, anaesthetics, Atebrin, Morphia, Vitamin preparations, antiseptics and dressings were only issued by direct application to the SMO. By this means it was amazing on what small quantities of drugs a large hospital could be run.'[19]

The work at Nong Pladuk was tedious; the hours were long but the great panic and drive of the speedo period was behind them. They had to form working parties to load and unload trains, move stores from dump to dump and dig defences and air-raid shelters for the Japanese. Toosey did not like the fact that his men were asked to handle war stores and ammunition but it was useless to protest, as they had discovered from past experience. The officer in charge of organising work parties for the Hashimoto railway workshops was Lieutenant Harold Payne. His difficult task was to balance the requirements of the Japanese engineers with the numbers of fit men in the camp available for work. There were many who were considered 'light sick', suffering from chronic conditions as a result of serious illnesses contracted in the jungle. Some men were partially sighted; others had lost their sense of balance, both as a result of vitamin deficiencies. More still suffered from chronic diarrhoea. Payne had fulfilled that role for many months and became expert in dealing with the Japanese, and as a result of his regular interventions, conflicts were often defused and avoided.

As 1944 wore on, ever more restrictions were introduced. Church services were limited to half an hour once a week and the padres had to submit in writing to the Japanese everything that was to be said or sung at these services. Toosey understood the value of the church to camp morale and he did everything he could for the padres, trying to protect them from the indignities and humiliations to which they were often subjected.

He was not unanimous in his praise for the churchmen, how-ever. It was his experience, and that of other men, too, that the Church of England padres were less effective than the Roman Catholic or Baptist. His own regimental chaplain was one such example. Toosey went up to him on one occasion and said: 'Look here, my boy, this is the opportunity of your lifetime. This is what you've been training for all your life, that is to get up and help save some lives. Whereas all you do is to lie on your backside on the bamboo and let it grow up your arse.' However, the Roman Catholic priests, with their rules and unflinching promises, accru-ing great benefits in the world beyond if adhered to, were wonderfully inspiring. 'The man who inspired us all at the camps I was in was a Roman Catholic Jesuit priest called Father Cowin,' Toosey recalled. 'He always wore his robes, he got badly beaten up, he wasn't in any way dogmatic but he was there all the time, to help us when we were in distress. He was really quite won-derful.'[20]

Father Cowin was constantly frustrated by the Japanese in Nong Pladuk. They took away his Bibles, hymn sheets, prayer books and sermon manuscripts. He wasn't allowed a watch or a pen and his sermons had to be scratched on bamboo and shown to the Japanese. He was forbidden to pray for the Allies or the royal family. What upset him more than anything was that they forbade him to visit dying men in neighbouring Nong Pladuk II to administer the last rites. 'With the result that hundreds of Catholics died denied the Sacraments, the supreme consolation of their faith, and burial by the priest. Throughout their captiv-ity', he concluded, 'the prisoners of war were starved – starved of food – starved of clothing – of medical supplies – of news – of letters from home and starved of spiritual consolation.'[21]

One of the things they were desperate for was news from home. When letters did eventually get through, often up to eighteen months late, there was great excitement. Letters had to be censored and at Nong Pladuk this was done by a Japanese who spoke no English. Louis Baume wrote in his diary:

> These letters have been here for months and those which have not been stolen by us, eaten by white ants or destroyed by damp, many have been burnt by the Nips as being the quickest way to reduce the number. Most of them are over one year old already, yet only about 20 a day are given out, and not even regularly at that. At last Toosey has obtained permission to censor them himself and he is doing several hundred a day. Occasionally he takes a perfectly innocent one to the Nip interpreter to ask his opinion – this flatters the Nip and maintains the pretence. All are happy and no face is lost. But what a comic opera situation – prisoners censoring their own mail! Is there any other race but the Nips who could be so utterly stupid?[22]

Toosey himself was concerned that the letters had a detrimental effect on morale. For some they were a reminder of a forgotten life, disturbing or even unwelcome. He had successfully compartmentalised his own life so that anything not to do with the camps was forgotten. He received three letters from home during his captivity and on each occasion, he admitted, he was shaken and depressed.

In Nong Pladuk the prisoners were dogged by a combination of boredom and fear. Louis Baume recorded his feelings on 6 June 1944: 'Our dull daily existence drags on in unrelieved monotony: gardening for the Nips, ballast carrying, swill pits, wood chopping, log sawing, with eternal stodgy rice and watery veg stew for meals; rice and stew, rice and stew, 3 times a day, 21 times a week, 1095 times a year for 2½ years. How much longer, O Lord?'[23]

In a move that perplexed and angered everyone in the camp, Nong Pladuk I had been sited only a few yards away from the railway line and close to the large marshalling yards, an obvious target for bombing by the Allies. Between Nong Pladuk I and Nong Pladuk II there was a Bofors anti-aircraft gun manned by renegade Indian troops and Toosey knew it was only a matter of time before the marshalling yards and anti-aircraft position would be attacked.

So he began a campaign to get the Japanese to allow them to dig slit trenches. He took a different tack from the one he had taken at Tamarkan over food, rest days and working hours. He demanded that they be allowed to dig them as it was against all military practice to place a prisoner-of-war camp near a strategic target. He told them that Japan would be shamed by the rest of the world when this came to light and that the very least they could do would be to let him move the camp back 200 metres from the sidings and to dig trenches. They refused on both counts. Over the spring and summer of 1944 he kept up the pressure until Ebiko had had enough and threatened to shoot him. 'Well, shoot me then,' Toosey told him curtly. He was not shot but nor were the slit trenches dug for the prisoners. However, they were for the Japanese.

In his camp report Toosey wrote:

It was quite obvious to me from the day of my arrival in Camp that sooner or later we should be bombed, due to the proximity of military objectives to the Camp. I made every form of representation and protest to the Japanese Authorities on many occasions regarding P.A.D. [Personnel Air Defence] measures. I received very little help, an example of their replies being, 'The British have no aircraft left; you have no need to worry.' They also informed me that our Air Force knew of the location of the camp, which I doubted.[24]

By September 1944 there was still no air-raid protection in Nong Pladuk and Japanese orders were that all men had to remain in their huts during air raids. This order was to be enforced at the point of the bayonet, Toosey was warned.

Meanwhile, despite the anxiety over air raids or perhaps because of it, rumours of their imminent release abounded. Their secret radio informed them at the beginning of September that Paris had fallen to the Allies and that good progress was being made on other fronts. In their excitement they held a raffle and drew lots for the last day of their captivity. Most people thought the war would finish by the end of September.

In September 1944, Toosey received a small consignment of American Red Cross parcels. This was good news. The Japanese gave him about half the supplies, which amounted to one box of comforts to ten men. It was a very small quantity but the effect on the morale of the prisoners was wonderful to see. Before handing out the Red Cross boxes to the men, Toosey got the medical team to remove and store all the medicines supplied. This consisted mainly of M&B 693 antibiotics and multivitamins.

The second half of the consignment was delivered at the end of September but not until the Koreans had stolen over 3000 M&B tablets and more than half of the remaining multivitamin tablets. This time each box had to be divided between twenty men. Dr Smyth's indignation can be well understood, not least as the Koreans were using the M&B 693 to cure venereal disease. 'Nevertheless', he concluded, 'the American supplies received were magnificent both in quantity and quality. I calculated, that continuing the usual POW restrictions on drugs, I could continue for 13 months provided the camp strength remained reasonably constant.'[25]

On Monday 4 September things took a turn for the worse. A recent visit by a Japanese officer from Tokyo had condemned

Nong Pladuk I as an unsuitable camp for the prisoners but the administration decided to close Nong Pladuk II and move all the prisoners into Nong Pladuk I. Toosey was horrified. He considered it a callous act that would almost certainly lead to disaster. The camp was now seriously overcrowded. There were 350 men per hut designed for 200 men, giving them about 1 square yard for eating, sleeping and living. Tempers were frayed as they pushed and shoved at night to find some respite from the sweltering heat.

The following day brought more bad news. Ebiko, the camp commandant, was to leave and Major Chida would take over. He was a man with a bad reputation, who had been in charge of Nong Pladuk when it started in 1942. He was unpredictable and refused, unlike Ebiko, to speak to Toosey directly. That day Toosey received orders to evacuate hut 1 because the Japanese wanted it. All the officers would move to hut 3, which was temporarily full of men from Nong Pladuk II. Such moves were not infrequent but they always had a dislocating effect and generally meant a search, which heightened anxiety. That same afternoon an RAF leaflet found its way into the camp showing a map of Europe with the latest fronts and the cheering message across the top: 'It's in the bag boys'.[26]

And all the time they were aware of the dangers from the bombers. Night-time, which had once brought them welcome relief, now brought fear. 'The moon: cold, hard, impersonal; punctual and relentless in its wanderings round the earth; subject of many a discussion, companion in our troubles, comforter in our secret sorrows,' mused Louis Baume in his diary. 'How often have we stood in the early hours of the morning, watching the setting moon, wondering that as it shone on us so too it shone on those at home. Constant friend, but now chilling foe. The bomber's moon.'[27]

Shortly after 2 a.m. on the night of 6/7 September 1944, Allied bombers passed over Nong Pladuk and attacked the railway sidings hidden in the trees half a mile away. A petrol train and an ammunition dump were destroyed as well as most of the sidings. Then it happened. 'Another plane approached,' wrote Louis Baume in his diary, 'we lay in the ditch among the red ants and waited. The stick of bombs crashed across the camp and the plane roared away to the north; before us on the padang [parade ground] rose a thick cloud of dust; against the starlit sky we could see the shattered roof of hut 3, and soon we heard the screams and moans of the wounded.'[28]

The bombers came back again and again, dive bombing the sidings. The prisoners could hear the bombs whistling overhead not knowing whether they would fall in or outside the camp. Splinters tore through the flimsy bamboo and attap of the huts. 'The earth shook and shivered as we lay in the shallow ditches, not knowing whether the bombs were in or only around the camp.'[29]

At 3:20 a.m. the raid was over. Toosey emerged from the badly damaged hut 3. It was one of the most gruesome sights he had seen. Injured men running around covered in blood, bodies and body parts strewn across the camp, huts on fire, splinters of palm and bamboo everywhere. And all around the hideous smell of burning flesh. No guards had been injured but they were in a panic. Some had run away, others refused to allow the men to have lights so they were fumbling around in the dark with only the glow from the fires in the sidings and the moon and stars to help them. A handful of the guards, however, helped the prisoners as best they could. Toosey took charge, giving orders for blankets to be handed over, for the dead to be moved and the injured to be brought to the hospital.

Dr Smyth's calculations about his medical stocks were

shattered by the air raid. He had 360 casualties, including some seriously injured men needing blood transfusions and a great deal of medical assistance. Men queued up to offer blood. Others attempted to assist but were hindered by the Japanese. 'One Japanese, however, preferred human duty to self-protection. Sergeant Watanabe proceeded at once to the bombed area, himself carried to the Hospital one of the first casualties and assisted generally in directing P.O.W. to drains while the raid proceeded.'[30] Other Japanese, Charles Steel wrote bitterly in his next letter to his wife, Louise, found it funny that the prisoners were being killed by their own side.

'The scene behind hut 3 was grim,' Louis Baume recorded, 'whilst in front of the hospital lay rows and rows of corpses, broken and bloody. Around the huts, in the grass and on the paths lay others, killed as they ran for cover; half in a ditch, for which he had raced in vain, sprawled a naked Javanese, his head smashed and the dry ground beneath dark with his blood. Alone, with his sword trailing in the dust behind him and with tears in his eyes, Chida drifted and paused, helplessly saluting the dead.'[31]

After the first shock had passed the cry went out: why? Why has it happened to us? Have we suffered and survived only to be killed by our own side? 'It was a terrible, terrible occasion,' Toosey said in 1974, his voice breaking with the pain of the memory, 'one hut was hit and we had nearly ninety killed and four hundred wounded in that one evening. It was a most terrible occasion.' Of all the things he saw and suffered in Thailand, the bombing of Nong Pladuk was for him one of the worst.

He had the bodies laid out on hastily made stretchers on the blood-soaked ground in front of the makeshift chapel. The Japanese gave them one day off to bury the dead. A Korean guard walked up to Toosey and told him to hurry up and move the bodies. 'I looked him straight in the eye', Toosey recalled, 'and told him in plain bold English "Fuck off". Which he proceeded to do. He was drunk and very frightened.'[32]

That day they were allowed to dig slit trenches.

The funeral for the 76 victims of the air raid was held on the evening of 7 September. Toosey had been allowed to organise a working party to dig a mass grave, and towards sundown they gathered together to bury the victims. Initially, the Japanese had promised them transport but then they changed their mind. They supplied no facilities for the hospital or the dead. 'About 350 men then picked up the bodies on the rice sack stretchers to carry them to the cemetery – a mile away,' wrote Charles Steel. 'This was the signal for a most tremendous rainstorm, which caused the stretchers to come to pieces and caused the bearers great difficulty in carrying the bodies, which slipped out. Overall was the realisation that if the RAF came back that night, many more would be in the same position the following night. It was ghastly. The Thais fled at our approach. The stench of the broken bodies was appalling.'[33] In the pouring rain they trudged through thick, sticky mud to the cemetery. The long dismal procession stretched down the road, down along the paddy-fields, under the dripping trees, and away into the mist and rain.

Padre Christopher Ross took the service and the gathered men listened as he read out the all too familiar words: 'I am the resurrection and the life, saith the Lord . . . For as much as it hath pleased Almighty God of his great mercy to take unto himself the souls of our dear brothers here departed, we therefore commit their bodies to the ground; earth to earth, ashes to ashes, dust to dust.' Those who had remained in camp could hear the stirring notes of the Last Post followed by the clear challenge of Reveille.

The men were anxious, angry and afraid. The Japanese continued to be deaf to demands to move the camp away from the railway and they threatened to shoot anyone who tried to escape.

The tension grew and Toosey and the other officers were worried; it was inevitable that there would be more air raids. The *Bangkok Chronicle* printed the Allied report of the bombing: '20 planes successfully raided a Japanese transit camp and railway sidings'. 'The word "successfully" is at least correct,' Louis Baume noted bitterly in his diary.

Mountbatten and his staff were aware of the existence of the POW camp at Nong Pladuk yet he ordered the pilots to go ahead because the strategic importance of the target should override any feelings of sentiment about bombing Allied POW. Toosey said

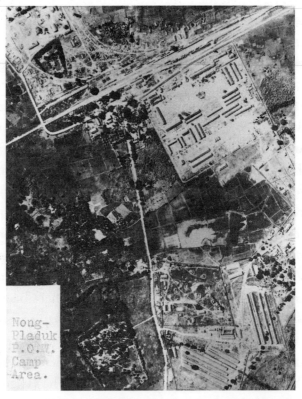

RAF photograph of Nong Pladuk I from the air. It shows the proximity of the camp to the railway line. Nong Pladuk II is in the bottom right of the picture.

later: 'I'm afraid you couldn't have blamed the American Air Force and the Royal Air Force, because the railway siding was precisely fifty yards from the edge of the camp and it was a vitally important one and they bombed it to ruins and they only hit us three times, which is really quite remarkable but my God when they hit us it was terrible, it was appalling.'[34]

A few days later the overall Japanese POW commander, Lieutenant Colonel Sugasawa, visited the camp. Toosey was in the hospital at the time visiting the wounded who were so many that they were lying all over the floor. He protested vehemently to Sugasawa and told him that the camp must be moved to a safer area. 'His reply, so far as I can remember it, was as follows: "You must remain in this camp and there will be many more similar raids. You are soldiers and must expect to die."'[35]

He did, however, permit the seriously injured to be taken to Nakhon Phatom, where the large hospital camp had much better medical facilities. Toosey sent Major Gill with the sick men along with the guard Watanabe who had helped them during the raid.

This was one of the most severe tests on Toosey's leadership. He could do so little for the men in the face of such arrogant denial from their captors and yet they looked to him for help. After several requests Chida gave him permission to address the whole camp. He spoke to the men on roll call: 'In order to put across what I really meant, and that was that every man should cease to think of himself and think of the community, I used that great quotation: "He who is greatest among you shall be servant of you all." This, I indicated, applied to everyone, some 6,000 in all. The result was extraordinary, everyone buckled to and did something to help their fellow men. As a result morale became higher than it had ever been before.'[36]

Life in camp began to return to normal. Working parties went out as usual, the canteen continued to function, they organised sports events and plays. Toosey visited the sick in hospital and one Dutchman remembered him patting him on the arm and saying: 'Cheer up boys, the allies have re-conquered half your country and are fighting near Arnhem.'[37] This statement was correct and must have come from the secret radio.

In November there was another bomb attack. Charles Steel wrote to his wife: 'My darling, they've done it again!! I looked up once and saw a huge 4-engine bomber pass across the face of the moon. The black silhouette seemed to represent all that was evil in the world – and yet – they are our own planes, with our own flesh and blood. This is a ghastly mix up.'[38] That night there were no deaths but the cookhouse was damaged and several prisoners were injured.

On 30 November they heard news that the night before there had been a raid on the bridges over the Mae Khlong at Tamarkan. A high-level American raid had caused splinter damage to three of the piers on the steel bridge but three bombs had overshot and landed in Tamarkan camp. Seventeen prisoners had been killed and several dozen injured.

For the Allies the bridges were a key target. Mountbatten explained to Toosey in a letter written in 1968: 'In my Intelligence Room in Headquarters SACSEA we kept track of the Burma–Siam Railway, its progress and the results of our bombing. I remember being worried when in the early summer of 1943 it was reported that the Japanese had completed an essential bridge, but it was not until we could get a new form of guided bomb that we finally were able to knock the bridge out much later on.'[39] Bombing on the bridges at Tamarkan began in 1944 but it was not until June 1945, when Toosey was back in Kanchanaburi, that the steel bridge was finally put out of commission.

Toosey stepped up the pressure on the Japanese to move the

camp. He wrote a letter, signed by himself and Colonel Scheurer, and sent it, over Chida's head, to Japanese headquarters:

> We, the undersigned, on behalf of the Officers and other ranks, British and Dutch, in Nong Pladuk Camp, desire to register the strongest possible protest against the maintenance of this Camp within 10 yards of an important military objective which has already been heavily bombed twice and is likely to be bombed with increasing frequency in the future.
>
> This policy is contrary to the rules of war, to elementary humanity and common sense.
>
> If the I.J.A. desire to keep the P.O.W. as an effective force to repair the ever increasing damage to the Thai–Burma Railway it is essential that they should be kept in a place where their necessary services, such as cookhouses and Hospitals will not be destroyed and where they will not suffer the perpetual strain of casualties and loss of sleep.
>
> No reasonable person thinks for a moment that the I.J.A. imagine they can stop a military objective from being bombed by keeping a P.O.W. Camp close by. But after a war people are not reasonable, and when it becomes known, <u>as one day it will</u>, that P.O.W. were kept in a Camp in close proximity to a military objective when there was another large Camp at a fairly safe distance from the railway line, and moreover that P.O.W. were transferred from the safe Camp to the dangerous Camp after the first raid, there cannot fail to be criticism and comment highly prejudicial to the honour of the I.J.A.
>
> We therefore request most strongly that all P.O.W. at Nong Pladuk be evacuated to a distance not less than 5,000 yards from the sidings or from any other military objectives; the new Camp shall be clearly marked as a P.O.W. Camp and that if possible its location shall be communicated to our air forces.[40]

Whether as a result of this letter or because of the casualties, the camp was finally moved back some 200 yards from the railway. But the protests annoyed Chida and he began to crack down on camp life. First sports were outlawed. Then church services were further curtailed. Curiously, Toosey observed, this had exactly the opposite effect than the Japanese expected; it simply made the prisoners all the more determined to stick together and fight the common enemy.

On the night of 3 December 1944 Nong Pladuk was bombed for a third time. Charles Steel was just finishing his tea when he heard the bugle call give warning of the raid. He ran outside and saw a sight that made his blood freeze: 'Approaching from the East, in perfect formation, in broad daylight and not more than 5,000 feet were 12 four engine bombers. The AA opened up and I dived. Then came the bombs.' Louis Baume recorded:

> Above the din rose the now terrifying roar of the bombs, . . . the piercing screams as they raced towards us; then complete silence for that fraction of a second as the whole world seemed poised, waiting for the impact and roar of the explosions, the hot blast of air – the whistle of the fragments flying towards us and the thuds as they embed themselves in the ground around us. The ground rose and shook itself in its fury and the earth cracked and crumbled as the bombs rained down.'[41]

They crouched in the trenches, praying, counting the bombs as they fell. 'It's not fair, sir, it's not fair!' Arthur Osborne yelled as he lay in a slit trench clinging to Toosey's leg, 'after all we've gone through and now we're being killed by our own side. It's not fair!'[42] It seemed that nothing could survive. Then it was over. Their hair and mouths were filled with dust, and the air was heavy with the smell of explosives. The camp was a broken shambles of half-ruined buildings. The hospital was partially burnt down. Two other huts were also destroyed. Charles Steel wrote to Louise: 'Men are walking about with just a ball bag on, having lost all other kit. Many men with mental disorders. The strain of being Aunt Sallies is rather great.'[43]

The damage to the railway was even worse than in the September raid. Louis Baume described the devastation: 'Railway wagons and trucks tossed in all directions, wrecked engines lurching drunkardly over the brims of enormous craters, railway lines lying like giant spirally twisted tendrils; and out of the wreckage, black smoke billowing and flames leaping and licking the Gargantuan feast.'[44]

The camp was ablaze and fires were raging in two of the huts and the new hospital wing. Toosey ran from one group of fire-fighters to the next urging them to use anything they could to stamp out the flames. They grabbed handfuls of mud and sand but what they needed was water. He organised a human chain to one of the deep ditches at the side of the camp and called for buckets and basins. This could only hold the flames in check so he rallied more troops to form more chains and eventually, after several hours, they put the fires out. Now it was time to assess the damage. Six bombs had fallen in the camp killing nine and injuring thirteen. This is compared with the September raid when five bombs had killed 76 men, injured 250, of whom 20 died later, showing the value of the slit trenches. But this time damage to morale was much greater. Part of the hospital was wrecked and a number of important drugs and dressings were lost. Two huts had been completely destroyed and hundreds of men had lost all their precious possessions. Paddy Sykes died of his wounds the next day.

He was sorely missed. 'A more generous, unselfish man never lived; always thinking of and working for others; bags of guts especially when dealing with these yellow bastards & absolutely tireless in energy. I & many of us have lost a most sincere friend & the camp a first rate officer,' David Davidson wrote in his next letter to the Gairdners. During the raid a bomb fell on a hut full of Japanese but it exploded on impact with the roof and none of them was hurt. In the heat of the moment the prisoners felt that very bitterly.

Yet as 1944 drew to a close it was not future bombings that bothered Toosey, for the workshops had been completely destroyed and the RAF would turn their attention to other targets, but news. His main concern was to ensure that the dissemination of news, which was all much in the Allies favour, was handled with great care. The Japanese had become increasingly nervous and the number of spot searches had increased. Sources of news varied from the camp radio to Thai newspapers smuggled in by men who had been out on working parties. All news came to Toosey's office and he worked out a careful distribution, entirely verbal, which would mean that if one or other of the guards overheard the men talking they would not be able to identify the source. Now that it was clear the war was turning in favour of the Allies, some of the Koreans were concerned to impress the prisoners, and thus gave them little bits of news also, so it was quite easy to mask the sources.

Despite all the agonies of the bombing raids of the last four months, Christmas 1944 was optimistic. There was a general belief that this would be their last in captivity and there was joy when the Dutch erected a home-made Christmas tree. It was made of bamboo and foliage and looked like a real fir tree: '. . . candles had been made from carefully hoarded grease and decorations from half egg shells, tin foil and bits of cardboard. That tree, more than anything else, helped to bring back memories of happier times.'[45]

Early in the new year, after weeks of speculation the prisoners learned that the officers were to be separated from the men. The Japanese had decided that the officers had become a motivating force among the men and were, as such, a potential threat. They hoped that by removing that leadership the morale of the men would crumble. What they had not bargained for was the iron determination of the senior NCOs such as Regimental Sergeant Major Sandy McTavish to keep the discipline and morale as high as it had been under the leadership of Lieutenant Colonel Toosey.

The move was scheduled to take place on 24 January 1945. The evening before there was a magnificent concert called Three Moods and many believed it was one of the best they had ever put on. On the day of the officers' departure the mood was sombre. Toosey spent time talking to the men who would take over duties from the various officers; without hesitation he put Sandy McTavish in charge of the 3000 men. His trust was not misplaced but it was a move that was later to prove controversial and difficult. He had overlooked the medical officers and given the jobs of camp administration to NCOs. Charles Steel wrote to Louise about the change:

> A sad day in our lives as POWs as all the officers have been taken from us and sent to Kanburi. RSM McTavish has taken over as Camp Commander from Colonel Toosey, CSM Stadden has taken over as Adjutant from Major Davidson, Staff Sergeant Sherring has taken over messing from Captain Boyle, while I have taken on the job of PRI from Major Marsh, the canteen from Lt Fullerton and the underhand work of the finance committee from Captain Northcote. The Colonel almost made me howl when he said 'au revoir'. He is a grand man![46]

The officers finally left camp at 8 p.m., through a throng of men who had gathered to line their exit. It was a moment of great emotion. Toosey wrote:

> I shall never forget the day we left Nong Pladuk Camp. The men had been told that they were not to demonstrate in any way at all as we felt it would only result in punitive measures being taken against them. However, they lined our exit route, every single man in the place who could stand on two feet, and shouted 'Goodbye, see you again sir' and all sorts of pleasant messages. It was a most heart-warming experience and a most wonderful demonstration of loyalty which will remain in my mind always.[47]

When they eventually got away they were loaded on to open goods trucks with their gear and were told if there was an air raid they should run for cover and then come back when recalled. It was a crisp night with a shining moon. They dozed fitfully on the train and finally arrived in Kanchanaburi, 50 kilometres away, at four o'clock the next morning.

9

THE OFFICERS' MESS

The Japanese realised that they had got all the officers where
they wanted them — and they gave us real hell.

Phil Toosey, autobiographical writings

Phil Toosey loved writing letters. When he travelled he always
kept a diary and would send home long, descriptive letters, full
of humour. They give an insight into the way he viewed the
world. So it is perhaps strange that he never kept a diary nor
wrote letters during his time as a prisoner of war. It would have
been wholly in keeping had he done so. But he did not. Nor did
he learn Japanese. He was a good linguist, he spoke German,
French and Spanish.

The Japanese forbade the prisoners from keeping diaries
and writing letters and the penalty for discovery was a severe
beating and, possibly, death. Toosey was prepared to help men
run the gauntlet of the guards and record their experiences but
he could not afford to keep one himself. He knew the Japanese

would have loved to have caught him and he had no desire to give them any excuse. He could not possibly have risked making notes about the existence of the V-scheme, the radios, or of the many illicit activities he covered up for. On one occasion, during a search of an incoming party at Nong Pladuk, a Scot he had known at Tamarkan called Alec Young gestured to him that he had a diary on him. Years later Young remembered how Toosey 'hovered in the background ready to take my diary almost under the very eyes of the guard'.[1] Alec Young and the diary returned safely to Scotland after the war.

The prisoners devised endlessly clever ways to hide their writings. A favourite was a piece of hollow bamboo that might be part of a bed or hut, but some went as far as stitching precious papers into collars or cuffs of their tattered shirts and shorts. When a move or a search was announced there would be a general panic as people desperately hid their material. Before a move to another camp men might bury their notes in tins in the ground. Louis Baume buried a part of his diary at Nong Pladuk but when he went back to find it after the war he found it had been burned to a cinder in its tin during one of the air raids. Dr Arthur Moon was more fortunate. He buried his hospital records and the 101 drawings he had commissioned in a tin with rat poison beneath a hut in Tha Muang. He managed to recover these safely after the war.

So it was a surprise when they arrived at their new camp that they were not searched.

At first light the officers from Nong Pladuk were able to see their new home. It was a depressing sight. The camp, known as Kanburi, was reputedly the oldest in Thailand. Situated on the south-east side of the town of Kanchanaburi, it was well away from the river but close to the railway. It was dirty, the huts were dilapidated and there was very little space. There had been an outbreak of cholera in the camp in 1943 and it had a reputation for being bad and unhygienic. Toosey wrote: 'We were put in before the camp had been extended or improved and for the first few weeks conditions were very unhappy.'[2]

The strength of the camp was 3000, consisting of all nationalities. It became clear after only a few days that the intention of the Japanese was to humiliate the officers and to attempt to break their spirit. 'The Japanese, up to a point, were cunning in their methods,' Toosey explained, '. . . in dealing with us they nearly always were able to prove that they were abiding by the letter of the Hague Convention, but by no means by the spirit. In addition they covered themselves by issuing orders, which included paragraphs that by the Hague Convention we were subject to the normal disciplinary measures of the Japanese Army and their penal code.'[3]

The Japanese camp commandant Captain Noguchi held a special place in the chamber of horrors that was the Japanese POW command. He was variously described in diaries and subsequent books as an ogre, an arch-swine and, by Toosey, as a sadist of the worst type. 'An arch bastard if there ever was one!' wrote Captain Frank Robinson. 'A fanatically patriotic Nip, sensing the war was going the wrong way, he did everything in his power to make life difficult by restrictions, working conditions and strict discipline, ably assisted by brother Shimojo with bamboo and whip.'[4] Jerry Coombes went further: '. . . the twin ogres Noguchi and Shimojo, ably backed by the Korean "Undertaker", enjoyed an orgasm of unfrustrated sadism'.[5] 'Noguchi's sole aim and interest', Australian Rohan Rivett wrote in 1946, 'was to persecute his prisoners by every interference with their liberty and amusements that his mind could conceive.'[6]

At first Noguchi's influence in the officers' camp was noticed only by way of negligence. Louis Baume wrote in despair in his diary on 30 January 1945:

> Chaos has reigned since our arrival. The camp is in process of being rebuilt – the huts are being lengthened to take the additional personnel and the two cookhouses, British and Dutch, both in a sad state of deterioration and filth, are to be rebuilt to enable the cooks to cope with the influx of hungry bodies. As usual no preparations have been made by the Nips to cope with the arrival of 3000 prisoners; no extra latrines dug, no facilities for drawing water, no bathing area, nothing. More parties are streaming in and were it not for our own efforts, complete confusion would reign.[7]

The Allied camp administration at Kanburi officers' camp was cumbersome and inefficient. With such a high concentration of lieutenant colonels – there were ninety-eight in all – it had been decided to have a committee comprising two liaison officers each from the British, Dutch and Australian forces and one American. All the lieutenant colonels were housed together in one hut, number 4. The senior British officer in Kanburi was Lieutenant Colonel Ted Swinton. Toosey, one of the most junior, played no part in the organisation at the outset.

The camp site was cramped and this aggravated the feeling that they were living on top of one another. The density at Kanburi was about two-thirds of that at Selarang barracks in September 1942. 'Total area of the camp appears to cover 84,000 square yards, approximately 400 yards by 210. Of this the Nips have about one third or an area approx 140 x 210, which is situated at the NW end of the camp. We are housed in a long row of 13 huts, each about 300 feet long and the first of which (No 4) is the Imperial War Museum (so called because all the field officers are there) and the last is the hospital. 200–250 Nips to guard 3000 prisoners. 2,000 Aus, UK, American; 1000 Dutch, 180 OR [other ranks].'[8] They were never further than six feet from another man.

The only areas for recreation were the parade ground, which had just enough space to accommodate all the prisoners, the space between the huts and on a broad strip that ran at the opposite end of the long huts for the whole length of the camp, some 150 yards long and about 20 yards wide: 'Many of us must have walked several hundred miles up and down this road in search of daily exercise during the ensuing months,'[9] Cary Owtram from Chungkai observed. Some of the younger officers rigged up a basketball pitch and started an inter-hut league that was popular. Noguchi allowed this but forbade cricket.

The camp had no trees and therefore no shade. It was too far from the river for bathing parties to be permitted and it was surrounded by a 10-foot-high fence with sentries in watchtowers on each corner. The Thais refused to supply wood for hut improvements so parties were sent out to the disused camp at Tamarkan to collect bamboos and attap for improvements to the huts in Kanburi. 'When we first arrived, there was already a fairly wide and deep moat all round the camp with a high barbed wire fence along the outer bank, and machine gun posts at intervals all round,' Cary Owtram wrote. 'However, the Nips evidently intended to take no chances with us and made us dig the moat still deeper and the soil was made into a high bank on the outer side and then surmounted by the barbed wire fence and machine gun posts as before. They then went one better still and made us build a bamboo stockade as well, so that we could not see out.'[10] They were told by helpful Koreans that the ditch that they had dug was to be used as their mass grave in the event of there being a final massacre.

Meanwhile the Allies continued to send bombing missions to the bridges at nearby Tamarkan. During February there were regular parties to collect the material from the old camp and this had given them the chance to see the destruction caused by the bombing. On 5 February the wooden bridge was partly destroyed and on 13 February there was delight when American high-level bombing damaged both bridges. To their amazement they were repaired within days. According to a Japanese account written in 1981 the wooden bridge was repaired at least four times, only to be hit in successive raids. It showed the durability of the Japanese wooden bridges that could be repaired quickly after bomb damage.

By the end of February the officers' camp had reached full strength and Noguchi began to exert his authority. On 28 February he announced that all valuables had to be handed in. This included pens, cigarette cases, walking sticks, wooden stools, notebooks, pencils, diaries, razors, rope, string, knives, scissors, forks, mirrors etc. The following day he made an inspection of the camp. He made a beeline for hut 6, the oldest and the most tumbledown hut. Louis Baume observed him: 'When he left the hut he wanted to show the inmates his disgust (and probably his wide knowledge of English too) and with a bamboo stick scratched the words BEGGAR HOUSU on the ground – we could not agree with him more.'[11]

In civilian life Noguchi had been a chemist and now he saw himself as something of an inventor. He ordered officers to prepare a dye works and there they dyed material that was then turned into shirts for himself and the other guards. 'Futile experiments on such a tiny scale as to be useless,' Frank Robinson recorded in his diary. 'Castor oil leaves and logwood chips dyed the ragged IJA uniforms a dirty khaki green but the patches still showed different shades.'[12]

The officers also made bricks from which they constructed a bread oven. This was very popular even though the bread was made from rice flour. They also enlarged the canteen so that feeding, if not rations, was improved. 'We were able to get rice bread for breakfast and could buy peanut stews, eggs (now 30–40 Ticals each), tobacco (5–6 Ticals) and other tit bits, some 1000% advanced in price owing to currency inflation and distrust of Jap notes by local Thai traders,'[13] Robinson wrote. Their pay was reduced from 30 Ticals to 20 Ticals a month so that with soaring prices their purchasing power was low. Since they were not allowed outside the camp they began minting their own money out of cardboard with a Japanese stamp so that they had a camp currency in order to pay each other.

There was no formal work required of the officers but there

Hu. 4552

Chopping wood for the cookhouse in the officers' camp.

were endless jobs to be done just to keep the camp going. There were gangs chopping wood for the cookhouses, digging latrines and slit trenches. Robinson complained he was on a heavy gang carrying half of Thailand from point A to point B in an effort to drain and level the camp before the monsoon. Toosey was a wood chopper for the cookhouse. Some jobs, such as onion peeling, were done by the older and more senior officers. A popular job was peanut bashing. Cary Owtram said it was 'quite a pleasant occupation calling for considerably more energy [than peeling onions] and having the advantage that when one had "bashed" the peanuts into butter, one was entitled to scrape off what remained sticking to the basher and eat it. Since peanut butter contained a high vitamin content, this had considerable value apart from the pleasure of tasting something other than rice.'[14] The results of their labours were sold as peanut-butter biscuits in the canteen for 5 cents each.

Toosey enjoyed the physical work and it gave him a break from the claustrophobic atmosphere of the 'imperial war museum'. With such a concentration of senior officers, rivalries and factions arose. The TA officers, in general, had been prepared to sweep away military codes and get on with commanding their camps, bringing their civilian experiences to bear on the situation. Housed now with regular army lieutenant colonels with years of service behind them Toosey felt uncomfortable. There were claims of seniority and rivalry between the different nationalities. But there was one regular officer, Lieutenant Colonel Harry Flower, 9th Battalion, the Royal Northumberland Fusiliers, who made efforts to bridge the gap between the TA and the regulars. Two days older than Toosey, he had been an inspirational commander on the railway. He had been responsible for plate-laying parties and had travelled with his men 237 kilometres up the railway to Tomajo. Flower had seen some of the desperate conditions of the men working so far away from the Base Camps. Like Toosey he had a reputation for standing up to the Japanese and they understood one another.

It was not only the atmosphere among the senior officers that was tense. Louis Baume had become increasingly concerned about the pressure from the Japanese secret police: 'Ever since the end of Feb. we have been going through a trying time. The Kempei discovered that we have been cashing cheques and buying newspapers from outside. Almost every day a handful of thugs arrive in the camp around Tenko time, armed with truncheons, whips and lengths of rubber tubing. They seize a few officers and take them away to HQ for interrogation, torture and imprisonment. The camp is on tenterhooks. . . . Some come back horribly beaten up; others have not been seen again.'[15] The officers who were accused of buying newspapers from the Thais were taken for trial in Bangkok and sentenced to five to seven years' hard labour.

When the officers and men were separated in January 1945 contact with the V-scheme was lost, although Boon Pong continued to supply the camps around the Kanchanaburi area. At the officers' camp the Kempei Tai began what one officer later described as a witch-hunt. Unknown to the Kempei Tai, four British TA officers, who had been involved one way or another in the V-scheme, were sleeping under one roof in hut 4 – Lieutenant Colonels Toosey, Knights, Owtram and Lilly. For some reason not readily understood by the other three, the Kempei Tai seized on Harold Lilly for interrogation. It seemed to them all extraordinary that Lilly had been singled out. As Knights wrote to Toosey later: '. . . as far as I knew, and I had kept my ears pretty close to the ground, Lilly had never been mixed up in any racket which justified his being picked out for the Kempei Tai's attention'.[16]

They concluded that it must have something to do with the changing of large denomination notes at Tha Muang and not the V-scheme itself. However, it was very worrying and, as Knights said, if the Kempei Tai had got on to that the fat was certainly in the fire.

Knights was able to speak to Lilly briefly before he was escorted to the Kempei Tai headquarters in Kanchanaburi, a house only a stone's throw and on the other side of the street from Boon Pong's store. Knights made him promise to deny any complicity whatsoever and, if tortured by the Kempei Tai, to put all the blame on him. This Lilly eventually agreed to do and under torture he named Arthur Knights but not until he had been so badly beaten that on his return to the camp people barely recognised him. 'Colonel Lilly came back, an old man,' Louis Baume wrote in his diary, 'and refused to speak of his experiences. How much can a man stand before he is forced to speak? With this in mind, it has been arranged who shall give who away; thus the Kempei will always go round in circles, never reaching the vital centre of our resistance. There is so much, so very much at stake.'[17]

The next day the Kempei Tai took Knights away and the atmosphere became more tense than ever. They had long since learned that the walls had ears and several of the guards spoke better English than they were prepared to admit. Noguchi used these men to spy on the prisoners day and night. There was no possibility of Toosey and Owtram discussing their concerns or even voicing opinions as to why Knights and Lilly had been detained. All they could do was to hunker down and wait. Of all the sleepless nights Toosey had in Thailand, he said later, this was one of the very worst.

During the course of his interrogation, which lasted eight hours, Knights was able to steer the conversation towards large denomination notes that he, as camp commander at Tha Sao, had withheld from the officers' pay for the hospital. When he had moved to Tha Muang he had taken this money with him. He admitted disobeying Japanese orders and the Kempei Tai now wished to know whether he had continued to do so. In the certain knowledge that he had found a red herring he talked. 'I frankly admitted disobeying Japanese orders, in fact in the circumstances I would not hesitate to disobey them in future. I considered that the callous and inhuman way in which the Japanese treated sick POW was a disgrace to their army and to their nation, a nation which prided itself on being civilised. As camp commander one of my prime responsibilities was to prevent unnecessary suffering and if this entailed disobeying Japanese orders then as far as I was concerned that was just too bad.'[18] This outburst had a disturbing effect on the Kempei Tai. They locked him up again but the following morning, to his surprise, he was released. He had been pardoned, he was told, by the 'Head Boy' of the Kempei Tai because he had disobeyed Japanese orders for the sake of his men. 'The ways of the Japanese were always something of a mystery to me and it was difficult to visualise how their minds worked, and I couldn't help thinking that even with the dreaded Kempei Tai there must be some thin streak of gold. There was also the thought that the age of miracles was not past.'[19]

When Knights and Lilly staggered back into camp that afternoon Toosey knew that there would be no discussion of what had happened but he knew that the V-scheme had not been unravelled. It was the closest of close shaves. Knights later told Toosey that he put Lilly's early death down to the torture he had received at the hands of the Kempei Tai.

Meanwhile the leadership committee was having ever more problems. They could seldom agree on anything, however small and petty. The Japanese became impatient and insisted on having one officer in charge. In the past the Japanese had not been guided by seniority in the British army when selecting individuals for running prisoner camps. Toosey recorded in his camp report: '. . . on the representations of Lieutenant Colonel G.E. Swinton, M.C., East Surrey Regt., the senior British Officer in Camp, I was put in by the Japanese as British Liaison Officer. Owing to the many difficulties of control and on orders from Jap H.Q., the P.O.W. Staff was changed and only one Liaison Officer was permitted, with two Adjutants – British and Dutch. The Japanese, who by now knew me well, selected me for this job. The task of attempting to run this Camp was one of the most difficult experiences of my life.'[20]

Louis Baume recorded in his diary: 'A week ago Col. Toosey was appointed CO of our camp much to everyone's delight. He had a hard tussle to get to the top as many of the older and crustier inmates of the Imperial War Museum insisted that seniority and not ability should be the qualification for the appointment; now we can expect some action.'[21]

If Louis Baume and others were delighted at the appointment of Toosey as senior liaison officer Toosey himself was far from pleased. In fact he only accepted the position because he was told to: 'I was ordered by Ted Swinton to take over the officers' camp. At first I refused because I was utterly weary after three years battling with the "Beasts" but he said it was an order, so I obeyed on the condition that he backed up any order I gave, which he did.'[22]

Toosey felt more caged in and more miserable than at any time since becoming a prisoner. He was surrounded by senior officers who were more concerned with jostling for authority and saving themselves than they were for the welfare of the camp. He hated his role there. Without his men to look after he felt at a loss. He mused on this when he wrote in 1974 to Harry Flower:

'The officers were much more difficult than the men. When I gave the order to clean up the camp, which meant the difference between a high and low death rate, which you knew only too well, they refused until being reasoned into doing so for their own sake.'[23]

For a while things ran fairly smoothly but there were constant niggling problems both with Noguchi and with the officers, young and old. Toosey suffered from a constant pulling of rank from some of the colonels jostling for the maximum of authority with the minimum of risk. There were times when he found himself at odds as much with the officers as with the Japanese. The prisoners were bored, living on top of one another and edgy about the outcome of the war.

Toosey wrote in his report in September 1945:

In this camp there were more incidents of a deliberately sadistic nature than I had met before. In the early days, all officers were severely beaten up for very minor offences and crimes, such as smoking outside the huts and failing to salute Jap officers. After heated protests against this method of punishment it was changed to an even more severe punishment – that of standing in the sun, in front of the guardroom without a hat, for periods of up to 48 hours, the first 24 hours being without food or water.[24]

He went on:

Every form of unnecessary restriction was imposed in this camp. Although we had no work to do we were only allowed to read between 1300 and 1500 hrs and after 1800 hrs at night. We were not allowed to lie on our beds except during these hours, all stools and chairs were removed, concerts were

frequently stopped for some minor infringement and the canteen closed. We were not allowed any form of mental
relaxation, lectures were forbidden, no one was permitted to
have any paper with any writing whatsoever, pay was reduced
from 30 Ticals to 20 Ticals per month – in spite of a sharp
increase in prices – and we were given every form of verbal
insult which could be thought of. In effect it was quite clear that
a deliberate attempt was being made to insult Officers.[25]

Now that they no longer had their men to think of, some of
the officers decided to take a stand against the Japanese. Toosey
was worried. He believed that the Japanese were spoiling for a
fight and he was right to be concerned. Noguchi had taken
a dislike to one of the Allied interpreters in the Kanburi camp.
This officer, Captain Bill Drower – six feet three inches,
Oxford educated, with a gift for languages and trained as an
artillery officer – found sitting about in Malaya waiting to inter-
rogate Japanese prisoners (only eight of whom were taken in
Malaya), a waste of time. Volunteering for an artillery posting he
was lucky enough, he said later, to be posted to Toosey's 135th
Hertfordshire Yeomanry Regiment shortly before the British
capitulation in February 1942. The British Army's regulation
expects 'escape' from captivity. General Percival, however, had
given out after surrender that officers should stay with their men
and not attempt to escape. Toosey heard of Drower's intention
of organising an escape party and 'promptly put me under "close
arrest" – movements restricted and under constant observation,
hardly a promising start to what later became in POW conditions
a fast friendship which would continue after the war.'[26] Drower
explained.

Two months later Drower, now back with Malayan command, where very few POW knew any Japanese at all, was

posted to interpret for the predominantly Australian 'A' Force, shipped to Burma to start work on the railway near Moulmein and down, over the Three Pagodas pass to Bangkok. Bill Drower worked closely with Lieutenant Colonel Charles Anderson of the AIF, 'an Australian farmer volunteer of rare courage and judgement'.[27] In December 1943 Drower was with various nationalities, British, Dutch, Australian and a few American who had been brought down, mostly in poor health, to the 'hospital camp' at Tamarkan.

On 28 May 1945 an incident occurred that became known as 'the Drower Incident'. Toosey believed Noguchi had been waiting for an opportunity to humiliate Drower, and when the opportunity arose he grasped it with both hands. Drower wrote: 'It was late May 1945 that I incurred Noguchi's violent displeasure. I was reported to have rebuked a Korean guard who was taking it out on a water carrying party without cause.' The situation in the camp was clear. The Japanese were losing the war and the Korean guards were, one by one, edging towards the Allies and distancing themselves from the Japanese. Drower reminded this guard that under the Geneva Conventions an officer should not be struck or punished. Unfortunately this Korean happened to be a friend of one of the Japanese guards close to Noguchi. 'Somewhat to my surprise', he continued, 'a summons to Noguchi's office was followed by a savage tirade, and a hefty beating up in the course of which I fell over his writing desk and broke it in pieces. The Emperor had been insulted. To make amends, I was accordingly thrown in solitary confinement "forever".'[28]

The following day Toosey was called to Noguchi's hut where the Japanese commander apologised for losing his temper and for beating Drower personally rather than delegating it to his underlings. However, when Toosey requested Drower's release, Noguchi refused to discuss it. The atmosphere in the camp was very tense. Bill Drower spent the first week or so of his solitary confinement in a crude, narrow underground shelter where he was awoken one night by a rat nibbling his foot. Then there was a change of scene and he was moved to a cell next to the guardhouse. Every time Toosey brought the subject up Noguchi became furious and eventually threatened to shoot him. So Toosey wrote a strongly worded letter to Colonel Sugasawa, the head of POW command in Thailand, but Noguchi refused to pass it on. Drower was allowed one meal of a tennis ball-sized riceball a day. To start with his food was prepared in the Japanese cookhouse but soon they passed over the responsibility to the British and Toosey asked the cooks surreptitiously to put extra vitamins into the rice. It was all they could do and the doctors believed it would help. Captain Peter Fane was asked by Toosey to risk punishment and deliver this daily riceball, which he did. He would certainly have been severely beaten if Noguchi had discovered what was going on. Drower maintains today that Toosey's repeated interventions on his behalf with the Japanese and Captain Fane's bravery saved his life.

At the beginning of June Noguchi restricted all the officers to their huts on the grounds that as some had refused to work they would all be banned from working. Stanley Gimson recorded the events leading up to this order in his diary: 'Col Toosey told by Nips to submit our proposals re work. He sent a letter saying we do not admit the principle of work for officers but in the circs, seeing no alternative, we would do camp fatigues. Nip No 1 angry – No officers to work.'[29] The only people allowed to work in camp were the 180 other ranks, the Colonel, the camp quartermaster and a few other officials. They were to be wood choppers. The medical officers were ordered to work the drains. Noguchi told Toosey that this treatment was expected to subdue the prisoners and break their obstinate spirit.

Hu. 4556

Bill Drower's prison.

It had, of course, the opposite effect and the more offensive and petty Noguchi's dictates became, the more spirits rose.

However, Toosey was as anxious outside as were those confined to their huts. Louis Baume wrote in his diary at the end of their first week of confinement:

> We have received a warning that the Nips are gunning for us and are probably trying to provoke the long-awaited incident that will give them the excuse to open fire on us; at present thank God the big ditch is full of water and the machine gun posts are submerged. Toosey has appealed to all to obey implicitly every new Nip regulation, however trivial, so as to give them no excuse at all – it will be difficult but the alternative will be worse. Roll on the end![30]

273

Every day brought new restrictions and then, as suddenly as the confinement had begun it ended. On 14 June the order restricting them was lifted. There was no explanation but the mood in camp was confident. They felt they had won a victory over their captors. The only bitterness was that Bill Drower remained locked up and no one was allowed to visit him apart from the medical orderly who took him his daily meal. By the end of June Drower was suffering from beri beri, malaria and eventually blackwater fever but no doctor was allowed to visit him.

It was in that guard house cell that I realised, as others have so often done in similar circumstances, the reserve value of an extended and liberal education. The hallucinatory realism of the plots of books and films I had liked or been gripped by; amateur dramatic parts once taken; walks through Germany, Austria, Italy and France and, of course, the British Isles all occupied my thoughts. Concerts conjured themselves up where I imagined playing the violin; singing in a choir – especially Handel. It seems that the guards afterwards reported that I annoyed them by singing. Probably this was the reason why, on more than one occasion, they threw into my cell, large, rattly centipedes which I could not see, but which saw me clearly enough to give me hostile and extremely irritating bites.[31]

By the summer of 1945 the news headlines were pointing to an Allied victory in the Far East. The news came principally from the camp radio that was operated in the hospital by two young officers of the Malay Regiment, brothers Max and Donald Webber. They had operated the radio in Chungkai for over two years without detection. When the officers left Chungkai in February 1945 Colonel Owtram, the camp commander, was against the brothers smuggling the radio into the officers' camp. They insisted they could do it. In the end it was agreed that they would tell nobody how they intended to do it so that if they did get caught, no one else could be implicated. Owtram was amazed at their bravery but it did not stop him being nervous both during the leaving inspection at Chungkai and the arrival inspection at Kanburi.

The Japanese found nothing but Owtram noticed that the camp provost, Robin Calderwood, was transported on a stretcher. The story went that he had had a nasty fall the previous day and badly hurt his back. Calderwood was carefully carried down to the river by a few friends who lowered him gently onto a barge and travelled with him on the short journey to Kanchanaburi. On arrival there they were equally careful taking him out of the barge and carrying him to the officers' camp. 'He lay on his stretcher while another thorough search of our kit was carried out by the camp guards, after which he was borne off to the hospital hut. On arrival there, his back became suddenly better and the bamboo stretcher was quickly dismantled and various parts of the wireless set removed from the hollow poles,' Owtram recalled. 'Furthermore, little did the Japanese know that the small wooden stool, which Max Webber carried with him, sported a false bottom in which the rest of the set was concealed!'[32]

The radio was reassembled and went into operation once again. It was known as the 'canary' and the batteries as 'bird seed'. The presence of the canary in camp caused great anxiety among the cloud of senior lieutenant colonels. As Noguchi stepped up his campaign of harassment they became more concerned than ever. The senior Australian, Lieutenant Colonel McEachern, ordered the radio to be destroyed. The Webber brothers protested that no one had consulted them; they felt that as they were taking the risk they should have the final say but this was not accepted and they were threatened with courts martial.

Toosey was sent along to talk sense into them. He explained that the real concern of the senior officers was that if the radio were discovered the Webber brothers, under torture, might name one of them as ultimately responsible. In his camp report he wrote: 'The handling of news was very dangerous since, as separately reported, two officers had been beaten to death for a similar offence and so great care was necessary.'[33] If, however, the brothers were determined to keep the radio going Toosey would permit it on the condition that if they were discovered they would name only him. Having agreed to take ultimate responsibility for the radio Toosey took over the dissemination of news from March onwards until the batteries ran out at the end of May and they were unable to acquire fresh ones.

The risks were indeed great and, as Toosey wrote to Harry Flower years later, some officers would gossip in front of the guards, even though they knew many of them spoke good English. At one stage he stopped circulation of information for several weeks and only when he was convinced that the news could be controlled would he allow the information to be circulated again. By this time it was clear that the tide was turning against the Japanese and this made them all the more difficult and unpredictable.

Once the batteries had run out, the prisoners were forced to rely on any scraps of outside information that they could glean and piece them together. Owtram recalled: 'An intelligence centre was formed consisting of a selected group of officers, most of whom had had some previous experience of this kind of work and from the meagre scraps of information brought in to them day by day, they managed to extract a surprising amount of interesting, cheering and, as was subsequently proven, accurate information.'[34]

The confirmation of Germany's surrender came through in a most unlikely way. Toosey had asked Noguchi to acquire some violin strings for the camp orchestra on a trip to Bangkok. Noguchi agreed and when he returned he handed over a neatly wrapped parcel. When they came to unwrap the parcel they discovered that it was a Thai newspaper from mid-May 1945. This source gave them not only concrete information on the end of the war in Europe but also the news that Rangoon had been recaptured. The news of Germany's surrender caused a ripple of barely suppressed excitement in the camp and lifted their spirits even higher. But it was dangerous, Toosey warned them, to show too much enthusiasm.

Noguchi grudgingly allowed the orchestra from Chungkai to regroup and perform. He was far less tolerant of the musical performances than those in command at Chungkai so that rehearsal times for the orchestra and theatre performances were limited. Sometimes he would cancel a concert at the last minute but on other occasions he would order the orchestra to perform. Their number was enlarged by some very able musicians from other camps and the orchestra was very proud of all its instruments including its homemade double bass.

'Somehow we survived it and had our laughs at the same time,' Toosey wrote. 'On one occasion we were told that some high ranking officers were coming from Tokyo to inspect the Officers' Camp and we were told we might stage our concert party, which had been stopped for some time, which we did, and the famous tune "Colonel Bogey" was played as the Japs marched into the Camp and that verse which we all know so well was sung out by all. "Bollocks and the same to you!" They stood firmly to attention and saluted as we cheered: they thought we were cheering them!'[35]

In early June rumours of a move of POW officers up country, to the eastern part of Thailand, began to circulate. There were two reasons for the move. For one, it would have been an embarrassment in the event of an Allied invasion to have the prisoners in the camps close to Bangkok but secondly the Japanese were concerned that the officers might be capable of being of military value to the Allies. A few days later Noguchi informed Toosey that officers were to be moved to a new camp, 'in order to provide us with more room and a better camp, this statement being quite inaccurate since the move was purely for strategic reasons'.[36] Stephen Alexander wrote: 'Helpful Koreans told us it was an officer bumping off camp.'[37]

Noguchi said that Toosey should lead the advance party of four hundred fit officers in order to prepare the new camp for the remainder. 'The senior Officers agreed to this suggestion since I could ensure that the new camp was built to some extent according to our wishes, and so on the 28 June I left Kanburi, my position as Liaison Officer being taken over by Lt.Col. Swinton.'[38] It was a relief to Toosey that he would be out of the officers' camp, and although the prospect of the unknown was unnerving it was a welcome change from the stagnant frustration and claustrophobia of the last few months.

He was told they would be taken by train as far as the line went, from Bangkok to Nakhon Nayok, and then they would have to march 41 kilometres to their camp in the jungle, the last part of this march being off road. The monsoon was about to break and this would add to the discomfort of their journey.

In order to prepare the officers for the forced march to come Toosey organised exercise on the 150-yard strip of ground outside the huts. Men walked miles every day carrying their full packs but months of inactivity had made them soft and the march would turn out to be a trial for those officers in later parties who were ill. Toosey still had one pair of boots that were in quite good condition, plus a pair of shorts that had only a few patches. These he determined to keep for the outbreak of peace he felt sure would come soon. He chose to make the journey in a pair of old shorts, a shirt and bare feet.

Four days before Toosey left Kanchanaburi there was a final air raid on the two bridges at Tamarkan. Low-level missions by the RAF and USAAF put both bridges beyond repair. Three spans of the steel bridge were blasted into the river, two piers were completely destroyed and a third badly damaged. The much-repaired wooden bridge was all but demolished. The prisoners had been allowed to dig slit trenches in the officers' camp and during all the air raids on the Kanchanaburi area in the spring and summer of 1945 they had five deaths, and several injuries.

The journey to Nakhon Nayok was typical of all journeys they made under Japanese arrangements. There was a great deal of hanging about and being shunted into sidings to make way for more important trains. Leaving Kanchanaburi at 10 p.m. they travelled thirty men to an open luggage truck in the pouring rain towards Bangkok. 'At 1300 hours we arrived at a blown up bridge across a river [the Tha Chin] east of Nakhon Phatom where we had to unload our baggage, carry it across a very dangerous foot bridge some 2'6" wide, over the river,' Toosey wrote in his report. The walkway was three planks wide and the river flowed swiftly some thirty feet below them. The whole structure swayed unpleasantly and they were all enormously relieved to get safely to the other side where they camped for the night in the open alongside the blown-up railway bridge. 'Fortunately it did not rain although the tide came up and flooded a large part of the camp.'[39]

They spent the following night in Bangkok station, which had been heavily bombed, and the next morning were packed like sardines into five barges and towed down the river to some go-downs, or warehouses, about 10 kilometres from the capital. Here they unloaded the barges and attempted to get some sleep lying on the concrete floor. 'Some of the buildings were partially open to the weather from bomb damage. Here we were well fed from the cookhouse of an O.R.'s [other ranks] camp, which was situated in a neighbouring go-down. We made contact with them and found them to be in good order, although nervous since they were forced to remain in the go-down during air raids.'[40] Once again Toosey was shocked at the callous attitude of the Japanese to the prisoners' safety. He was so indignant that he and David Boyle went to seek out the Japanese officer in charge of the camp to see if anything could be done. They were met by complete indifference.

From Bangkok they travelled by train and arrived at Nakhon Nayok late at night. It was a journey of some 100 kilometres and they felt they were a very long way from civilisation. For those men who had been up jungle in 1943 there was something familiar about their journey; for Toosey and others it was an unwelcome surprise. The rain poured down as they heaved their heavy baggage on to two lorries. At two o'clock in the morning they started a 41-kilometre march in fifty-minute stages, resting for ten minutes and then continuing. For the first four hours they marched in a monsoon deluge. 'We had some 25 blister casualties; most Officers had not marched for some considerable time, but generally speaking the party was quite fit,'[41] Toosey wrote. 'Our new camp consisted of a piece of virgin jungle at the foot of a long line of hills, 17 km from the nearest village, approached from the road by a 3 km jungle track just wide enough in most places to permit moving in a single file.'[42]

The party was split in two. Two hundred officers cleared a patch of lalang grass where they were to live temporarily and erected the dozen tents they had brought with them. These were the outer coverings of three-and-a-half-year-old Indian-pattern tents. 'They made no pretence at being waterproof,' Toosey wrote, adding: 'The whole of this expedition was made in the middle of the monsoon season, but fortunately for us we had four dry nights out of the first fourteen. Had this not been so, conditions, to put it mildly, would have been chaotic – or tragic.'[43]

Their first task was to prepare a road to the camp, which was vital as a lifeline for everything had to be carried manually into the camp until the road was completed. It involved the hardest type of manual labour and took three weeks. During this period there was no time to make any improvements to their living quarters. Those who were not working on the road spent their time clearing the area for building huts. Meanwhile they continued to live in their leaky tents, 29 or 30 to a tent measuring 6 feet by 18 feet. The road they built was not suitable for motor traffic until the end of July. 'During that period every piece of building material and all stores were carried into camp on our backs. We had one holiday in the first three weeks.'[44]

At the end of four weeks they had finished the road and built two huts sufficient to house themselves, but the Koreans announced that all four hundred officers could have one hut while they, thirty guards, would have the other. After a good deal of heated discussion the Koreans agreed to let Toosey use one third of their hut for his officers. This gave them about 2 feet by 6 feet of space per man. There was no time to build sleeping platforms so they had to sleep on the damp floor.

Before the camp was ready other parties began to arrive from Kanchanaburi. 'Generally speaking their journey had been worse than ours since the party consisted of some unfit, and all parties contained some older officers. On the journey the treatment by the Korean guards was just as bad as in 1942 and 1943,' wrote Toosey.[45] Officers who fell out through sickness or exhaustion were forced along by rifle butts and bayonet points and were kicked in the face. 'In one case a Korean guard urinated on a Dutch Officer's face while he was lying on the ground. Every form of protest was made with little result.'[46]

Typically the parties would arrive in the early hours of the morning. As it was still the monsoon season they were often soaked to the skin and exhausted. Toosey made every attempt to greet them and to have prepared at least a cup of tea and a rice cake. Then they would be allocated a space in the huts. George 'Dutch' Holland had been a medical orderly in Tamarkan and the officers' camp. He remembered arriving at Nakhon Nayok with the second party. 'There was nothing there,' he recalled, 'just broken down huts.' [47]

For the first fortnight they had no cookhouse of their own. Their food was prepared at another prison camp eight kilometres away. It was brought by lorry to the end of their road where it was dropped off and a party of officers would carry the food on their shoulders back into camp. Naturally a proportion was spilt in transit and they received on average one eighth of a pint of stew and one pint of rice per man three times a day. It was hardly adequate for men who were working so hard. There was no canteen at Nakhon Nayok so there was nothing to supplement their meagre diet and deficiency diseases began to emerge again. Quite soon one section of the newly constructed huts had to be used as a hospital. It measured just 3.5 by 6.5 metres (11 feet by 21 feet) and at one stage the doctors had over fifty sick men.

Toosey had enjoyed exceptional good health for the past three and a half years, suffering from a mild attack of pellagra and from scrub typhus in Tamarkan, as well as mild beri beri. He seems to have been one of the lucky few immune to malaria and claimed he had never spent more than half a day sick on his bed. This is born out by the accounts of other prisoners. However, in Nakhon Nayok the physical hard labour, the monsoon rains that left everything soaking, the poor diet they were subjected to for the first ten days, coupled with three and a half years of unrelenting pressure, took their toll. In mid-July he contracted bilateral pneumonia and lay for nearly a fortnight, a very sick man, in the hospital hut. Fortunately the doctors, who were alarmed by his rapid deterioration, had some M&B 693 which they gave him and slowly he made a recovery. Several diaries and books record that he lost some of his sparkle, some of the Toosey magic in Nakhon Nayok. He had very nearly lost his life.

Stanley Gimson arrived at the end of July and was immediately enlisted to work:

In the afternoon it poured and we had to work on, shivering with cold in the dark, dripping, unyielding jungle, hacking away with hopeless tools. The huts are fairly small and we are lying in three rows on the very damp ground. Each of us has about 6 feet by 27 inches with a fifteen inch gangway between rows. We have no lights at night. It is just work, sleep, eat. Heavy sick had to do grass (lalang) cutting. Tagasaki wanted them for general work, but Toosey managed to prevent this. One day, sick figures went up from 42 to 54 and Tagasaki said he would inspect them. Toosey intervened, and instructed the MO to turn out the 18 fittest of them. This caused much bad feeling – in fact Col Toosey has lost much of his reputation – (partly because he himself is too keen on hurrying forward the construction work) – even though he himself works hard. There are no soft jobs – everyone is working.[48]

For a handful of officers this was the first time they had had to do any serious manual work since being taken prisoner. Those who had been in camps with Toosey knew that he expected everyone to pull their weight and work hard, not only for their own sake but for the sake of the whole camp. Stephen Alexander, who had been with Toosey in Tamarkan, had quite a different reaction from Stanley Gimson. He arrived in Nakhon Nayok in the second week of August worn out and jaded. He was greeted by Toosey who was neatly dressed and quite the man in charge again. He told the incoming party there was a cup of tea, a bun each and a space in a hut for them. 'A day later I joined them on the eleven hour working parties carrying bamboo, and though the discomfort was extreme there was a pioneering spirit about the new camp that came as a relief after the more circumscribed life of Kanburi.'[49]

Stephen Alexander described Nakhon Nayok as a schizophrenic camp: '. . . in squalor and working conditions it was like going back to square one on the railway in the worst days of 1943, yet just around the corner was the road to freedom – or, of course, extermination.'[50] The camp was situated in what was subsequently discovered to be one of the Japanese lines of defence. 'We were right in the middle of this line where there were about 30,000 Jap fighting troops who had marched from China, taking a year and three months to complete the journey,' Toosey wrote. 'The hills behind us were being prepared for a defence line. Had the war gone on we should have caught trouble.'[51]

Toosey had been approached by a Korean guard called Haria, who warned him that the Japanese were planning to massacre the prisoners. Stanley Gimson told the story in 1999:

Toosey arranged that on the order being given for the massacre, Haria should bring all the Koreans with all the weapons in the guard-hut (probably only about twelve rifles and one or two light automatics) to a rendezvous. There, selected POW marksmen would take over the weapons and do what they could to hold off the attack while the rest tried to disperse into the nearby jungle. Each of us was ordered to prepare a sharpened bamboo spear to be hidden in the thatch above our bed space. At some stage it became known that two Japanese machine-gun companies were stationed near the camp to carry out the massacre. The weapons in the camp would have been of little use against them.[52]

According to Gimson, very few of the other prisoners knew of this plan to defend themselves but, seeing the spears being prepared, imagined that the Colonel anticipated trouble at the end of the war. Toosey was ever anxious about the spread of news which might provoke the Japanese to retaliate.

In early August Tagasaki, who had travelled up with the first party and had been in overall charge of the camp, was joined in Nakhon Nayok by Noguchi. This was a turn for the worse and sure enough he began once again to mete out punishments for the most minor infringements. At the go-down in Bangkok a Thai lorry driver passing the door threw in two packets of cigarettes. 'A British Officer opened one packet in which there were two messages, and gave the other packet to his friend. They were observed by the Jap guard. They were taken by the Kempei, laid naked on the concrete floor and thrashed, one receiving 24 strokes and the other 10 on the backside,'[53] Toosey wrote. The message read: 'I'm your friend. I will be back tomorrow'. When these officers arrived at Nakhon Nayok Noguchi forced them to stand in front of the guardroom without food or water even though they had received punishment from the Kempei Tai already. Toosey protested but to no avail. These two prisoners were joined in front of the guardroom by a Dutch officer who had fallen out on the march through exhaustion. Noguchi told them they had all behaved like beggars and they would be treated like beggars for the rest of the war which, he added, would be over by Christmas, when Britain would surrender. It was Thursday 16 August 1945.

That afternoon they received sufficient Red Cross medical stores to last them for three years, most of them dated 1942.

A major problem for Toosey at Nakhon Nayok was the lack of concrete information from outside. Kanburi officers' camp was on the edge of the town of Kanchanaburi so that in the event of the war coming to an end the prisoners would hear of it quite quickly, which they did. Boon Pong cycled by the camp several times waving V signs and shouting 'War finish!' At Nakhon Nayok they were far from civilisation and had to rely on news brought to them by incoming parties which was, inevitably, days out of date or based on rumours pieced together from the locals which was often unreliable. Anticipating this Toosey had consulted the Webber brothers before he left Kanburi. They had volunteered for the party scheduled to leave on 10 August and said they would bring the radio with them. The next question was how? Every time the prisoners moved, a full inspection of luggage was made and there was no excuse this time to use the stretcher trick as the officers going to Nakhon Nayok had the long trek from the railway station to camp. In the end they decided that the safest way was for the Japanese to carry it for them. One of the prisoners was acting as a batman to Noguchi; he was therefore responsible for packing and unpacking Noguchi's belongings at either end. In a move of the utmost audacity and risk — death would have been the least feared outcome if he had been discovered – he packed the radio in Noguchi's personal luggage.

The radio arrived, with Noguchi, on 14 August. They had no batteries and no means of acquiring any but they were desperate for news as the rumours of the end of the war were spreading. 'Eventually, on the night of 16 August, the operators "borrowed" the battery from Noguchi's car at about midnight, and tuned in to All-India Radio. The first thing they hear was part of the News: "General MacArthur has flown to Tokyo to take control". From this it was obvious that Japan had surrendered. Toosey was told immediately, and ordered that no one else, other than anyone whom he considered must know, should be told lest there be any form of demonstration.'[54] Toosey found himself in a very tricky situation. He knew now that the war had ended the day before but he also knew that the Japanese were unpredictable and would not believe the news until they received orders from their own high command.

The camp was rife with rumour. 'There is obviously something most unusual in the air,' Louis Baume wrote in his diary for the morning of 16 August, 'some of us begin to think that the war is over and we are all asking ourselves whether it could possibly be so. Later again – Toosey is said to have stated that he thinks it is quite probable. Furious discussions now – especially as Toosey has a reputation for jumping to optimistic conclusions.'[55] The next morning the working parties went out as usual. They saw Thais showing them the V sign for victory and heard them calling out 'War over. You go home' but their guards said nothing. Noguchi left the camp for Bangkok and Tagasaki was once again in charge. At lunchtime the working parties came back into camp. That was unusual and the feeling of anticipation grew. At about five o'clock in the afternoon on Friday 17 August Tagasaki sent for Toosey.

Toosey went with David Boyle to the guard hut where he saw a new mat laid out on the floor and cups of Chinese tea on the table. Tagasaki told Toosey that a weapon of such magnitude such as had never been seen before had been used against the Japanese and that the Emperor had had no option but to order them to surrender unconditionally. Neither Toosey nor Tagasaki knew what an atom bomb was. At that moment it meant only one thing for him and the prisoners. The war was over and they had been spared the massacre that he had feared.

'Now we are friends we can shake hands. The war is over,' Tagasaki said to Toosey.

Toosey replied, '"Before I do that I want to know what happened to those officers and men who escaped from Tamarkan Camp. Did you shoot them and cut off their heads on your own initiative, or had you orders from above?" And, since he was a brave man, he replied that he had done it on his own initiative. So I had to refuse to take tea with him.'[56]

Toosey ordered Tagasaki to stay in the hut and he posted a guard on the door. Then he called the camp together and told them that the war had ended. They sang the British, Dutch and American national anthems followed by a prayer of thanks. And then they drifted towards their huts and their bug-ridden beds.

That night Louis Baume wrote:

Yes, it is all over and we have reached the bitter end. We are free. O God, can it really be true? 3½ years of eternity and at last we have reached the end. All those weeks, those months, that suffering and now it is all finished. All that agony, bombing, diseases, hunger, death and we have lived to see the end! We have vainly hoped, prayed, planned for this day for how long – and now it has come, suddenly, unexpectedly, quietly, just like this. I suppose we ought to sing, to dance, to go mad and scream with joy but we cannot. The going has been too hard and, anyway, the magnitude of the event is so great that it is quite beyond us to fully appreciate it.

It is a particularly beautiful night: the stars are glimmering bright and ghostly wisps of white cloud are lazily drifting round the dark hill tops.[57]

10

CLEAN SHIRTS AND SHORTS

My reaction? I was stunned. Stunned. You have to remember
what we'd gone through. And then to be told, just like that, out
of the blue, the whole thing was over. My mind was stunned.
Completely. My feelings had been so numbed by some of the
dreadful things that had gone on that I wasn't particularly easily
moved by anything by then. But gradually my mind reacted to
it and then it was a feeling of tremendous joy.

Phil Toosey 1974

Once the news of the surrender had begun to sink in Toosey's
first reaction was that he had to get back to his own men. It took
four days to get transport organised and during that time he acted
as Liaison Officer while Colonel Lilly took over command of
Nakhon Nayok. Several of the Korean guards, fearing reprisals,
asked Toosey for protection and advice. There was nothing he
could do officially but he gave them 150 Ticals each and told
them to make their way to Bangkok where they might be able to
find their way home.

On 22 August Toosey packed up his small bag of possessions and set off to Ubon where his men of the 135th and the Argylls and Gordons, 1500 Dutch prisoners and a handful of Australians had been imprisoned since they left Nong Pladuk. Ubon was situated on the Indo-China border some 600 kilometres east of Bangkok. Knights and Lilly were also leaving that day to join their men. Toosey's journey was to take him via Bangkok and he travelled with thirty-one fellow officers including Reggie Lees, David Boyle, Malcolm Northcote and Louis Baume. They made the trip in three lorries driven by Japanese soldiers. As they left the camp they passed a column of dejected, exhausted Japanese soldiers shuffling along, pushing wheelbarrows and handcarts piled high with paraphernalia. Some of the men were leading half-starved mules who tottered pathetically behind. What a level they had sunk to since 1942, Toosey thought.

The lorries sped along the straight rough roads through the rice fields, and although they were cramped for space the mood in the party was very cheerful. There were several breakdowns as a tyre burst or a wheel came loose. On one occasion the steering on one lorry failed. However, it was quickly repaired and they were back on the road. They wanted to get to Bangkok before nightfall, which was a full day's drive, but they also wanted to savour their freedom. On arriving at a larger village in the late morning, Toosey ordered the drivers to stop and they went to a Chinese café for their first meal 'on the road' as free men. Slowly their sense of freedom began to sink in; they ordered milky coffee, biscuits and cigarettes. Before long a Japanese soldier approached them and offered to buy them a drink. It was an awkward moment but Toosey accepted. The young man was polite and friendly. They chatted away in their own peculiar Anglo-Japanese pidgin until they had finished, whereupon they stood up, wished each other good luck and went their separate ways.

As they drew closer to Bangkok they began to see the signs of the capital city. The roads were good and lined with trees and houses of all descriptions, interspersed with magnificent temples. Soon they crossed the river over the Ram L Bridge and passed the Royal Palace with its great coloured temple and extensive buildings with their familiar pointed and curved roofs. There was more colour here than Toosey had seen in months – gold, red, blue, green and saffron. The roads were full of vehicles of all descriptions. Cars, lorries, buses crammed to overflowing with passengers clinging on the outside, oxen-drawn carts, hand-carts, and everywhere there were trishaws weaving in and out of the chaos. Captain Newell observed on his own journey into Bangkok that:

> On the slow flowing river the traffic seemed to be as dense as on the roads. There were tugs, motor-boats of all shapes and sizes, sampans, some square rigged, others with latten sails and in the midst of them all were the smaller but heavily laden sampans being propelled by sculls crammed to the gunwales and above with all manner of produce. There appeared to be no right of way rule, some craft asserting their progress upstream, some downstream, while yet others simply seemed content to try and cross straight over from one bank to the other.[1]

They arrived in Bangkok just before nightfall and ahead of a tropical storm. Toosey had been told to go to the go-downs at Smut Prakan where, two months earlier, he had slept on his way up to Nakhon Nayok. What a difference there was in the atmosphere. 'It was strange to visualise again the long grey ranks of prisoners on the concrete floor, the Nip guards with fixed bayonets at the doors and Noguchi strutting around like a tin god,' Louis Baume wrote. 'Now it was full of happy, laughing soldiers all intent on smoking, chatting or eating a jolly good meal.'[2]

It was here that they caught up with what had happened at other camps at the outbreak of peace. To his delight and relief, Toosey heard that Bill Drower had been pulled out of his prison alive, if only just. Colonel Swinton, who was then in charge of the officers' camp, led the Japanese field officer to the wooden cell attached to the guardhouse in which Drower had been in solitary confinement since mid-May. The Japanese officer looked into the cell. 'In the half light, with the assistance of a lantern, he saw the emaciated, bearded, half-demented figure who had been the tall, broad-shouldered, cultured figure of Bill Drower, and said, "We know nothing of this."'[3]

On his release from his cell Drower was seriously ill. 'The cooks, all officers of course, did what they could to help by secreting broken up vitamin tablets in my daily rice ball, which probably saved my life. So there I stayed until the Atomic Bomb, to which presumably I owe some debt of gratitude, brought the Pacific War to its dramatic end. By then, malnutrition and Black Water Fever had made time of no importance. Vague memories linger of the doctor and other friends breaking into the cell and hauling me out. Another few days, they said later, would have made their action of little use.'[4] He was treated briefly by the doctors in camp and then sent down to the big hospital camp at Nakhon Phatom where he received intensive antibiotics and nursing. From there he was transferred to hospital in Bangkok where he recuperated before being flown to join his parents in Baghdad.

Toosey spent the following day relaxing in the go-down and getting used to the idea of being a free man again. He was lying on the floor snoozing in the afternoon when suddenly he heard his name being called: 'Does anyone know where I will find Colonel Toosey?' He sat up and looked at the man who was standing right next to him. It was a tall, thin Englishman who turned out to be Peter Heath. He had heard that Toosey had arrived from Nakhon Nayok and was waiting to join his men at Ubon. 'I am Colonel Toosey,' he said. 'Well I am V of the V Organisation,' Heath replied and told Toosey to get ready as they were to go out for a meal that evening with Boon Pong. 'There was a fight going on in Bangkok between the Chinese and the Thai element', Toosey recalled, 'and going round one corner to my horror I saw a soldier at the very far end of the road sitting with his legs astride a machine gun and firing down the street.' Fortunately his taxi driver took evasive action and reversed out of trouble. He eventually arrived at the restaurant where he had a meal with Boon Pong and Peter Heath. It was a real celebration. Peter Heath told him more about how the V organisation had worked and about the extraordinary risks that had been taken by the people involved. Toosey heard about Boon Pong's family and the way his daughter and sister had been used as decoys, how the girls had smuggled radio batteries into the camps in their skirts, and how his wife had at all times been civil to the Japanese when they came into their shop so no one would suspect him or his family of helping the prisoners. It had been a dangerous game and Boon Pong was still at risk from those who had supported the Japanese and did not like the fact that some Thais had helped the prisoners of war.

Toosey returned to the go-down that night full of good food and Thai whisky. 'I have to admit', he said later, 'that I was as tight as I have ever been in my life. I was driven home in a rickshaw that night in the pouring rain, virtually unconscious from the first application of alcohol in 3½ years, singing loudly and I could not have cared less that I was soaking wet.'

Two days later Peter Heath arrived at the go-down and told Toosey he had managed to lay on transport to get him and the other officers to Ubon. Having found the Japanese unco-operative and unwilling to help, Peter Heath had approached the Thai authorities about organising a special train. The Thais had immediately offered him a diesel locomotive and two coaches. On hearing this the Japanese were furious. They insisted that the British officers should travel by their diesel engine and two metal trucks. Toosey and Peter Heath decided, according to Louis Baume, that 'whichever train proved the faster and arrived at Korat [station] first, we would continue on that train as far as Ubon. We informed our Thais of the arrangement and the driver promised to prove to the Nips which was the better train. We had no doubts whatsoever.'[5]

They left Bangkok at midnight on 25 August 1945 with Thai transport. They were travelling in barely recalled luxury: sixteen men to a coach sitting on wooden seats rather than thirty-two men to a metal truck. They clattered along, averaging 40 k.p.h., in high spirits but wondering if it was all real.

The following day they arrived at Ubon station at 5 p.m. where they were met by an official reception party comprising the governor of Ubon province, the military commandant and several other dignitaries. In their dazed and travel-weary state they found such affairs bewildering. The Thais were resplendent in crisply ironed uniforms adorned with sparkling medals. Toosey was still dressed in a pair of over-patched shorts and a crumpled shirt. His DSO ribbon was almost threadbare. However, they had been able to shave and wash before arriving so that they, as the honoured guests, were as clean as possible.

The governor offered them the use of their military barracks but Toosey and the others were impatient to get to their men, having heard rumours of hardship in the camp at Ubon. So they were driven to a wide river, which they crossed in little boats. There they were met by 'an extraordinarily smart soldier',

Toosey recalled, 'one of my men dressed in full uniform he had borrowed from everybody else, and there he was to welcome me and bring me back to camp. I was driven there in something called a jeep, a vehicle I had never heard of before.' The other officers boarded two lorries and the little convoy sped through the town and out, northwards, eleven kilometres to the prison camp.

To his relief, Toosey found that the rumours he had heard in Bangkok were wrong. The camp was clean and the men looked quite fit and well although few of them had any clothes left. The welcome was one of the most emotional that Toosey could remember: 'On arrival at camp I received the most wonderful reception you could believe possible. It took me quite some time to get through the large cheering crowd.'[6] Louis Baume found the meeting equally moving: 'Our reception on arrival was terrific. That they were genuinely overjoyed to see us was obvious – they seemed as happy to see us as we were to see them.'[7]

Sergeant Major Sandy McTavish had survived several bashings by the Japanese during his time as commander of Ubon. He was even beaten on his birthday when some of the men sang Happy Birthday to him. When the rumours of the atomic bomb reached Ubon McTavish knew the war was finally over. He was summoned by the Japanese commandant, Major Chida, who told him that this was the case but that no one else in the camp knew it. Chida offered him his sword and the leadership switched quietly and peacefully to the British. McTavish instructed the Japanese to go to the Korean guards and get them to hand over their weapons and lock them in a shed by the guardhouse. He insisted that the men should go out to work as normal and that the announcement that the war was over would not be made until the weapons had been handed over and locked away. He did not want any violent reprisals. Later that morning the men returned from work and the camp commander stood in front of them and announced: 'War is over. You go home.' The mood swing was dramatic. The Australians started a conga through the camp and a small group of men smashed down the camp gate, but there was no serious retaliation. McTavish continued to command Ubon until Toosey arrived.

He had done a great job of keeping morale and discipline in camp and it was not only Toosey who was impressed. David Smiley wrote: 'The camp seemed clean and efficient. The inmates had improvised bamboo pumps to draw water out of the ground. Most of this was thanks to McTavish, a remarkable man who had managed to keep up a surprisingly high morale among the prisoners.'[8]

It was only the following day that Toosey first met Lieutenant Colonel David Smiley of the Blues. Smiley was a member of SOE (Special Operations Executive) Force 136. He had been in Ceylon from January 1945 where he trained at the school of jungle warfare and in April 1945 was sent to Thailand. He had a wireless operator and two detectives and their brief was to gather intelligence on the Japanese and to train Thai guerrilla bands to be ready for the day Mountbatten gave orders for the attack on the Japanese. Smiley was injured by the premature explosion of a booby-trapped briefcase and convalesced in India. He returned to Thailand and after the ceasefire moved about a thousand guerrillas near to the Ubon POW camp in case the Japanese decided to massacre the prisoners. When Toosey arrived at Ubon, Major 'Soapy' Hudson, the SOE officer in charge of the adjoining Korat area, came over to help accompanied by Major Alec Griswold, an American OSS officer.

Toosey suggested to Smiley that he might like to see all the prisoners together. Smiley agreed, so Toosey asked McTavish to call a parade of all the men. Toosey described the scene: 'With his help and that of Reggie Lees I organised a full parade. When Smiley marched on to parade they were called to attention and Reggie Lees came up to me and reported the number on parade. It was a most inspiring sight to see these splendid men together with their discipline still intact after 3½ years of absolute hell and I was extremely proud of them. Colonel Smiley spoke to them from a box and then walked round the ranks talking to a very large number of them. He was deeply moved himself and at one stage I noticed he was in tears.'[9]

Smiley spoke years later of this episode: 'Toosey sent me a message saying come along at 11 a.m. "I am going to have a big parade and I want you to take the salute." It was a most impressive parade too. The best part of 4000 men standing in strict lines singing "God Save the King", the Union Jack going up, and they'd been prisoners for 3½ years. I didn't cry but I felt like it. It was a very emotional thing altogether.'[10]

Ubon Camp parade: RSM McTavish handing over to Toosey.

The men had been living on starvation rations for three and a half years and the doctors were concerned that they should be reintroduced to protein-rich food slowly. Toosey organised food drops by the RAF and bought local food, including cattle on the hoof, and gradually the men's diet was improved.

With improved food the men's interest in sex was reawakening and the prostitutes of the town were known to be full of venereal disease thanks to the presence of Japanese soldiers over the last few years. Toosey then addressed the men:

> I propose to keep the discipline exactly the same as I have done throughout three-and-a-half years and I am in charge and you will, I am sorry to say, still have to do as you are told. I warn you against two things: that is indiscriminately going out of camp to get food for yourselves or getting mixed up with women, because the last thing I want is to get a lot of you full of venereal disease before we go home. Before I am going to let you make contact with women I am going to make proper arrangements to have an air-drop and get some proper supplies so that if you wish sexual intercourse you can do it in safety.[11]

Toosey asked Smiley to cable Delhi for him. A cable was duly sent which read: 'Please send 10,000 French letters at once'. 'They arrived the next day,' Toosey remembered, 'I believe that the message was received by a girl wireless operator in the Royal Air Force. She must have been astonished at our virility after so many years in captivity!'

The air drops continued and the prisoners received clothing and Players cigarettes, which were very welcome. The drop on 5 September was eagerly awaited. They had visions of tinned fruit, baked beans, razor blades and other such luxuries falling like manna from heaven. 'But on opening the containers, what did we find?' asked Louis Baume, 'Cadbury's milk chocolate, picture magazines? No . . . RICE!! My God! If the planes had not been so fast, we would have thrown it back at them again! Here are we, been living on rice three times a day for over three and a half years, and what do they send us? RICE, bloody rice! But still, we had to laugh.'[12]

As each day went by they became more accustomed to the sense of being free but they still found themselves surprised by

Rice Again *by Jan Van Holthe.*

everyday events. One evening David Smiley invited Toosey and a handful of other officers to dinner at his headquarters in the police chief's house. There they had a Thai meal, which they remembered particularly for having a white tablecloth on the table, white napkins and real glasses with real drink inside. And an electric light. It was too good to be true.

By day they learned about all the things that had been introduced into the world over the last three and a half years. 'We will be returning to a strange world, full of strange and unknown things,' Louis Baume wrote in his diary. 'We are completely foxed by expressions such as D Day, VE Day, VJ Day, SEAC, Alligators, Ducks, Pythons, RAPWI, buzz bombs, atom bombs, bazookas etc. Neither do we know who are Montgomery, Supremo, Ike or Bill Slim. I suppose we shall find out bit by bit.'[13]

Anxious to get his men repatriated as quickly as possible Toosey made a number of trips to Bangkok by light aircraft and had meetings with officials in charge of RAPWI – the Recovery of Allied Prisoners of War and Internees – the body responsible for getting the 36,000 British, Australian and Dutch prisoners home. He was frustrated at the lack of movement and discovered it was due to the fact that his men were well-disciplined and not causing trouble. The authorities were focused on getting prisoners out of Bangkok where discipline had collapsed and troops were making up for lost time in the city's restaurants and brothels.

Toosey requested an interview with General Clague in Bangkok. The first thing Clague did was give Toosey a new DSO ribbon to replace the worn one. He agreed that it was unfair that Toosey's men were being penalised for good behaviour and he agreed to speed up their repatriation. He also asked him to write a report on the prison camps. Toosey was given a small office where he sat with Captain Ewart Escritt and wrote the story of the prison camps he had commanded from Bukit Timah on Singapore Island in 1942 to Nakhon Nayok in August 1945. When he returned to Ubon he asked various people to supply appendices to the report. Dr Smyth submitted a long and detailed medical report; Staff Sergeant Sherring wrote an extensive summary of his experience of the food and ration swindles at Nong Pladuk; David Boyle wrote about the role of the interpreters. There were short pieces by the padres, both Roman Catholic and Protestant, and reports on individual atrocities witnessed. It took some three weeks to write and ran to over 20,000 words.

What Toosey saw in the capital city reinforced his belief that he had been right to insist on maintaining the same standard of discipline he had during captivity. Jack Leeman of the War Graves Commission observed this too and wrote: 'The ex-prisoners really let their hair down with a bang. They drank anything at all regardless of taste, cost or effects. The girls in the extensive red light district were kept fully employed day and night.' Night after night trucks were sent into the city to find the men who were due to be repatriated the following day. On one such journey an ex-prisoner was shot in the cross-fire between Chinese and Thais: 'A pointless tragedy,' Leeman wrote. 'After surviving 3½ years of brutal savagery it seemed a dreadful waste for him to get killed while salvaging drunks from brothels.'[14]

Violence had nearly claimed the life of Boon Pong in Kanchanaburi. Toosey heard that he was shot outside his shop in front of his wife and father at the beginning of September. A British officer of Force 136 in Kanchanaburi, Captain Newell, heard the shots and rushed to the scene. 'He had a shot through his neck and left arm and he had also been shot clean through the back. There was a large hole in his chest where the bullet had emerged and spent itself. He looked up at me. "Thai police kill me." That was all he said.' Newell and Boon Pong's wife bundled him into Newell's car and drove him to Tha Muang where there was a British medical team headed by Major Barnes. They managed to get him to the hospital hut where they gave him blood transfusions and a surgeon operated on the wounds. Arthur Moon had been sent to Tha Muang to see Boon Pong and he reported back that although he would be in hospital for months he expected him to make a full recovery. On that visit Moon was able to recover his medical records and drawings buried under his hut in a tin for safe keeping in January 1945. All 101 drawings and his notes were in perfect condition.

On another visit to Bangkok, Toosey was asked to give evidence about war crimes. All the Japanese guards were to be screened to see whether they had been guilty of any particular crimes. When asked about this later, he said: 'I had no thoughts of revenge. The only thing I was determined to do, which I did, was to bring to justice cold-blooded murderers. I felt that these men had got to be dealt with.'[15] Toosey gave evidence against Tagasaki and Kaneishero, who were implicated in the murders of the escapees from Tamarkan in 1943 and in particular in the bayoneting of Pomeroy and Howard. He also indicted Noguchi for his attempted murder of Bill Drower. The British hanged 265 war criminals.

It was during the screening that Toosey came face to face with Saito for the last time in his life. The two men met in Bangkok. To Saito's intense surprise, now that their situations were reversed, Toosey showed no acrimony. He shook Saito by the hand and they exchanged friendly greetings. According to Peter Davies, who interviewed Saito in the 1980s, they discussed the reasons for the deaths of so many prisoners. 'Before leaving, Toosey remarked: "God would decide who was in the right." This was a phrase that Saito, who knew little English, could still remember forty years later.'[16] Toosey had spoken up for Saito, saying that he had been strict but fair in his dealings with the prisoners and this was reflected in his camp report. As a result, Saito, who would in all probability have been cleared in the normal way, had his case accelerated.

The Dutch prisoners had more serious problems than the British and Australian. Those from the Netherlands East Indies had no home to go to. Thousands of Dutch there were held by extremists and their safety was not guaranteed. As news and rumours continued to flood into Ubon via their new wireless sets, distressing stories of the fate of Dutch families on Java and Sumatra began to emerge. The British were deeply sympathetic. Former Dutch prisoners had to remain in camps in Thailand where they were trained to fight. One of Toosey's closest Dutch friends, Hans Tillema, wrote to him ruefully: 'You won the War. We lost it.' A few months later the situation was still desperate for them. Padre Hamel wrote to Toosey: 'Alas for us the war is not yet over. We are here in Java still in the midst of serious trouble. Almost half of the women and children are still in the hands of the extremists, and some of my best friends have been murdered and some others kidnapped. When will this trouble be over?'[17] Many Dutch were still in Thailand twelve months later.

A job undertaken by the Dutch after the war was care of the Asian labourers, 23,000 of whom were still working along the Thailand–Burma railway in August 1945. The Allied forces who had taken over the running of the railway were clear that they had a responsibility to help with the repatriation of the men, particularly the Malays, and they were anxious in the immediate aftermath for their safety. A mixed party of Dutch and British officers visited all the camps along the railway to reassure the men that they were to be cared for. They told them not to run away and ordered the Japanese to feed them until they could be brought down to base camps in the Kanchanaburi area. This happened during September and members of the Federal Malay States Volunteer Force remained there to help.

On 18 September an Australian, Major Evitt, returned to Ubon from Bangkok. He brought news. Louis Baume recorded:

> He informs us that the Aussies are leaving on the 22nd. He also brings us news that Shimojo is in jail; the Aussies have been chucking Nips and Koreans out of cafes; there is trouble between the Thais and the Chinese in Bangkok; Jap working parties are out; Gurkhas, jeeps, Dakotas, Spitfires and General Slim are in the capital. He also confirms that Nakhon Nayok was to have been bombed out of existence by the R.A.F. on August 18 and that all officer-prisoners were to have been shot by the Japanese on September 7th – the day of the invasion of Malaya and Siam. Three days, or three weeks at the most, was all that we had left. [18]

The same morning that Major Evitt returned with the news of their lucky escape, Toosey was asked by Smiley to accompany him to disarm the Japanese division that was situated in the neighbourhood. There were 83,000 Japanese troops and they were still armed. 'Having been on the other side of the fence for so long I regarded this new mission with a certain amount of trepidation,' Toosey confessed, 'but Smiley gave me two revolvers and said, "We will go together and if we get any opposition, draw both your revolvers and slap them on the table in front of the general."' [19] They arrived at the headquarters and met the Japanese general, who was wearing a blood-stained bandage around his head and who turned out to be very obstinate and difficult. Smiley gave the sign and he and Toosey took out their revolvers and banged them down firmly on the table in front of them. 'His attitude changed immediately,' Toosey recalled. 'He sent his servant for a bottle of good Scotch whisky – something I had not tasted for 3½ years – and we sat round the table and made the necessary arrangements. Once having done this one has to say that the discipline of the Japanese was immaculate. They brought all their arms to a certain place and there they piled them and they went back to form a POW camp where they caused absolutely no trouble at all. Apparently once the Emperor had said the war was over they reacted at once and behaved in a very highly disciplined manner.'[20]

The troops stacked their weapons in one pile and all the officers were ordered to pile up their ceremonial swords in another. Smiley invited Toosey to help himself to a sword as a memento. He took one for himself as well. The Japanese were proud of their ceremonial swords and would not permit them to be taken by the enemy. Smiley knew that a great many of the Japanese officers had ceremoniously thrown their best swords into the river and the ones that were piled up were of a lesser quality and thus importance.

Under his command Smiley had two Thais named 'Pluto' and 'Red Ant'. Red Ant was one of the two Thai cabinet ministers to oppose Thailand's submission to Japan in December 1941. As a result he had had a high price on his head and had been forced to escape to the hills. He eventually found his way to the USA where he was trained for guerrilla work. He was dropped by parachute into Thailand in September 1944 and had been working underground ever since. He and Toosey got on well; Red Ant presented him with a revolver which he wore proudly and kept for many years after the war.

Plans for the evacuation continued and finally the day was set for Monday 24 September 1945. Toosey and Reggie Lees had been to the Japanese camp with Louis Baume and Barney Dutton to get lorries. Initially the Japanese had been unwilling to help and denied having any working transport at all. However, having worked with the Japanese for so long Toosey reckoned he had heard all their excuses and demanded they hand over their vehicles. Eventually, after a stand off, the Japanese conceded and supplied six lorries and two brand-new cars. 'By the time we had finished, the Nips, amazed and impressed by our flow of impolite language (picked up in captivity), were bowing and scraping and presenting arms at every opportunity!'[21] Louis Baume recalled.

The Dutch, who would be remaining behind, had planned a big send-off for the Australian and British prisoners. They prepared a concert with speeches and a presentation to Toosey of a

Toosey by Jan Van Holthe.

drawing by Jan Van Holthe. Suddenly the plans to evacuate the first men were brought forward by two days and the concert had to be cancelled but the Dutch medical officer, Dr den Hertog, presented Toosey with a copy of the speech and the drawing the night before he left. In the speech he said:

> Many of us have been under your command for more than two years. I do not want to use the common place that you have been a father to us. You are too young for that and it would be an awkward idea for you to leave behind so many children. But you have been one of us, you watched our games, you were with us when the bombs fell, you visited our sick in hospital, you shared our joy and sorrow with us, you stood at the grave of many of our comrades and on New Year between 12 and 1 you appeared in our huts, not as a ghost but as your very self to wish us a Happy New Year: in short you were our comrade and we loved you for it.[22]

The first consignment of men – the Australians plus 250 British – left on the night of 22 September. Toosey, Lees, Dutton and Baume accompanied them as far as the station. The journey involved crossing the Menam Moun River, which was now swollen by monsoon rains, in little dugouts. Fortunately the moon was bright that night but they all realised it was dangerous to move the men at night, particularly as the river-crossing took forty-five minutes now rather than the fifteen during the dry season.

The logistics of getting the men home was complicated by the fact they had to be divided into fifty-eight planeloads of twenty-five men each for the flight from Bangkok to Rangoon. They also had to get all the men across the river in dugouts in order to catch their train on the 24th. The whole exercise took eight hours with the last party of men crossing at 5 p.m. including Lees and Toosey.

As the groups left the camp they passed by the old guard-house where Major Chida, who had been with them in Nong Pladuk and then Ubon, was standing. He was dressed in his best clothes but without his sword; he saluted each lorryload of prisoners for the last time as they left the camp. This extraordinary action elicited a confused response. Louis Baume recorded the scene in his diary:

> He kept this up throughout the day and ordered his old camp staff to do likewise. We felt a certain amount of pity mixed with contempt for this senile and ineffectual old man who did such extraordinary and unexpected things; but, though at times almost paternal in his actions, we had come to despise him for refusing to use the authority that went with his rank and for being unable, or unwilling, to control the excesses of those under his command. We felt contempt that anyone could lower himself to such servility and cringe before those whom he so recently treated like slaves; but we appreciated too what this complete and utter loss of face must mean. I could see again Major Chida in his best uniform, standing on a table to address the prisoners of Nong Pladuk – standing, rifle in hand, before a mutinous camp and ordering the Nip guard to load their rifles and face the officer prisoners – wandering around on a clear moonlit night, saluting the rows of shattered corpses – indeed, the once arrogant and conceited Japanese are truly humbled. That Major Chida will have to bear some of the blame for the killings at Kanchanaburi, the crowding of Nong Pladuk during the bombings, and the two murders at Ubon, there can be no doubt.[23]

The first leg of the journey home began with a formal send-off on the platform of Ubon station by the Thai military. It could not have been in starker contrast to the journey they had made to Thailand in the autumn of 1942. At every station along the way to Bangkok the train stopped and was met by an official welcome committee with food, flowers and drink for the prisoners. Tables heaped with delicious Thai delicacies, which the men struggled to eat so as not to insult their generous hosts. Scores of school-children danced and sang songs of welcome on the platforms and at every halt bunches of flowers and fruit were pushed through the open windows so that the carriages were soon filled with the overpowering, cloying scent of tropical flowers. There were messages of good luck and presents from groups such as the local boy scouts, the Chinese traders and the local schools. It was at once wonderful and overwhelming. The men, whose stomachs were unaccustomed to such rich food, eventually took it in turns to get down at the stations to show gratitude to the generous Thais. It was with some relief that nightfall signalled the end to festivities.

They reached Bangkok station at nine o'clock the following morning where they were greeted by Lady Mountbatten's lady-in-waiting. She was the first Western woman the men had seen since the fall of Singapore.

From Bangkok they flew by Dakota to Rangoon where they were all examined in hospital. The very sick had been evacuated from Ubon in late August, so the majority of them were mod-erately fit although some were still having trouble adjusting to the new diet. This continued to cause problems as European food was introduced in Rangoon. Here Toosey slept in a bed with springs for the first time. He also received his first letters from home and ate his first meal of bread and butter. If arriving at Ubon had been a shock after Nakhon Nayok, it was at least famil-iar as it was still Thailand with Japanese milling around. Here in Rangoon the Allies were in charge. There were nurses in crisp, white uniforms folding crisp, white sheets on squeaky, springy beds. Toosey was given a clean shirt and shorts.

He learned from the officials at RAPWI that the men would be split up into small parties and sent home on a number of ships. 'This to me, having been with these splendid men for the last 3½ years, was a very grave disappointment, as it was to them. But I knew that my great friend John Nicholson was head of shipping in Delhi.' A cable was sent to Delhi and Nicholson organised for them to come home on one ship. At 5 p.m. on Wednesday 11 October 1945 the SS *Orbita*, a 16,532 ton-ship of the Pacific Steam Navigation Company, on which Toosey had returned to Britain from South America in 1929, weighed anchor and sailed downstream. A glorious sunset lit up the golden pagoda of Shwedagon which shimmered in the distance. A silvery moon rose in the sky; it was another perfect tropical night.

It was not only the bar steward and one or two other members of the ship's company that Toosey recognised from his South American voyage some seventeen years earlier. The man commanding the ship was Arthur Ratcliffe, an ex-member of the Liverpool Cotton Market, and from whom Toosey and Alex had bought their home, Heathcote, in 1937. As Toosey came on board Ratcliffe welcomed him, and shaking him warmly by the hand, said: 'How wonderful to see you, Phil. We all thought you were dead, but I am so sorry about your brother Arthur.'[24] This was the first Toosey had heard of this tragedy. Arthur Toosey had been killed on 15 July 1944, five weeks after D-Day. It came as a terrible shock, not least because he had already received a letter from Alex with all the family news. She had not told him of Arthur's death, he learned, because she was worried it would upset him. He wrote and asked her to tell him the whole truth, whatever it was.

As they left the Burma coast and sailed towards their new

lives there was a sense of completion. Toosey was not alone in feeling that an immense chapter in his life had closed – a chapter that was remote and known only to those who had been involved in it. He welcomed the opportunity to be able to talk about those times during the voyage home. They talked about the good times as well as the bad and Toosey knew that what he had lived through, what they had all lived through, had been an experience the like of which they would never see again and which, in retrospect, he said he would not have missed for anything in the world. When asked about his experiences later he said:

> It got my values right and I hope they remained right. People say to me 'what a ghastly experience' and I say, 'My dear friend, it was nothing of the sort. It was an experience which I could not go through again but I wouldn't have missed it for anything. It taught me so much about human beings.
>
> 'You see one thing one learned was this panoply of rank – Lords and so forth: once you were made equal in a POW camp the real man came out. It didn't matter what his rank was, if he was a man he was a man, and that's all there was to it.'[25]

Many men did not come home. According to Toosey, of the 701 men from the 135th who had gone out to Singapore from the UK, only 346 came back. A tenth of those had died in battle, the remainder had perished in Thailand. The Argyll and Sutherland Highlanders, who had sustained heavy casualties in the campaign, brought back just 230 men from the original 900. Overall 27 per cent of the men who went into captivity in Japanese prison camps died. This compared with 4 per cent of men imprisoned by the Germans.

During the first half of the voyage the ship was commanded

by Arthur Ratcliffe and run by the RAF, which led to complaints of inefficiency and general grumbles. However, after leaving Port Said a number of articles were stolen from the captain's cabin, including some silk stockings as a present for his wife. Toosey was consulted and he knew what had happened. He told Ratcliffe that he could sort this out if he was allowed to take command of the ship until they got home. Ratcliffe was only too happy and Toosey was allowed to broadcast a message through the tannoy system: 'I am going to empty the alleyways for half an hour,' he announced. 'If the Argylls do not return the silk stockings and other things they have taken from the Captain's cabin in that time, they will get no more beer for the rest of the voyage. You know who is speaking to you and you know that I mean what I say.'[26] The booty was returned within half an hour and the ship continued on its way with Toosey in charge. They had no more trouble.

As the ship got closer to home, various domestic tragedies began to emerge. Some women sent cables telling their husbands that they had thought they were dead and had found new boyfriends, others had died, some had even divorced the men and married again in their absence. After Suez 'The Jilted Lovers' Club' was called into being, comprising the hundred or so men who had learned that they had no wife to return to. At their first meeting they passed a resolution to ask the captain to turn back to Bali or somewhere else where love was cheap. But below the jollity and high spirits there was a real sense of despair and sadness. Toosey was asked to join The Jilted Lovers' Club as an honorary member and he went along to their meetings and commiserated with them as they attempted to drown their sorrows. He recalled one of them coming to him in great distress: 'It was really very sad. I remember a Gordon Highlander – a great big man – coming to me and showing me a cable from his wife, which read: "It is no good you coming back to me. I have married an American soldier." He was obviously very upset so I did my best to console him. But he had been a regular soldier in India before the war broke out and they had been separated for a great length of time.'[27]

Over the next fortnight the weather began to get colder and as they sailed into the Atlantic thoughts focused impatiently on home. On 5 November they were given battledress for the first time. Nurses on board were busy sewing ribbons, badges and buttons on the uniforms. The clothing felt strange, heavy and unfamiliar after all these years. Reggie Lees, who had continued to wear his patched-up shorts, rather than the new ones offered to him in Rangoon, at last had to admit that his tropical attire was unsuitable for the climate. Toosey learned that the ship was to sail into Liverpool on Thursday 8 November 1945 but that they would not dock until Friday at 2 p.m. There was some frustration on board as the men were by now eager to get away. Most of them were not interested in the celebrations that had been prepared.

On the Thursday afternoon the ship picked up her pilot at Port Lynas, off Anglesey. They were guided to the Mersey where they anchored and spent their last night aboard ship. There was a small party that evening. The following day dawned cold but fine. The *Orbita* was dressed and sailed up the Mersey towards Princes Dock. Louis Baume recorded what he saw: 'We passed up the river, gazing at the shipping and the forts, acknowledging the salutes and sirens of all the ships. We received a terrific welcome. Finally we docked at 15.00 hours. The cycle is completed. Altogether, we have covered some 8,027 miles on the *Orbita* and taken 29 days for the journey from Rangoon.'[28]

Alex was at the quayside with the children. Patrick, Toosey's eldest son, remembered a woman running up and down the quay in front of the eager crowd screaming out: 'Has anyone seen Johnny? Has anyone seen my Johnny?' She was desperate and he felt very sad for her. Alex was allowed on board the ship and in his cabin Toosey was able to greet his wife for the first time in more than four years. He gave her a gold watch he had bought for her in Bangkok and the two of them walked down onto the quayside together into the throng of friends and wellwishers. Alan Tod, Alex had told him, had arranged this reception for him. He was nowhere to be seen. Eventually Toosey found him, 'hiding behind a pillar on the staging at Princes Landing Stage. I went up to him and thanked him and he said, simply: "Phil, I am absolutely delighted to see you."'

11

THE CAPTAIN REVIVED

I have no doubt in my own mind that those whose background enabled them to withstand this experience have benefited immensely by it. The difficulty is not to throw away such a wonderful experience by being overwhelmed by the difficulties and complexities of life in England today.

Phil Toosey to Sir John Hobhouse 1960

Alex drove Toosey home on Saturday 10 November 1945 and as they turned in to the drive at Heathcote he saw an enormous bonfire burning on the lawn where his beloved tennis court had been and a huge sign across the front of the house saying WELCOME HOME. The house was decorated with Union Jacks and all the locals seemed to have turned out to celebrate his return. It was a wonderful and heartening homecoming, although he hadn't prepared himself for the fact that of his three children only Patrick recognised him, and he only just. Alex told him that Nicholas, the youngest, 'was heard discussing with his elder brother and sister what they were going to do with me when I arrived. He suggested that I should live in Bromborough (4 miles away) but they said no they thought that was rather far. He then said what about him living with Mr Fergusson next door whereupon my eldest son, Patrick, being by then a man of the world, said: "Don't be a fool, Nicholas, Daddy lives here and what's more he lives in Mummy's bed."'

The initial surprise of the changes at Heathcote — the tennis court dug up for potatoes and a family of three children all six years older than when he had left the house in 1939 — was followed by further discoveries. Patrick, now twelve, was in his first term at Winchester. Toosey perhaps would have hoped he might follow him to Gresham's but he had not been around to consult. Gillian, at ten, was painfully shy and found she could barely talk to her father. She remembered him coming home and hugging her: 'I just backed away,' she said. 'I was very wary as I had no recollection of any man showing me affection. It honestly took me years before I was relaxed with him. Now I think how sad that must have been for him.'[1]

Nicholas was five and a half and had grown up in exclusively female company. He too took time to adjust.

This was not a problem limited to the Toosey family. Patricia Mark, daughter of Dr Jim Mark from Tamarkan, wrote of her father's return: 'I was four years and three months old when my father came home. Old enough to realise that there were serious changes afoot, and not old enough to understand the underlying dynamics. I can remember quite clearly when I met this man, who was with my mother, walking into the porch which always smelt of geraniums. He smiled down at me and I glared up at him, brows down in the scowl for which I had become famous. There and then I told him that he should go back to Siam. We didn't want him here.'[2] It did not last long. Jim Mark soon won his daughter over but what a shock it must have been for him, that first encounter.

Gillian, Patrick and Nicholas Toosey in 1946.

Gillian found it difficult to talk to her father. She loved his energy and enthusiasm, she even did not mind it when he told her off but she could not bring herself to open up. It was not until she was in her late teens that she first felt at ease with him. When she was seventeen Alex went into hospital and she was left at Heathcote to hold the fort. On the first evening she cooked a meal of boiled rice and stew. When Toosey had finished he looked up at her and said: 'I swore I'd never eat rice again but this was delicious.' She was horrified when his remark sank in. His prisoner-of-war experiences were never discussed at home so she had no reason to understand the significance of rice to him, but he handled the situation so kindly that she couldn't help but relax her guard a little, 'then by the time I was nineteen', she said, 'I was totally at ease and from then on our relationship was wonderful'.[3]

This situation was mirrored in many families. It seems that the returning men often found it easier to establish an understanding with their daughters than with their wives. One daughter wrote: 'My mother seemed to become more and more frozen in her emotional distress, for distress it surely was. He was the one who showed affection to her, with gentle teasing and laughter and hands out to touch and hold. I can't ever remember seeing her respond.'[4] Several daughters of former prisoners talked about having problems with their mothers who felt that the prisoner-of-war experience had ruined their marriages and that the friendships between fathers and daughters had rubbed salt into already open wounds. Some wives even made their daughters scapegoats for their own grudge against the war: 'As the years went by, it became increasingly difficult to talk to my father about anything because she became so angry and vituperative, interrupting and shouting us down. I learned to keep quiet and let her talk about what she wanted to talk about, all too often a tirade about something, and when I got my father alone, we could enjoy each other's company and discussions. He was a wonderful person to have discussions with, so philosophical and so wise. I miss him to this day.'[5]

Patrick did not share his sister's early inhibitions. He was delighted to see his father come home and they got on famously. Patrick was keen to learn to shoot and Toosey was an enthusiastic teacher. At the weekends they would shoot at Bodorgan on Anglesey and for further practice Toosey would station Patrick on the newly restored tennis court at Heathcote and get Tig (Walter Duke, the gardener) to drive birds from the trees of the next-door neighbour's garden. Patrick remembers Mrs Fergusson howling with indignation as they took pot shots at 'her' birds.

Patrick was a keen sportsman and once the tennis court had been repaired to its former glory he, Gillian, Alex and 'the

Captain', as they called him, played regularly. 'My father was *quite* a good tennis player,' Gillian said, 'he was wildly enthusiastic but when he served he invariably foot faulted and more often than not the balls went way out but if they did land inside the court they were winners. My mother had been a county player in her youth and she had a deadly underarm serve.'[6]

Toosey found it difficult to sleep in a bed. It was too soft and for the first few months he slept on the floor in their bedroom. Eventually he had his own separate bedroom. This was, he explained, on account of his nightmares that troubled him for years after the war. He would dream that he was trapped in the corner of a room, penned in by huge, black panthers with enormous teeth and yellow eyes, and would wake up screaming. The children all remember hearing piercing screams in the night but when Patrick asked him about it the next morning Toosey would reply that he did not know what he was referring to. Eventually the panthers metamorphosed into Labrador dogs, and that was almost more terrifying for him. He loved his Labradors and hated their association with his nightmares.

When Toosey first came home he like thousands of others found a Britain that was no longer familiar. He was completely out of touch with the changes that had taken place, knew little of the course the war had taken, of the changes in the country and the way people lived. 'The vocabulary was new, the developments enormous and we had much ground to make up physically. It was not too difficult to acquire a veneer; it was less easy to take our places with any assurance in the new world of 1945 and 1946.'[7]

Alex Toosey had spent the war at Heathcote with the three children. She had no certainty of her husband's whereabouts until a telegram arrived from the War Office dated 21 December 1942. It read: 'Official report received that Lt Col P.J.D. Toosey

R.A. is a prisoner of war. Letter follows shortly.' Barings Bank had been assiduous in following the war careers of their various employees and sent eight letters, copied to all servicemen and their families, between September 1942 and March 1945. In the first of these letters Mackintosh of the London office wrote: 'Lieut Col Toosey, who survived Dunkirk, was with the territorial division which arrived in Singapore just in time to be snaffled by the Japs. Sgt Major Rutherford, also of the Liverpool office, was with him. So far there has been no official news of either; though there are grounds for thinking Toosey is all right but a prisoner.'[8] It was a further year before Alex received a pre-printed postcard from Toosey and not until September 1945 that she had a letter.

Alex was an independent spirit and she coped during the six years she was on her own with typical determination and grit. She had had some help with the cooking and landgirls had been sent to cultivate vegetables in the garden. She kept hens and rabbits, they grew potatoes and green vegetables but nevertheless they were short of food like everyone else. The children had memories of rabbit stew with little bits of unappetising meat floating in it. Alex was an excellent organiser but not a great cook. Patrick and Gillian were old enough to help with outside jobs like chopping wood and cleaning out the hens which they did when the gardener, Walter Duke, joined up and went off to spend the war as a driver in Africa. Walter, whom the children nicknamed Tig (The Incredible Giant) because he was four feet eleven inches, was a dearly loved member of the household. With his departure there were no men about, apart from visitors, for five years.

Alex's relations had tried to encourage her to leave the Wirral with its dangerous proximity to Liverpool, target of fierce bombing by the Luftwaffe in May 1941, and take the children to the

USA. Toosey's older sister, Patsey, tried very hard to persuade her as well. With a husband in the Navy, Patsey took advantage to send her three children to the United States where they would be safer. The Tooseys' next-door neighbours, the Fergussons, also sent theirs away. Alex had refused. In fact she refused even to hide with the children during the air raids, announcing curtly that if she was going to die she would die in her own bed. When the bombing started the children and Greedles, the nanny, would be bundled into the 'Bogey Hole' under the stairs where Alex believed they were safe. But it was uncomfortable and the children were afraid. The dining room was then reinforced with pillars and sandbags were layered outside the window, and the children and Greedles would sleep in there during the raids. Alex remained resolutely in her bedroom. Patsey's daughter Susannah was homesick in America and eventually persuaded her parents to let her come back to Britain in 1945. Tragically the ship she was sailing on was torpedoed off Ireland with very few survivors. Susannah died.

Despite her gruff manner Alex was a caring and considerate person who was as anxious as Toosey to do her duty. Throughout the war she corresponded not only with the families of the men from Toosey's regiment, the 135th Herts Yeomanry, but also with families of men in the Argyll and Sutherland Highlanders and the Gordon Highlanders. At first she wrote to them in response to news of deaths and injuries received from Singapore. However, towards the end of the war, when information about the prison camps was filtering slowly back to Britain, she would receive letters asking about men who might or might not have been in a camp with Toosey. This was a responsibility she took seriously but one that she conducted privately, so that the children were unaware of it, even in later years. It was only when families of the men wrote to thank Toosey for his part in the lives of their sons that he learned of her activities, for they would frequently ask him to extend to her their grateful thanks for all the work she had done on their behalf during the war.

Alex also worked in a canteen in Little Sutton, a couple of miles down the road, serving tea and coffee to the troops. When there was no petrol she pedalled on a bicycle nicknamed 'the percher'. She only ever rode the bicycle on the flat and as soon as she came to a hill she would get off and, to the children's delight, push it both up and down hill.

She was resourceful and took advantage of the black market that built up on the Wirral. If some petrol was to be had at the local garage, Mr Evans, the garage owner, would ring Heathcote and say that 'the bicycle had been repaired'. Alex would know that she could drop in and fill up. She was also a squirrel when it came to storing tinned food. In 1953, when Patrick prepared her dinner in bed one evening as she was recovering from an operation, he found a tin of shrimps which he added to an omelette. He took it upstairs and when Alex asked what was in it Patrick told her he had found the shrimps. She shrieked in horror – she had purchased those shrimps before the war. Over the period of the six years Alex was on her own she built up an impressive routine and she coped with everything, including eighteen months without Toosey's army pay. Barings were aware of the problem and in the third of their report letters they wrote: 'If through the mischances of war a member of the staff were to be survived by a young family, it is in the mind of the partners that where necessary the firm would help with the education of the children.'[9]

On his return Toosey was a different man. On the one hand a hero and on the other a troubled spirit. Alex was deposed. She no longer had to fulfil the role of head of the family. But she was not able to accommodate this change quickly. It lead to strains in their marriage and it was a very long time before the two of them found a way of living comfortably with one another. Their friends appeared unaware of the difficulties they were experiencing but the children recognised the strain. Other wives found their men had returned greatly changed. One woman observed: 'He was a different man. The experiences he had on the railway obsessed him. It affected our whole way of life and I could no longer accept him as a lover. It almost came to divorce.'[10]

It has been said that there were more broken marriages and broken engagements among former prisoners of the Japanese than in any other group of people after the war. A high number of suicides and deaths by accidents occurred in the first five years among this group of men.

There were those who had survivor's guilt and more who were simply confused by what England had become. Everything had changed. They came home to children who had grown older, wives who had found a degree of independence, girlfriends who had often married another man and a government preoccupied with reconstruction.

Younger men struggled to find work, older men slotted back into their pre-war jobs uneasily. 'We thought we had come home to freedom,' Ernest Gordon wrote. 'While we were prisoners we had been free to contribute to the general good, to help create order out of disorder. Here, in a society which paid lip service to freedom, we were prohibited, apparently, from applying the lessons we had learned. Impersonal laws, red tape, regulations in triplicate, were hemming us in like the jungle with invisible walls.'[11]

It was not until the late 1940s that any research was carried out into the medical or psychological condition of the prisoners. The official line was that the men should not try to talk to their families nor the families attempt to question them. It would lead to nothing but bitterness and misunderstanding, they were told.

Instead the men were encouraged to assimilate and keep their past to themselves. Malcolm Northcote, Toosey's adjutant from Macclesfield in 1941 to Ubon in 1945 summed it up when he wrote to thank Toosey for his letter: 'I shall keep your letter as a memento of "four years" of life which was a compartment all of its own, and only those few that were together can ever realise its joys and sorrows.'[12]

The most common complaints that Toosey heard from the men who wrote to him were anxiety, restlessness and nightmares. Ernest Gordon wrote: 'If we dreamed of the day's events in our new environment the guards would be there, walking unnoticed among the people in the street. If we strolled past with a friend they'd reach out and grab us. If we dreamed of open fields or rolling moors our old hosts would be there, advancing, closing in on us from every side.'[13] Ewart Escritt, who went back to work immediately on his return had to take time off after a few weeks: 'I began to feel as if fingers were clawing at my cheeks,'[14] he wrote later. Toosey heard of one officer who became so obsessed with understanding what he and others had been through that he went as far as naming rooms in his house with camp names and Japanese expressions. A second built a little shrine in his study on which he piled the carefully salvaged objects from his prisoner existence – his mess tin, some scribbled notes, an old razor and various Japanese notices and instructions.

No sooner was Toosey back home than he was inundated by letters from former prisoners and their families. There was a steady stream of correspondence for the next thirty years with everything from congratulations to pleas for help. Toosey was not alone in this. Malcolm Northcote wrote to him on 27 November 1945: 'My home has not been my own since I got back what with moving back to the flat, the office, the ruddy army forms, relations and ex-POW friends visiting, I have not had a moment. I am alone today and commenced at 8 am and only stopped for a slight band of hope at lunch time and it's now 4 pm and I still have plenty of letters to answer.'[15] However, he took his responsibility towards the ex-POWs very seriously and when Toosey asked him to find out how he could contact and write to each of the families who had lost men in Singapore and Thailand Northcote got to work. Toosey not only wanted the names and addresses of the families but information as to how, when and where the men had died. It was, Northcote wrote to him, a huge task but the colonel at the War Office had given him every encouragement.

There were letters from Dutchmen, Australians, British and Thais; many were full of anecdotes concerning individual events that stood out as turning points. But among the praise and gratitude there was also an undertone of depression. Arthur Osborne, who had been Toosey's batman, wrote in November 1945: 'I really do feel lost, now, without you to look after. I am a little bewildered when it comes to thinking out a career, because I do so want to avoid getting back into the pre-war rut. England rather depresses me after the bright and sunny East, but I expect that you, like most other people, think I'm crazy.'[16] Toosey was full of sympathy and he sent him a cheque and suggested he take his parents away for a week so that he might have time to rest and recuperate before working out what he wanted to do with his life. Osborne corresponded with Toosey for months after this, always asking advice and fretting about settling down. In 1951 he visited Heathcote and Toosey gave him a Labrador puppy as a gift. He had found work and some peace of mind. The two men continued to correspond and meet until the end of Toosey's life.

On the face of it Toosey appeared to be fit and well. He had gained two stone on the voyage home so that by the time he arrived in Liverpool he weighed just over ten stone. Even so, the years in Thailand had affected his health. Initially, the most noticeable problem was with his teeth caused by lack of vitamins in his diet in the camps compounded by little in the way of dental care. The dentist wanted to take all his teeth out but he refused saying that he would not give the Japanese that satisfaction. With some difficulty but iron determination he kept almost all his teeth until the day he died.

News of rationing and food shortages in Britain reached friends in Australia and Thailand. His Australian friends sent him huge food parcels regularly. He joked with Arthur Moon that he would have to get the letterbox at Heathcote enlarged in order to take the packets. However, their generosity became embarrassing and he asked them to stop sending him food, which they finally did in the early 1950s. Some of his Thai friends, including Red Ant, sent him fruit and this was very welcome at Heathcote although Alex regarded foreign food with suspicion.

When he was demobilized in early 1946 Toosey found himself demoted. That hurt. 'Our grateful government has now reduced me to Major to avoid paying me a Lt Col's gratuity,' he wrote to Alan Tod. 'No wonder Winston Churchill believes there is some discontent about. It is all so petty, particularly when one sees London full of useless Red Tabs [staff officers who had stayed in Britain – the civil service of the army] who have had a most successful and comfortable war.'

Barings granted Toosey six months' leave on full pay. They realised, better than he, the need for him to have a break and get back on his feet. He agreed but after three and a half weeks at home, answering piles of correspondence, he decided he wanted to go back to the office. Alan Tod would not let him. In January 1946 he took a short holiday with Hubert Servaes. The holiday ended with a visit to London where the two men had dinner with Arthur Villiers of Barings who told ACT (Alan Tod) that he found them to be in good form and delightful guests. ACT however was far from convinced that Toosey was in as good a shape as Villiers thought.

He knew Toosey better than almost anyone else. He had helped to guide and develop his career for nine years prior to the war and now, six and a half years later, he could see a striking change. Toosey's world had been turned completely upside down. The things he had previously held dear had been replaced by a far simpler but more deeply understood appreciation of the value of human life and dignity. ACT could see that Toosey's strength lay in the remarkable leadership he had shown in the prison camps in Thailand and for which he had become renowned. He saw great potential but before this could be developed in a business context he had to help Toosey overcome the turmoil of captivity. The problem Toosey had, apart from his nightmares, was a sense of dislocation, uncertainty and lack of confidence.

ACT let Toosey restart at Barings Liverpool in the middle of February 1946. He and the secretary, Mrs Crummock, who was known affectionately by Toosey as Mrs Stomach, had manned the office in the Tods' dining room during the war. Toosey's first project was to move them all back into the Cotton Exchange building.

At the beginning of April, ACT went to London and talked to Evelyn Baring about Toosey. They concluded he needed a complete break, the opportunity to get right away from everything so that he could get some perspective on his 'old' life. This was shrewd thinking on their part, and considering the complete lack of interest shown in the mental state of men returning from the Far East, a stroke of good fortune for Toosey. Barings needed to have a presence in South America and ACT told Evelyn Baring that he thought Toosey should be sent. Evelyn Baring was not convinced. He wrote to Toosey: 'You have had a pretty tough four years and may be looking forward to a summer in England, and indeed your wife might be sad to see you going off again and this is the last thing we should want.'

Toosey replied: 'As far as Alex is concerned, she naturally does not want me to go anywhere at the moment but she fully understands that it may be necessary and so long as I am back in time to take her and the children away for a summer holiday she is perfectly content.' And then, to underline his determination to show no weakness, he went on: 'As to the tough times of the last 4½ years I seem to thrive on them since the doctor at the School of Tropical Medicine in Liverpool said that I was one of the fittest men he had met for some time, after a most careful examination.'

Alan Tod followed up Toosey's letter with reassurances that they had discussed it between them. The arrangements for the trip were made by Barings in April and May 1946. Evelyn Baring sent over twenty letters of introduction, some short and others with a longer explanation. To a business contact in Argentina he wrote: 'Toosey is a particularly good chap with a very fine war record and I should be very grateful if you would be good enough to be kind to him. He was a POW with the Japanese for 3½ years and therefore he deserves all that we can do for him.'[17]

Toosey arrived in Rio de Janeiro on 23 May 1946 feeling, in his words, mentally breathless. Brazil was not the same place it had been eleven years earlier. There was no longer hostility towards the English. Toosey too felt a change in himself. He wrote to Alan Tod two days after his arrival: 'You can probably imagine how sharp is the contrast between POW days and England today compared with Brazil, for this reason it is important not to form opinions until one is acclimatised to the new world.'[18] To Evelyn Baring he wrote a few days later: 'This has been a very hectic week. When I first arrived the contrast in conditions was so sharp that my head spun, but I think I am now beginning to make sense.

Incidentally, my very tiny drop of Irish blood is a great help with the Brazilians. We get on famously. Fortunately as I spend most of my time with Brazilians, I am not expected to drink, as they are very abstemious – this is a great relief.'[19]

At a cocktail party at the end of May, Toosey experienced a flashback to his earlier life. He was introduced to Donald Beary, the American admiral who had been the commander of the SS *Mount Vernon* on which he sailed to Singapore in 1941. The two of them had been together in the captain's cabin when they learned of the bombing of Pearl Harbor. Beary had turned to Toosey on that occasion and assured him that they, the Allies, would be all right now as America would be in the war and they would win. Five years later there they were standing and reminiscing in a smart drawing room in Brazil. 'A curious coincidence . . .' Toosey mused in a letter to ACT.

Toosey's tour took him to São Paulo, Buenos Aires, Santiago and, finally, to Lima. Here he met up with Dum Tweedy with whom he had been firm friends since his first visit. Tweedy worked for ICI and lived in Peru all his life. It was he who had held Toosey's jacket when he ran and won the 'mile' on Empire Day in 1929. He was delighted to meet up with him again and arranged to take him on a trip into the Peruvian interior.

They made the 950-mile journey by car which was not without incident. 'We climbed the sierra, crossing the top at just under 16,000 feet, crossed the high plateau, going through Oroya and Cerro de Pasco,' Toosey wrote. 'At this stage the driver passed out completely, and I had to drive, which made me also somewhat breathless.'[20] He described this journey as one of the finest in the world for its contrasts of scenery and climate. Dum Tweedy was a cultured man with a wealth of experience, understanding and knowledge about Peru. He was a great travelling companion as well as a good friend and the trip seems to have had a restorative effect on Toosey. The letters back to Britain after the journey are less breathless and more reflective. 'It was a wonderful experience,' he wrote to Evelyn Baring, 'I recognised and felt I knew the jungle well and it reminded me most vividly of my experience in Thailand, the great difference being that when I passed a native hut, instead of envying the inhabitants I felt sorry for them and realised how lucky I am.'[21]

A problem with the South American visit was that it took twice as long as the planned six weeks. Alex and the children went on holiday without him and she was understandably furious. 'Alex airmailed me a very severe rocket for outstaying my leave,' he confessed to Evelyn Baring. 'I sent her a cable last night confirming my final dates, which now cannot be changed.'[22] In fact he did not get home until the end of the first week of September.

'I feel I have done one thing during my trip, which is to convince people that England is by no means finished. So many Englishmen have come out to South America with sad tales and long faces which do no good at all.' Not only did Toosey succeed in convincing people that England was 'not finished' but he also developed a new impetus in himself and it was clear that he too was not finished.

This was picked up by Dick Lockett when he wrote to Evelyn Baring after Toosey's visit was over: 'I am writing you these few lines to tell you what a real pleasure and a tonic it has been to have Phil Toosey out here. After all his grim experiences, his energy and enthusiasm is quite astonishing. He has certainly made a great many Peruvian friends and is a real diplomat; if more people like him could come out to South America, people would soon realise that there is nothing wrong with the Old Country.'[23]

Of great value and importance to Toosey's self-esteem was the Brazilians' insatiable interest in hearing about his life in captivity. People were fascinated and sometimes they seemed to want to touch him physically to see if he really had survived. On one occasion he was invited to speak to the local British Legion about Thailand. He wrote to Evelyn Baring: 'I only hope that I can put across the extraordinary contrast of my menus one year ago as compared with the present time.'

On his return Toosey felt a great deal better. The trip had given him the space and time to put his past into perspective and Alan Tod had the satisfaction of seeing him newly invigorated and well adjusted.

In October 1949 Toosey made his first visit to Africa. He went to Nigeria to inspect the business interests of one of Barings' Liverpool clients, Holt & Company. Over the next seven weeks he travelled 2000 miles, almost entirely by car on dirt roads, and went to eleven towns in Nigeria and the Gold Coast. He visited coal mines, medical stations, veterinary projects, markets, harbours and even attended the first degree ceremony at Achimoto College in Accra. He was invited to this presentation by the Dean of the College, Padre Noel Duckworth, one of the most respected of the padres on the Thailand–Burma railway.

In all sorts of places he came across echoes of his prisoner-of-war existence. In Lagos he visited a small factory that made notebooks for schools. He noted in his diary: 'Wholly owned by Holts. This should be a very profitable business, particularly in view of the rapid expansion in education. The man in charge, Carr, was a POW with me and a very good man.'[24]

Travel became a feature of his business life. He loved it and it provided him with a periodic escape from the confines of Heathcote. Toosey and Alex had little in common and she did not take part in his work life nor indeed in his leisure pursuits. She tolerated his shooting but he always had to undress in the back kitchen on newspaper and clean his gun and boots outside in the cold. She had her own forms of entertainment that did not include him. She played bridge and, once they had a television, watched horse racing. Her social life revolved around Willaston village, the WI and the family rather than round Toosey's life in Liverpool. Nevertheless there were some of his friends that she really liked. Hubert Servaes was close to both of them and she greatly enjoyed his company. The three of them and John and Vera Bromfield had several holidays together including a cruise around the Norwegian fjords. Of the former prisoners of war she was fond of Hugh Peacock, Malcolm Northcote and Arthur Moon.

Toosey and Alex were so different in every way. He was tidy and organised. He had a large cupboard in his dressing room in which his collars, stiff and soft, his shirts, handkerchiefs, socks and scarves were beautifully ordered. Alex stuffed her stockings and other clothes untidily into her drawers, something he could never understand because she never appeared untidy in public. Her desk was always swimming with letters, spare envelopes and pieces of paper. His was neatly ordered and tidy.

In autobiographical notes written in 1971 Toosey summed up his marriage:

I do not think that two people could be so diametrically opposed in character and life interests as my wife and myself. I am an extrovert, she is an introvert. My interests are catholic and very widespread; I love business, the open air, gardening, shooting and meeting people. She loves her children and grand-children and the home which she has run in a quite admirable manner. She is a very strong character and is known to all her family as Mrs T. or the 'Regimental Sergeant Major'. We all deeply respect her. I fear I must have been a great trial to her, like a hen with a duckling when it first takes to water.[25]

Off duty and to his family Toosey was affectionately known as the Captain, named after a character called Bush in the Captain Hornblower series. He was the man in the city suit and a bowler hat cycling to Hooton station with his umbrella under his arm to catch the 8.05 to Liverpool; he was the upright figure standing at number eight, the silhouette at the end of the line of guns waiting for the next drive, his Labrador Dinah sitting expectantly at his feet; he was the enthusiastic tennis player who teamed up with Patrick to give his old friend Vernon Maxwell and his son Tim a run for their money. He was the one cracking jokes, enjoying himself in the company of good friends. To the children and their generation the Captain was not a war hero but a wonderful, colourful character with a zest and love of life they found infectious.

Heathcote was always buzzing with activity and by the mid-1950s there was a menagerie which included Gillian's ponies, Toosey's gundogs Dinah and Topsy, cats, geese, ducks, chickens, rabbits and three turkeys. He was passionate about the garden and all visitors to the house were given a tour and introduced to Tig. They grew all kinds of fruit and vegetables but what he really loved were his roses and would not let Alex cut them for flower arranging. She was eventually given a patch for her cut flowers which Tig tended for her.

At Heathcote the Labradors were treated as part of the family. Toosey trained them himself and he was very proud of them. Dinah was his favourite and was known as the WTD (well trained dog); he was especially proud of her although occasionally she would let him down. On one occasion he saw a dog running off into the distance and shouted at a young man who also had a black Labrador that he should 'keep his bloody dog under control'. A son of a friend, Colin Mather, stepped aside to show that his dog was sitting at his feet, as good as gold. The WTD had got over excited and run off. Toosey was covered with embarrassment and apologised but told the story against himself afterwards with a grin.

Often after shooting in North Wales the men would go back to the Mather family home at Nannerch. Banter and teasing between Jack Mather, John Bromfield and Phil Toosey could get quite out of hand, much to the delight of the younger members of the shoot who were eager to see what would happen next. Once Poppy Mather walked into the sitting room at Nannerch to find her husband and Toosey boasting to each other loudly about how well trained and obedient their gundogs were. They would do anything they were told, the two men exclaimed. Poppy looked round and saw Jack's dog balancing on the mantelpiece and Dinah, looking very sheepish, on the baby grand piano.

One of Toosey's party tricks was to show off Dinah's velvet jaws. When guests came he would send her to fetch a fresh egg from the sitting room carpet. It drove Alex to distraction but the children loved it when he behaved 'badly'. He invariably got into trouble from Alex but he would wink at them and try to suppress his mirth. On one occasion after a very lively dinner party at Heathcote he decided to show off his accuracy by shooting through the croquet hoops on the lawn with the pistol he had been given by Red Ant. That earned him a serious rocket, he recalled years later. 'When minded to Alex could put the fear of God into anyone, even Toosey,' one old friend observed.

By the late 1940s Toosey's business career was taking off. Lord Ashburton offered him his first directorship, standing down from the Trafford Park Estates Board in 1946. This was followed by the Birkenhead Brewery Company, who later employed more than one of his fellow prisoners of war; Liner Holdings, of which he became Chairman when ACT retired; Coast Lines, later taken over by P&O; Cammell Laird and some of its subsidiary companies, which became a real headache for him. Then there were the banks and trusts. He worked first as a director and then as chairman of the Albany Investment Trust and was on the board of Martin's Bank, which subsequently became Barclays Bank Liverpool, occupying the magnificent Martin's Building designed by Charles Rowse in 1927.

Although Toosey worked full time for Barings he seemed to have an insatiable hunger for work or activity. 'I am very conscious', he wrote to his friend John Hobhouse in 1960, 'of having done probably the only job of my life so far that was worthwhile and carried with it immediate rewards of loyalty and comradeship, the like of which I do not expect I shall ever experience again. I think all of us who enjoyed "our captivity" so agree with me in hoping that further adventures, not of a similar but of a parallel nature, await.'[26]

In 1947 Douglas Crawford asked him to rejoin the Territorial Army with a view to helping him to reform the 368th Medium Regiment. He accepted and found that he enjoyed the TA postwar quite as much as he had done in the 1930s, although the emphasis was different from the time when war was looming. Toosey was promoted to Honorary Brigadier and was given command of the 287th Medium Regiment and then the 87th Army Group Royal Artillery (AGRA) in 1951. He resigned in November 1954 and was awarded a CBE for his outstanding services to the Territorial Army in 1955. This time he kept his rank.

Arthur Moon was with Toosey in London in 1960 watching the review of the Territorial Army by the Queen in Hyde Park. He wrote, 'It was with pride that one watched these men march with heads erect, banners waving and drums beating. They were of the same breed and type as many of those soldiers who staggered into Tamarkan in May–July 1943 – sick, wasted and exhausted but not defeated.'[27]

He was invited to Heathcote where he spent what he said was a most enjoyable weekend with Toosey and Alex. 'Phil looked healthier than when last seen in Thailand and obviously was as keen and dynamic in civilian life as he had been during the war. The passage of years and the distance of 12,000 miles had not weakened the bonds of respect and friendship forged during the Tamarkan days.'[28]

One of the most time-consuming of Toosey's activities was his work on behalf of former prisoners of war. For the first eighteen months after they returned to Britain they went their own ways and settled down as best they could. An organisation called the Returned British Prisoners of War Association had been formed immediately after the war with Lady Mountbatten as its president. The organisation concerned itself with prisoners of war both under the Germans and the Japanese; the latter body of prisoners had had quite different experiences in captivity and it was they who showed the greatest enthusiasm. It soon became clear that they would need a body which would represent their special situation.

The National Federation of Far Eastern Prisoners of War (FEPOW) Clubs and Associations of Great Britain and Northern Ireland came into being in 1947. It began simply enough. Two men wrote to Toosey in early 1947 proposing that they start an ex-prisoners' association in order to help the wives and dependants of men who had died and also to get fair compensation for those men who had returned home broken. Toosey was both supportive and cautious. 'It smelt of a communist cell to me,' he said later, 'but they still trusted me and had come to me for advice so I wrote back and said that I would be glad to help them to set this thing up but that they needed a figurehead as the President.'[29]

He suggested General Arthur Percival which, on the face of it, may have seemed a strange choice, but Toosey was clear on two things: first he felt that Percival had been the wrong man in an impossible position in Singapore and secondly Percival had returned from the Far East himself a broken man. Through no fault of his own, he had been separated from the men for the duration of his captivity. Presidency of an association of former prisoners would, Toosey felt, give Percival something to be proud of. It took Toosey's considerable powers of persuasion to convince him but once he did it became an absorbing interest and Percival was a well-liked president. Toosey believed that it prolonged Percival's life by not months but by years. He remained president until a year before his death on 31 January 1966.

The motto of the Federation was 'to keep going the spirit that kept us going' and its purpose was to give assistance to former prisoners and their families. The organisation was not a single body but a collection of groups and clubs. There were local FEPOW organisations all over the country, from the Isle of Wight to Blackpool, with strong branches in Merseyside, Manchester, Blackpool and London. A separate organisation was set up for the Scottish FEPOWs. In addition to making donations and offering assistance to those in need, the FEPOW clubs met regularly to exchange news and catch up with what was being done on a national level. Toosey used to attend every local meeting he could as well as the annual reunions.

Initially, the Merseyside branch meetings were held in The Boot, which was owned by Birkenhead Brewery, a company of which Toosey was a director. The pub sign was a replica Wellington boot. It was run by George Downes, the amputee whose life was saved in Tamarkan when Toosey managed to buy him a chicken with money from the V-scheme. Downes had written to Toosey shortly after their return asking for advice on work and Toosey had been able to encourage the brewery to employ him.

At about the same time as the FEPOW Federation was set up Toosey heard that Boon Pong, who had recovered from his gunshot wounds and set up a bus company in Bangkok, had got into financial difficulties. Toosey, Lilly and Knights, three of the senior officers who had been involved in the V-scheme in 1943, wrote to all the ex-POWs asking them to contribute towards a collection for him:

> We realise that in looking back on our P.O.W. days one likes to forget the bad times, but we ask you, for a few moments, to cast your mind back to the camp hospitals. You know what they were like, and how necessary it was to provide drugs, medicines and extra food for the unfortunate patients. You may have been one of them yourself. The Medical Officers and Orderlies did wonderful work but we wonder if you know how they were assisted from outside sources with money for purchasing additional food and supplies of invaluable medical requirements.
>
> Mr Boon Pong was the main contact between certain officers commanding camps and an organisation in Bangkok. The movement started in the early stages of our jungle experiences in Thailand and continued until Officers and other ranks were separated. During this trying period Boon Pong continually ran the risk of torture and death at the hands of the Japanese. Fortunately, in spite of the efforts of the Kempei Tai, this underground traffic was never discovered and a sum of £40,000, in addition to large quantities of medical supplies, was safely delivered to the various camps which undoubtedly resulted in the saving of thousands of lives.
>
> We who sign this appeal, know only too well what Boon Pong did and the risks he ran. We are members of the 18th Division Association, but there are other Officers outside the Association, particularly Lt.-Col. Owtram, who also knew the inner workings of this invaluable aid at a time of serious need.
>
> Owing to the difficulty of transferring money from this

country to Siam, it is of the utmost importance that NO mention of this subject or appeal appears in any type of local or national press. If any public announcement is made it may well make it impossible to obtain permission to transfer donations to Thailand.

To end as we began, time effaces memories but surely we owe something to this foreign trader who risked his life and did so much to help us.

Will you please send a donation, however small, to Lt.-Col. A.E. Knights. Please pass this appeal on to any of your friends who are Ex-P.O.W.

Yours sincerely

Arthur Knights

Harold Lilly

Philip Toosey

The appeal raised £38,000 and this was transferred via Barings to Boon Pong in Bangkok. With this money he was able to run a successful bus company, the line 6 in Bangkok. Eventually the bus companies in Bangkok were nationalised and Boon Pong used the proceeds from the sale to start up a body-shop mending buses. It was called 'Dents Done by Boon Pong' and it still runs in Thailand. Toosey never saw Boon Pong again but both his sons met him on visits to Thailand. Boon Pong received any number of visits from grateful former prisoners and he enjoyed their visits very much. Boon Pong died on 29 January 1982.

At the height of the FEPOW Federation's activities there were seventy-five clubs and associations. Over the years Percival, encouraged by Toosey, visited as many as he could. He was a regular guest at Heathcote as he criss-crossed the country on these visits and the children remember him bolstering his confidence with a glass of whisky and talking earnestly to Toosey. He had a nervous cough which, Toosey explained to them, was due to the terrible ordeal and humiliation he had suffered in Malaya and Singapore.

Not every man who had been a prisoner of the Japanese joined their local FEPOW club. Many preferred to put the past behind them and to keep in touch with just the men who they had been close to in the camps. This was particularly true among the officers and caused Toosey and the other active officers in the Federation concern. One outspoken critic was Jack Marsh who felt passionately that the officers had a duty to keep faith with their men who had suffered. He thought the number of officers who did so was far too small.

Toosey talking to the Bishop of Liverpool at the FEPOW
Remembrance Day parade c.1967.

Many men still preferred to write and talk directly to Toosey rather than go through the clubs and associations. There were daily letters with requests for advice and men turned up in his office or even at Heathcote expecting to see him. He always saw them if he could. Alex was less charitable; understandably she saw it as an intrusion into their private life and she could not accept it. She told Ian Tod (ACT's nephew) on one occasion: 'I can't understand why people want his advice – he's the stupid-est person I've ever known!' When Geoffrey Pharaoh Adams and his wife arrived at Heathcote, having driven from Poole in Dorset, to deliver a copy of a medical report to Toosey, Alex greeted them on the doorstep. She announced that her husband was out and she would hand him the envelope when he returned. With that she closed the door and Adams had to drive back home. Mrs Adams might have liked some hospitality after the long drive but none was offered.

John Ashburton also remembered Alex as a cool but not un-kind figure. He spent the night at Heathcote on the way to Scotland for a shoot with Toosey and his overwhelming recollection is of the arctic conditions of the spare bedroom which felt as though it was about -10°C. At that stage Toosey was recovering from TB and he told Ashburton that it had affected his balance and no one was to worry if he fell over backwards while taking a high bird. 'He was tremendous fun to be with,' Ashburton said, 'hugely loyal and hardworking but too nice to be a top class businessman.'[30]

One of Toosey's secretaries remembered men walking in off the street and asking to speak to 'the Brig'. 'One minute we'd have Lord so and so and the next some fellow with a dirty rain-coat would ask to see Brigadier Toosey. He treated them both with equal courtesy.' One man who came had committed murder and he wanted Toosey's advice on what he should do. Toosey told him to go straight to the police but reassured him that he would help him by finding a good lawyer who would act for him. At that time Toosey was High Sheriff of Lancashire.

Another FEPOW, Les Martin, was a plumber in Liverpool. He called in to see Toosey one day: 'The Brig asked me, "How's business?" "Bloody awful," I replied. Then he asked me who my bank was, who's the manager? "I don't know," I said, so the Brig said, "Leave it to me" and he arranged for the manager to ring me and discuss what I needed. The Brig guaranteed me a £1000 overdraft. Turns out he was a director of the bank.' Les put his prices up and his business went well from then onwards.

Toosey had limited resources and his help was always targeted. He knew what it took to make a real difference but he never gave too much, he wanted people to stand on their own two feet. If he helped people, his son Nicholas explained, he did it in a way that did not make them dependent upon him and he never wanted any credit for it. Often donations or assistance were given without anyone else ever knowing about it. Arthur White, who worked as a company secretary for Liner Holdings, met Toosey when he used to come to board meetings. They became friends and White told him that his daughter had got a place at the Royal Ballet School but could not go because he could not afford the fees. Toosey paid the fees and his daughter went. 'Phil Toosey helped my daughter to enjoy her life in ballet and that was a great thing,'[31] Arthur White said.

Soon after the FEPOW Federation was formed a special sub-committee was set up to deal with the question of compensation from the Japanese. The purpose of this was to press home the abhorrence that was felt in the civilised world at Japan's deliberate flouting of the Hague and Geneva Conventions in their handling of prisoners of war under their control. Percival was on the committee and so was Toosey. They were invited to the House of Commons in early 1951 to put their case. Toosey's friend Sir John Smyth was Conservative MP for Norwood and he became a leading light in the compensation claim. He arranged for an all-Party meeting in the House of Commons to put the FEPOW case. The meeting was packed. Percival and Toosey both spoke, as did others. Percival ended his statement: 'If we forget or condone the atrocities committed against our prisoners of the Japanese then we lose something that is vital to our humanity.'[32] The MPs were told that the Australian and United States governments had already made strong protests to Japan on behalf of their prisoners and they pressed for a motion to be put before the House of Commons.

On 10 May 1951 Toosey sat in the public gallery along with dozens of other FEPOWs and heard Selwyn Lloyd, his old friend and MP for the Wirral, supporting the motion to get a clause in favour of the prisoners' compensation claim put into the peace treaty with Japan. As evidence, he held up a copy of the camp report that Toosey had written in September 1945.

Despite the support of the House of Commons, things moved frustratingly slowly and eventually Toosey seized the initiative himself and contacted the Japanese Foreign Minister to demand a meeting with a representative from the Federation. This was agreed and Percival asked Toosey to represent the FEPOWs. Toosey remembered the meeting well. He walked into the room where the minister was standing, with his silver-topped ebony cane in his hand. Toosey's step didn't falter but his heart missed a beat. However, the minister was charming and put him at his ease, a role reversal if ever there was one. The meeting was brief but helped to accelerate the unfreezing process of the Japanese assets.

When the money came through each prisoner received just under £100. Toosey spoke out against the per capita payments preferring the idea of building up a fund that could help those men and families who had the greatest need. In 1959 a further sum was paid and this time it was put into a trust for the benefit of the FEPOWs. The initial value of the fund was £326,000 and with careful stewardship and wise investment the fund rose in value by 1972 to £434,000 with payments in the interests of FEPOWs totalling £500,000. In total, the Japanese had paid £4,816,473.15s 6d to the FEPOWs by April 1961. Toosey was proud of this but he was even more proud that the compensation had not cost the British taxpayer a penny.

Through his various contacts Toosey became increasingly concerned with the health of a number of former prisoners. Often the men were suffering from tropical diseases with which many British doctors were unfamiliar.

There were specialists in tropical medicine available; it was just a question of channelling the former prisoners to the right hospitals. Percival asked John Smyth, who was a governor of Queen Mary's Hospital at Roehampton, to persuade the hospital to extend its work to encompass the FEPOW community and, over time, several thousand former prisoners took part in a survey into their health. More than half were diagnosed with chronic complaints directly attributable to their captivity. Many men had learned to live with their irreversible disabilities, some even to overcome them. The doctors were constantly amazed. 'The best example of the latter is the man whose visual acuity is below 6/60 and J.12, but who earns his living as a cinematograph film cutter. He does this by twisting his head through 90 degrees, so that he gets adequate service from the peripheral parts of his retina – but what a life!'[33]

Toosey approached the Liverpool School of Tropical Medicine in 1947, initially on a case by case basis. Soon this became onerous as increasing numbers of men heard of the benefits their friends were feeling after proper treatment. The school's head, Professor Brian Maegraith, told Toosey that the only thing to do was to put the agreement on a formal footing. In 1955 a close relationship between the School of Tropical Medicine and the northern FEPOW community began that continued for the rest of Toosey's life and beyond.

In 1965 Toosey was appointed President of the school. It was the first time in the school's history that a non-academic president had been chosen and he accepted the position with his characteristic mix of humility and enthusiasm. The school expanded dramatically during the seven years of his presidency. One of the changes he brought about was to introduce a committee of vice presidents, all men with power and influence. This included Lord Cohen of Birkenhead, Lord Cole who was then Chairman of Unilever and Chairman of the Trustees of the Leverhulme Trust, Sir Douglas Crawford, and Selwyn Lloyd who was responsible for raising £175,000 for the Maegraith Wing for which David Sainsbury had given £110,000 from his personal charitable trust. These eminent men were all personal friends of Phil Toosey. They had two roles as far as he was concerned: they were expected to give to the school themselves and to open doors to further funding. This would leave the doctors and professors at the school free to concentrate on their research. It was completely successful and Toosey was proud of the Liverpool School of Tropical Medicine and his association with it. Under his presidency they formed close links with schools in Ghana, Nigeria and Thailand.

Towards the end of his presidency he was particularly keen on the development of tropical paediatrics and child health. At the time the senior lecturer at the school was Professor Herbert Gilles, an expert and world authority on malaria; he had many conversations with Toosey at the school in Pembroke Place. 'We found him approachable, modest and friendly,' Gilles said. 'He was always interested and asked intelligent questions. The staff really appreciated his passionate commitment.'

In October 1957 the film *The Bridge on the River Kwai* was released. It was an instant box office hit and the critics in both New York and London fell over themselves to find superlatives to describe it. When a group of prisoners eventually got to see the film at a special screening in London in June 1958 there was a widespread feeling of anger. They were incensed at what they saw as a travesty of the real truth behind the building of the bridge over the River Kwai but also as a gross slur on the integrity and intelligence of their commander, Phil Toosey. General Percival criticised the film bitterly for being a close but distorted copy of the real bridge incident at Tamarkan. He wrote to Sam Spiegel and asked him to state clearly on screen that the film was fiction. Unsurprisingly Spiegel refused to do this. The prisoners' chief complaint was that the film showed British POWs working willingly, eager to do a good job to further the Japanese war plans.

Toosey first saw the film in Liverpool and as Alex did not go he took Gillian. She remembers him coming out of the cinema having found the film entertaining. 'A good piece of fiction,' he had remarked. He did not see that the role of Colonel Nicholson had anything to do with him. 'He never associated himself with Alec Guinness,' she later explained. 'It never entered his head he was being portrayed. He knew what he had done in the Far East and the film bore no resemblance to that.'[34]

The problem is that certain elements are close to the truth. When Pierre Boulle wrote the novel he had information from accounts by George Swanson and other ex-prisoners. Boulle cleverly mixed fact and fiction in order to give his novel authority. One example of this is the question of escape. In the book Colonel Nicholson refuses to attempt to escape at the fall of

Singapore and, controversially, he forbids his officers and men to do so. Toosey did the same thing and ended up having to place Bill Drower under 'close arrest' when he made clear his intentions to escape. Nicholson refuses to let the men form an escape committee in his camp; however, Toosey helped six men escape from Tamarkan and hid their disappearance for three days. Two facts, one historically correct the other not so. Another example is the episode when Nicholson takes a stand and refuses to allow his officers to work for the Japanese. Saito threatens to machine-gun them but Nicholson is obstinate. Toosey, when faced with the same situation in November 1942, consulted his officers who took his advice that they would have to work anyway so it was better to be seen to do so willingly rather than under duress. The inspiration for the scene in the book appears to have come from the stand some officers took in the prison camps at Chungkai and Nong Pladuk.

When the director David Lean came to rewrite Carl Foreman's script in 1956 he went back to Boulle's novel and naturally he cherry-picked the best stories for inclusion. Then factual and fictitious events were given equal weight. References to historical events gave the novel and the film authenticity. Other, more fanciful features, such as the escape of Shears, the capitulation of Saito, and the building of the bridge on a different site from that stipulated by the Japanese surveyors, were added and fiction melded inextricably and imperceptibly with historical reality.

Toosey later admitted he saw one or two parallels in the film to his captivity and he found those moving. 'The first was when the POW's marched into the camp. This was myself and my Regiment, and the 2nd Battalion of the Gordon Highlanders. We had marched a long way. The Japanese Colonel tried to dismiss the parade. The men just stood there stubbornly and refused to move. This went on for half an hour and eventually he said to me in perfect English "You carry on". So I gave the order "Fall out the Officers." They came forward and saluted and fell out behind me. Then I turned to the Regimental Sergeant Major of the Gordons and said "Dismiss the men." And of course the Colonel Bogey tune was fascinating. Actually it didn't happen there at the bridge as they played it in the film. It happened in the officers' camp where they segregated us six months before the end of the War — and treated us abominably.'[35] He saw no parallel between himself and Nicholson. The thought that people might begin to believe he could possibly have co-operated with the Japanese and helped their war effort was laughable. It was only when he realised how upset the ex-prisoners were and that the public had swallowed the film whole believing it to be the truth that he became concerned.

Toosey drafted a letter with Percival, which was published in the *Daily Telegraph* under Percival's signature:

> It is with regret that I find it necessary to write in critical terms of a film which has been acclaimed throughout the world, and which has won such honours as *The Bridge on the River Kwai*. As far as technique and drama are concerned, it is of course in the highest class. My criticism is that the story in the film, whilst being fiction, has a factual background, for it is based on the events which took place on the notorious Burma–Siam railway in World War II.

Percival and Toosey were most concerned that the fictional account would come to be accepted as historically true. Arguably, the film made millions of people think they were seeing something realistic when they were not. It gave no inkling of the terrible conditions along the railway. And gave the impression that the Thais were just waiting around for white boyfriends and 'worst of all', wrote Ian Watt, a former prisoner in Chungkai and later a Professor at Stanford University, 'it promoted the political delusion that the people of these poor villages are merely marking time until they are given an opportunity to sacrifice their lives on behalf of the ideology of the Western Powers'.[36]

Percival's letter provoked a stream of correspondence to the newspaper, most of it condemning the film and in particular its treatment of the British colonel. Toosey received letters of support as well. It was not long before the press tracked down the 'real-life' Colonel Nicholson and they tried to get Toosey to talk about the film and his own feelings about it. He refused point-blank. 'I have always been very frightened of publicity,' he wrote to Ian Watt, 'and particularly for films, since my experience has been that in order to sell the thing they have to appeal to the public and this is rarely done by telling the truth. In addition to that, personal publicity always makes me feel exceedingly uncomfortable. Perhaps this also is an aftermath of being a prisoner when I did a number of things which, if found out, would have had disastrous results for me and maybe I have an inbred wish to keep everything to myself.'[37]

He resisted all pressure to be drawn on it and it was a full ten years after the film was released that he made any public comment about it. He gave an interview for the *Cheshire Life* to his old batman, Arthur Osborne. Toosey had been asked to appear on television opposite Alec Guinness to defend his role as commander of the British and other Allied forces who had built the bridge at Tamarkan, now known by its film name as the Bridge on the River Kwai. In an article entitled 'Myth and Reality in an Asian Jungle', Osborne wrote that Toosey had confided in him: 'You know Old Osborne, I really don't know what all this fuss is about – wanting *me* to appear on television! I only did my job. To look after all you chaps, and see that as many of you as humanly possible got back home safely. I only did my job.'[38]

Alec Guinness told Patrick Toosey that he also had refused to appear opposite Toosey. He wrote in 1991: 'I vaguely remember some notion of a TV interview with your father. I probably turned it down because I thought the film likely to be indefensible and also, if it was to be defended that should have been done by Lean, Spiegel and Co.'[39]

On 1 September 1968 the *Observer* published an article by Ian Watt called 'The Myth of the River Kwai'. Watt examined the similarities and differences between the film and the reality, between Colonel Nicholson and Colonel Toosey. It was the first scholarly article on the subject: 'Boulle based his story on two startling paradoxes,' Watt explained, 'that Colonel Nicholson, a prisoner of the Japanese, should finally become their master; and that, though a loyal British officer, he should devote all his energies to building a strategic bridge for the enemy. But both these unlikely actions can actually be traced back to some of the unique historical circumstances of the war.'[40]

Watt described the unusual situation where captured officers were forced by the Japanese to administer the prison camps owing to the unexpectedly large number of prisoners of war and the lack of Japanese personnel to run the camps. The other element was the building of the bridges across the Khwae Mae Khlong at Tamarkan under the command of the Japanese Army railway engineering units. From these two historical facts Boulle created his story, which David Lean turned into the Hollywood fiction.

Watt concluded:

Colonel Toosey was led, not by what he wanted to believe, but by what he knew. He didn't beat the Japanese; he didn't even think of designing his own bridge; he merely noticed what was going on around him, and took all its unpleasant meaning in. The situation was not covered by the rules of war or the Geneva Convention, but standing on principle would have been giving up the struggle. If things were as intractable as they looked, the outlook for the years ahead was hopeless. The only thing worth working for was the possibility that tenacity and imagination could find a way by which we might decently survive. It was a modest objective; but in our circumstances at that time it was quite enough to be getting on with.[41]

Toosey was delighted with Watt's article, a draft of which he saw in 1967, and he wrote back: 'You describe, as far as I am concerned, exactly what I was trying to do. To put it in other words – which I do not want you to repeat to anyone – I felt I had a mission not only to save as many lives as possible but also to maintain human dignity in those ghastly circumstances.'[42]

This article provoked another flurry of letters including one from Alec Young of Glasgow, whose diary Toosey had hidden during a search in Nong Pladuk in 1944: 'What I had never dreamed of was that there could be any connection between yourself and Colonel Nicholson – the connection was just too absurd to be entertained – yet I suppose there must be many who were "taken in". The propaganda being what it is a kind of "legend" is already surrounding the idea of the bridge.'[43]

Lord Mountbatten also wrote to Toosey:

I realise that the film *The Bridge on the River Kwai* was wildly inaccurate, but I had also heard that it was based on a legendary British hero. The film was so interesting that I had it down here at Broadlands to show the Queen, who was thrilled. I must confess that it was not until I had read this article that I realised that the true hero was yourself, and in a way that made much more sense than Alec Guinness' hero. I feel, as the Supreme Allied Commander of those days, I really ought to write and thank you on behalf of the Command for all you did to keep morale going, and to save so many prisoners.[44]

Epilogue

BORROWED TIME

This is indeed a man, the like of whom this generation will not
see again. Those of us who are his friends, and many, many
others, regard him with respect and admiration, and when we
think of what he suffered and achieved, we salute him with
affectionate wonder.

Selwyn Lloyd in a tribute to Phil Toosey, 1972

Finally, Toosey's health began to fail. In 1968 he and Alex visited
their son Nicholas who was working in Tehran. Nicholas's fiancée,
Jane, worked for the British ambassador and as he was away she had
arranged for them to stay at the embassy and to have use of the facilities there. It was a wonderful treat and Alex was at her most relaxed
and happy. Toosey was delighted that she was enjoying the luxury
he felt she deserved and he described it as the happiest holiday of his
life. So successful was it that they decided to go again the following
year. On this second visit he became ill. He complained of chest
pains and the doctor informed Nicholas that he thought his father
had had a heart attack. However, he recovered and flew home.

A few months later, in June 1969, he was on his way to Africa for a meeting. He went for a routine check-up at University College Hospital in London, as he had been doing every six months for years. The doctor put him on the couch, as usual, but this time Toosey noticed that he spent a great deal of time on his heart. He straightened up and said: 'I'm afraid you've got a bit of heart trouble, my friend. You will have to go back up to Liverpool and have a cardiograph. They have an excellent unit up there.' 'I can't possibly do that,' Toosey replied, 'I'm going to Nigeria at six o'clock tomorrow morning. I've appointments with all sorts of senior people. The Prime Minister . . .' 'Well,' the doctor responded, quietly, 'if you go you won't come back alive, that's all I can say.'

Two days later Toosey was admitted to the heart unit at Sefton General Hospital in Liverpool where it was established that he had a serious heart condition. The condition was one that the surgeons came to see in other patients who had been in captivity in the Far East and they described it as 'bamboo heart', a disease that resulted from a lack of protein in the diet causing the heart to dilate and the valves to leak.

Toosey went in and out of Sefton General Hospital during the summer but by the autumn he was very unwell. He was admitted in October 1969 and there he lay for four months, his condition deteriorating daily. He could see his life slipping away as his strength ebbed. 'It nearly drove me mad,' he said, 'I was gradually getting worse and worse and they wouldn't do anything about it.'[1] One day, when Alex was visiting him, he burst into tears and said, 'I can't stand this. I'm dying slowly.' The following day, after Alex had asked to see the consultant, Dr Norman Coulshead, things began to move. Coulshead brought a cardiac surgeon, David Hamilton, to see the patient but he was not optimistic. Toosey was lying with his head slumped on his shoulder, he was short of breath and his lips and fingers were blue. They thought he would be dead within a few days. After a discussion they agreed that, if there was enough strength in the heart muscle, it was possible that he could survive the first critical days after the open-heart surgery and make a recovery.

Toosey was the oldest patient Hamilton had performed this operation on by several years. There was a tenuous link between the two men that Toosey was unaware of. Hamilton's uncle, Edward Kirk, had served as a missionary surgeon before the war in South China. He was living in Hong Kong at the time of the Japanese invasion. After evacuating his family to Canada he elected to stay on and was put in a civilian internment camp where he worked tirelessly for four years as a surgeon in the most primitive of conditions. This, David Hamilton admitted, was a motivating factor in his determination to get Phil Toosey back on his feet. 'I was prepared to take on high risk patients provided they understood the situation they were in and the likely outcome with or without surgery,' he said. 'I knew technically I could do the operation. Whether the heart had the strength to take over its vital function after surgery was the question. I felt he deserved the chance that open heart surgery would offer him, given his unique background.'[2]

After initial tests Hamilton spoke to Toosey and Alex. 'I'm prepared to do this operation,' he told them, 'but I must tell you that the odds of him living through it are 3–1 against.'[3] Shortly afterwards the operation was carried out at Broadgreen Hospital. When Toosey was on the operating table Hamilton revised the odds to 6–1 against. During the next six weeks Toosey suffered two cardiac arrests, renal and liver failure. Hamilton and his team battled to keep him alive; he needed twenty-four-hour nursing care during which time his life hung in the balance.

Six weeks after the operation he was out of Intensive Care

and back on the ward. He was still desperately frail but something of the old sparkle had returned. Hamilton went to see him one morning and was greeted with: 'Television sets, David, TV sets in this ward is what you want.' 'Be quiet and when you are better', he replied, 'then I'll tell you what we need in this unit.'

Hamilton had been appointed as the first full-time cardiac surgeon in Liverpool in April 1968. Due to the lack of beds for the Intensive Treatment Unit he could only treat two or three cases a week. He had to turn away patients he knew he could treat and who would die without an operation. It was both frustrating and depressing. He told Toosey he needed £30,000. 'So', Toosey explained, 'like the stupid old ass that I am, I said, "Alright, I'll raise it for you."'

By the end of March 1970 he was well enough to return to Heathcote. He was weak and the doctors had ordered bed rest but the delight that he felt in being at home, of lying in his own bed and looking at the tops of the oak trees through his own window was one of the most wonderful things that had ever happened to him, he said. He felt completely peaceful. After a fortnight he was allowed to come downstairs and slowly but surely his strength began to return. The doctors had warned him it would be a long process and he was not to do anything strenuous for the first twelve months. By now the grandchildren were allowed to visit and found him sitting up in his chair, with a rug over his knees, looking very gaunt but he was always so pleased to see them. He had a gold watch that Barings had given him on his retirement. It wound itself when he moved. He explained to his granddaughter Stephanie that he was very fed up as the watch kept stopping because he could not move his arm enough.

However, total inactivity was not in his nature. Having retired from all but two of his directorships, he decided to begin raising the money required for Broadgreen. Firstly he enlisted the help of his old friend Douglas Crawford. They approached industry but got little help there, apart from £5000 from Barings. The rest of the money had to come from individuals. Toosey joked to a young man, John Shone, who came to ask him for advice on fund-raising: 'What can I tell you? My friends all cross the road now when they see me!'

In six months he and Douglas Crawford succeeded in raising £50,000. The construction of Gunner Ward took eighteen months. According to Hamilton there is no doubt that Phil Toosey was the key to the expansion of cardiac surgery in Liverpool. He and Alex were present at the opening of the ward on 6 June 1973 as was Douglas Crawford. Toosey was proud of the ward at Broadgreen but saw it as nothing more than repayment for the debt he owed to the nursing staff, and to David Hamilton and his team in particular, for giving him the gift of a second life, his borrowed time as he called it.

As his fund-raising work continued during the early 1970s so did his work for the Far Eastern prisoners of war. His heart condition had forced him to limit the number of appearances he made at FEPOW functions. His deputy was Harold Payne, the officer who had been responsible for organising working parties in Nong Pladuk. Harold Payne took over most of his duties but Toosey remained in overall control. On one notable occasion in May 1971 he intervened.

It had been announced that Hirohito, the Emperor of Japan, had been invited to London as a guest of the Queen and was to be made a Knight of the Garter, the highest order for chivalry that Britain could bestow. There had been rumblings of discontent among the FEPOW clubs and the press, having heard about the visit, was speculating that there would be demonstrations against Hirohito. The Ministry of Defence received anxious enquiries from Tokyo about possible disruption. The 19th Annual

Conference of the National Federation was held at Buxton on 21 to 23 May 1971. Toosey arrived and received a tumultuous reception from the delegates. First he was able to thank them for their support and prayers during his long illness. He told them that the doctors were agreed 'that it was as much the love and esteem he had from them as the skill of the medical profession that had pulled him through'.[4]

He had told the FEPOW executive that he wanted to address the delegates on the forthcoming visit of Hirohito. Many of them were very upset about the visit but also about the decision that the executive had made that under no circumstances would they demonstrate against Hirohito. Toosey told them that it was not their position to object over what was Her Majesty's private business even though he, personally, thought that she had been ill-advised. Harold Payne explained that he had told the Ministry of Defence that as a highly respected ex-servicemen's organisation they would do nothing to jeopardise their standing in the country. There was further discussion and unrest continued among the delegates.

Toosey stood up and brought matters to a close. The delegates must make up their minds, he told them, whether to support him and the executive or not. He made it quite clear that if they did not, he would resign forthwith. John Smyth described it as 'the old Toosey magic again'. The vast majority agreed to support the executive and the decision was greeted by a collective sigh of relief in Whitehall. Sir Alec Douglas-Home wrote to Sir John Smyth on 27 August 1971: 'I warmly welcome the decision of the Federation of Far Eastern Prisoners of War not to be associated with any demonstrations or protest which may take place during the State visit of the Emperor of Japan in October. I have the most sincere sympathy for those who suffered at the hands of the Japanese during the war and I understand and respect their feelings about the proposed visit of the Emperor. Perhaps you would kindly let Brigadier Toosey know how much I appreciate his attitude.'[5]

Lord Mountbatten wrote to Toosey after the visit telling him he had told the Queen of his success in discouraging any demonstrations. 'I thoroughly understand how frightfully bitter most of the FEPOWs must still be feeling. At all events I feel I must write a line to express my deep appreciation to you and all FEPOWs for their statesmanlike attitude.'[6]

The effort of appearing in Buxton and the emotional energy required to carry out his duties as president on that occasion was almost too much for his frail body. His heart began to give him trouble again and further lengthy bed rest was needed. At one stage there was a suggestion that further surgery might be necessary but Toosey said that David Hamilton vowed, 'I am never opening up that man again.'[7]

By 1972 he was feeling better and he began to resume a more normal, if quiet, life. The School of Tropical Medicine was thriving and he visited Pembroke Place and enjoyed spending time talking to the academics and learning about the school's expanding activities. In 1972 he was awarded the Mary Kingsley Medal for services to the school, the highest honour the board could bestow. He spent a lot of time in the garden, although he could no longer do any heavy work. Tig was still working at Heathcote and when Alex went out he and Toosey would often sit in the study and chat about old times, about Africa and the war. Tig was always careful to leave his Wellington boots by the French windows so that when he heard the car crunching on the gravel he could nip back outside without getting caught by 'Mrs T'.

There were some things that could still make Toosey very angry. Once Stephanie complained about the smell of the dog mince in the back kitchen, saying she'd rather die than eat it. She was only about eight but he turned on her and spoke sternly: 'Young lady, don't you ever let me hear you say something like that again. Where I have been this would have been a feast for my men.' She was pretty shaken. The grandchildren were never allowed to leave food on their plates at Heathcote nor say that they were starving before lunch.

In 1973 there was a reunion of the Far Eastern Prisoners of War Federation at the Winter Gardens in Blackpool. Prince Philip, as their Patron, was the guest of honour. There were 3500 men present. It was the largest reunion outside London. The Prince gave a speech in which he recalled his own part in the last war when, as a young officer in the Royal Navy, he witnessed the rescue of two prisoners in August 1945 off the coast of Japan. He went on to praise the FEPOW Federation as one of the most out-standing ex-servicemen's organisations in Britain. Emotions were running very high in the Winter Gardens. Wives and sweethearts were watching proceedings from the balcony and Gillian remem-bered the extraordinary scenes below in the main hall. The Prince, her father, Harold Payne, Ted Coffey and other members of the executive were to be presented to the Mayor of Blackpool and various other dignitaries after the brief walkabout among the prisoners. But it was not to be. The men did not want to let their guests go. Then a man stepped forward and identified himself to the Prince as one of the two men he had picked up on his ship in 1945. The ten-minute walkabout became forty-five minutes; the Prince had to leave, and the Mayor had to miss out on the pres-entation.

At about this time Toosey was warned by the police that as a prominent figure in Liverpool he was probably on the IRA's list of 'legitimate' targets. One morning, an unidentified parcel arrived at Heathcote, wrapped in brown paper, with unfamiliar writing on the front. Alex immediately became suspicious. She fetched the fire tongs and carried the offending parcel very carefully out into the porch where she placed it on the stone wall. He watched her from his window thinking how sensible she had been. She went back inside and was out a few moments later with the poker. She hit the parcel with all her strength. There was fortunately no explosion but a hard-backed cookery book had a severe dent in the cover.

In July 1974 the University of Liverpool awarded Phil Toosey an Honorary Doctorate of Law for the eighteen years' service he had given on the University Council. On 12 July 1974 his honorary degree was conferred, just six days after he attended a FEPOW bowling match at which the Colonel Toosey Cup was awarded.

He received a knighthood that year in the Queen's birthday honours' list. This brought a rush of letters to Heathcote, over five hundred in less than a month. At first he had refused a knighthood but the FEPOW executive made it clear that they wished him to accept it this time so he did, writing to all the clubs and associations: 'I have not sought nor would I accept a Knighthood had I not known that this was recommended by the FEPOW, and I would like all to know that this is no personal honour, but a tribute to the spirit, discipline and loyalty of FEPOWs, not only in the Far East, but also in the 30 years since the war.'

Alex was not forgotten in the congratulations, although she took no pleasure or pride in Toosey's knighthood. 'Everyone knows about your war', her cousin E wrote to him, 'but few, perhaps, appreciate Alex's part. I had the privilege, on several occasions, of seeing her in action – and by jove, it took a bit of beating. Never a moan or grumble – she was magnificent, bless her.'[8]

There were congratulations from all the charities he was associated with, from the Hooton Village Hall Memorial Fund to the Personal Service Society. The station master from Hooton station in the 1950s wrote to congratulate him, as did the postmistress in Willaston.

Lord Mountbatten joined the chorus of congratulations. 'My dear Phil,' he wrote. 'At last, at last you have got long overdue recognition of all you have done for the Far East Prisoners of War. How delighted they must all be, basking in your reflected glory. Very very best congratulations.'[9]

Bertie Ogden wrote: 'What a far cry from those dark days of 1942. I wonder if Suzuki, Ichikora or any other of our erstwhile hosts have heard of your honour. When you become Lord Toosey, have you considered Toosey of Nong Pladuk or perhaps Lord Bridge maybe?'

Probably the oldest memory of Toosey came from Joyce Boston who wrote: 'My mind goes back so many years ago to that house in Upton Road when Nurse Robertson (who <u>you</u> will not remember!) showed me the new baby who had just arrived – little did I imagine he would achieve so much.'[10]

Dum Tweedy wrote a heartfelt letter from Peru:

My dear Old Phil, During the interminable, sleepless vigil crossing from Lisbon to Caracas through a prolonged night, I had ample time to think of many things and one of the happiest was of how, finally, your knighthood has been officially recognised. For years now you have been galumphing about through the dark forests of other people's pessimism, comforting the sick at heart, succouring the needy of spirit, taking their troubles on your own shoulders as should a very parfait, gentle Knight. Everybody who has ever been in touch with you has known about this for years, so it is no wonder that soon or later somebody would put a flea in Her Majesty's ear and she'd do the right thing – when she smacks you on the shoulder *do* remember to say 'thank you'; although she should really apologise for not having done it long before.[11]

Patrick, who understood his father better than many, wrote:

I know you hate praise, I know you have never sought honour but it is a supreme confirmation to me that an ordinary life is still a good one. You wouldn't get the honour for being out-standing in any one way but to me it is marvellous to see a normal man honoured . . . You have shown the value of being human and of getting on with and understanding people. Believe you me I am so thrilled that it's happened not because I want to hear you called Sir Philip but merely because you bloody well deserve it. To me and to hundreds, thousands of others you will always be 'the Captain', 'the Brig', 'Toosey', that old bugger, or whatever. Long live 'Sir Ancient and Crusty Bugler'.[12]

The next twelve months of Toosey's life were full of a new sort of activity. As he could no longer travel he decided that the time had come to record his memoirs. Originally he planned to record his life just for Patrick and Nicholas but he was persuaded by his friend Harry Chrimes to publish a book. Prolific letter writer though he was, he was no author. His unpublished auto-biography is typically self-effacing and although it offers a good insight into his early life, it does nothing to paint the bigger pic-ture of what happened in the Far East. He asked Sir John Smyth to take the manuscript in hand but it did not turn out to be the book he wanted. 'I do *not* like it, too much Phil Toosey. I have always disliked publicity,'[13] he complained and refused to allow it to be published in his lifetime. He then made a series of tape recordings over eighteen months with Peter Davies, Professor of History at Liverpool University, with a view to writing a full biography. Although his memory was patchy and some of what he remembered belonged to the collective memory of the period, it is nevertheless a remarkable record of his experiences and there are occasional glimpses of pain as well as humour. In October 1975 he attended his final FEPOW reunion in London. He asked Peter Davies to attend so that he could interview some of the prisoners who had been with him in various camps. Davies recalled the ceremony: 'My wife and I arrived a little late, just as the guests of honour were being presented on the stage. There was cheering and clapping for Harold Payne, Weary Dunlop and Mrs Beckwith-Smith, the General's widow, but then the Brigadier stepped up and the place erupted. It was like a scene in a film. Men threw their programmes, caps, even walking sticks into the air. They clapped, cheered and whistled for five minutes. For us going in "cold" it was extraordinary.'[14]

In November 1975 Patrick arrived at Heathcote to present his father with some railway spikes and a piece of sleeper that he and Peter Davies had brought back from a trip they had made to Thailand the year before. He was standing in the kitchen when he heard Toosey shuffling down the hall and was shocked and worried. His father had always been a stickler for picking up his feet. It was only then he realised how ill his father was. Toosey was delighted with the present and wrote to Peter Davies on 18 November 1975: 'Patrick yesterday brought me that most attractive piece of my railway beautifully mounted. I have to say that I was extremely moved by this present and the ideas behind it. It has a high nostalgic meaning for me, in fact, I nearly burst into tears.'[15]

A few days later he was admitted to Sefton General Hospital. He was breathless and his heart was giving out. He wrote to Alex, who was herself in hospital in Broad Green, on 24 November

1975: 'Food deplorable — Coulshead very good but I've never been so lost or mixed up in my life. I do so long to see you again tho' God knows when that will be.'[16] Four days later she came to visit him and he was delighted, writing to her that evening: 'we have been married so long that these occasional separations are more and more difficult now'.[17] Over the next weeks his organs began to fail and it was obvious that he would not live much longer. Among the many visitors to his bedside in December was his dear friend Reggie Lees, the only man to have called him by his Christian name in the three and a half years of captivity.

On 21 December Gillian went to the hospital. Her father was lying propped up on pillows. He smiled when she kissed him. She sat down and took his hand and told him that Alex would be coming to see him after supper, Patrick would bring her. She could hear his breathing and she looked at his frail figure outlined under the hospital blankets, his long, thin hands lying limply beside him. The minutes passed. Alex and Patrick arrived shortly after 8 p.m. and stayed for a couple of hours. Then Alex got up and kissed him gently goodbye. Patrick asked Gillian to keep him informed. He intended to spend the night at Heathcote. A nurse came in. She removed the pillows that were propping him up and made him comfortable for the night. He thanked her and closed his eyes for a few moments. The noises in the hospital began to grow quieter. The hustle and bustle of the day was replaced by the peace of the night-time. Lowered voices, the occasional trolley rattled by. A door opening here and closing quietly behind. Footsteps. Then almost complete silence except for the breathing of the man on the bed. The room was dimly lit. Gillian sat beside him holding his hand and talking quietly. His voice was barely more than a whisper.

Sometime after midnight the hospital chaplain arrived. A woman chaplain. Toosey turned to Gillian and said: 'It's all right now, darling Too Too, you can leave me.' She got up, kissed him on the cheek, and quietly left the room. A nurse appeared and showed her to a little room where she sat, frozen with sadness. A few minutes later the nurse came back. 'Gillian, your father has died,' she said. He had slipped peacefully away.

Phil Toosey was cremated on Christmas Eve at a small, private ceremony at Landican Cemetery. There was little time for preparation but Alex did not wish the funeral to be delayed until after Christmas.

On 31 January 1976 a memorial service was held in the parish church of Our Lady and St Nicholas, Liverpool, a modern church built on the site of a church bombed during the war. It overlooks the River Mersey and I remember it was bitterly cold. The church was packed and so many people had come that the service was relayed by loudspeaker to a crowd in a marquee outside. We were there to celebrate Phil Toosey's life and remember him with happiness. My father turned to me and Stephanie and said sternly: 'Now you are not to cry, girls.' We started with 'Abide with Me' and I failed to sing a note. Douglas Crawford read the lesson and John Bromfield, probably my grandfather's oldest friend, gave the address and began by saying: 'Phil packed about three men's lives into his seventy-one years and his activities were so numerous and varied that it just isn't possible to do more than touch on a few of them.' He then quoted a piece written by Sir John Smyth that I think we all felt summed up better than any other what he had achieved:

> Phil Toosey was with his men all the time, fought for them, worked for them, suffered for them, starved with them, was beaten up with them – and for their own good, sometimes bullied them and tore strips off them – with the result that their

morale remained high and their spirit was never broken: and they loved and respected him as few leaders of men can hope to be in their lifetime.[18]

I remember leaving the church after the service and walking with Stephanie through a seemingly endless crowd of men who had gathered in silence outside. There were hundreds of them, the press put the figure at 700; ordinary men whose lives had been touched by Phil Toosey – former prisoners of war, dockworkers and cotton merchants, young men who had benefited from his charity work, even the retired railway guard from Hooton station, from where Toosey had commuted to Liverpool for thirty years. There was a real sense of the passing of an era and the sadness which hung in the air has imprinted itself on my memory.

Sir John Nicholson wrote a short piece about him for the *Ocean Mail*:

One could never recapture the magic of his company or describe the unique blend of sympathy and enthusiasm which instantly warmed everyone who met him. But the greatness of his character and the measure of his achievement were summed up by his lifelong friend, Selwyn Lloyd: 'a wise and prudent leader never forgetting the suffering of individuals but always remembering the wider national purpose'. Yet for all the pleasure that tributes like this gave him and the sustained adulation of his fellow prisoners it had no effect on his selfless modesty. Nor was his life distorted by memories of his extraordinary past. And we who were privileged to work with him remember that despite his habit of unchallenged command even his strongest convictions were cheerfully subordinated to the attainment of our common good.[19]

One person had unfinished business with Toosey and that was Saito. He had written to him in 1974:

For long period of time I have been harbouring the wish to meet you and express my thanks to you. I especially remember in 1945 when the war ended and when our situations were completely reversed. I was gravely shocked and delighted when you came to shake me by the hand as only the day before you were prisoner. You exchanged friendly words with me and I discovered what a great man you were. Even after winning you were not arrogant or proud. You are the type of man who is a real bridge over the battlefield.

Saito, who had converted to Christianity after the war, had a great feeling of obligation towards Toosey and he would not be happy to die until he had discharged this obligation. In 1984 he came to Britain. Patrick took him to see his father's modest grave with Peter Davies. It was 12 August and it would have been Toosey's eightieth birthday. Saito expressed surprise that there was no grand monument. He asked to be left alone for a few minutes at the grave. On his return to Japan he wrote to Peter Davies and Patrick: 'I feel very fine because I finish my own strong duty. One thing I regret, I could not visit Mr Philip Toosey when he was alive. He showed me what a human being should be. He changed the philosophy of my life.'

APPENDIX I

MAJOR GROUPS EMPLOYED ON
RAILWAY CONSTRUCTION

Civilians	Total Employed	Deaths
From Malaya	75,000	42,000
Burmese	90,000	40,000
Javanese	7500	2900
From Singapore	5200	500

POWs		
British	30,131	6904
Dutch	17,990	2782
Australian	13,004	2802
American	686	131
Japanese and Koreans	15,000	1000

Courtesy: Rod Beattie of the Thailand–Burma Railway Centre, Kanchanaburi, Thailand

APPENDIX II

TOOSEY'S WAR

31 August 1939	Phil Toosey leaves his home, Heathcote, and does not return full time for six and a half years
October 1939 to May 1940	Exercises in France during the Phoney War
10 May	Germany invades Belgium
2 June	Toosey evacuated with the British Expeditionary Force at Dunkirk
End August 1941	Takes over command of the 135th Herts Yeomanry
26 October	Sails for the Middle East
7/8 December	Japan attacks Pearl Harbor, Singapore, Hong Kong; launches her invasion of Malaya and the Philippines
10 December	Sinking of the Royal Navy's Capital ships HMS *Repulse* and HMS *Prince of Wales*
14 December	Toosey learns he and his men are to be diverted to Singapore
29 January 1942	*Mount Vernon* arrives Singapore and Toosey takes part in the battle for Malaya and Singapore

13 February	Toosey receives order from General Key to evacuate to India. He refuses
15 February	General Percival agrees to surrender; nearly 90,000 Allied servicemen in S.E. Asia become prisoners of war of the Japanese
17 February	Toosey moves to Roberts Barracks, Changi
5 May	Moves to Bukit Timah camp with 500 men from his regiment
June	Senior officers of the rank of full colonel and above moved to Formosa and Japan; Toosey takes over command at Bukit Timah
26 October	Toosey arrives in Ban Pong, Thailand after a four-day train journey from Singapore
27 October	Moves to Tamarkan where he takes over from Major Roberts as camp commander and is ordered to build two bridges over the river Mae Khlong
30 April 1943	Bridges more or less finished. All fit men are sent up the railway to work. Toosey ordered to stay behind
1 May	Tamarkan becomes a hospital camp. Dr A.A. Moon arrives from Hintok to take over as senior medical officer from Dr Jim Mark
14 December	Toosey and David Boyle move to Nong Pladuk camp
16 January 1944	Toosey takes over running Nong Pladuk
25 January 1945	Officers separated from men and sent to Kanburi officers' camp
28 June	Toosey moves to Nakhon Nayok
8 August	Atomic bomb dropped on Hiroshima
15 August	Japan capitulates
17 August	Toosey told of end of war

7 October	Sails home on the SS *Orbita*
10 November	Toosey is driven back to Heathcote by his wife, Alex after an absence of 2263 days
1946	Phil Toosey is awarded an OBE for leadership in captivity
1957	*The Bridge on the River Kwai* is released and shown in UK cinemas

Phil Toosey aged thirty-one.

NOTES

CHAPTER 1 – THE BRIDGE ON THE RIVER KWAI:
NOVEL, FILM, REALITY

1 Natasha Fraser-Cavassoni, *Sam Spiegel*, p. 195
2 Pierre Boulle, *Le pont sur la rivière Kwaï*, p. 30
3 Ibid., p. 33
4 Pierre Boulle, *Source of the River Kwai*, p. 46
5 Ibid., p. 46
6 Pierre Boulle, letter to John Charles Sharp, 1953
7 Kevin Brownlow, *David Lean*, p. 347
8 Natasha Fraser-Cavassoni, *Sam Spiegel*, p. 179
9 Kevin Brownlow, *David Lean*, p. 350
10 Ibid., pp. 350–51
11 Ibid., p. 381
12 Alec Guinness, letter to Patrick Toosey, 26 April 1991
13 Alec Guinness, quoted in *Focus on Film*, autumn, 1972, p. 20
14 Alec Guinness, letter to Patrick Toosey, 26 April 1991
15 Natasha Fraser-Cavassoni, *Sam Spiegel*, p. 190
16 Kevin Brownlow, *David Lean*, p. 366
17 Ibid., pp. 368–9
18 Ibid., p. 377
19 Ibid., p. 378
20 Natasha Fraser-Cavassoni, *Sam Spiegel,* p. 194
21 Ibid., p. 194
22 Kevin Brownlow, *David Lean*, p. 386
23 Kazuyu Tsukamoto, 'The Mae Khlaung Steel Bridge', p. 32

CHAPTER 2 – AN HONEST BEGINNING

1 Toosey tapes, reel 2
2 Phyllis Rimmos, letter to Phil Toosey, June 1974
3 Toosey tapes, reel 10
4 Ibid.
5 Ibid.
6 Ibid., reel 3
7 Ibid., reel 2
8 Ibid.
9 Graeme McFarlane, letter to Phil Toosey, 29 June 1974
10 Bill Dennison, letter to Phil Toosey, 26 July 1974
11 Toosey tapes, reel 12
12 Ibid.
13 Ibid., reel 4
14 Ibid.
15 Ibid.
16 Ibid.
17 Ibid., reel 5
18 Toosey, letter to Arthur Villiers, 6 February 1935
19 Toosey, letter to Alan Tod, 18 February 1935
20 Toosey, letter to Arthur Villiers, 6 February 1935
21 Toosey, letter to Alan Tod, 19 March 1935
22 Ibid., 23 March 1935
23 Ibid., 19 March 1935
24 Ibid., 23 March 1935

CHAPTER 3 – SPIKE THE GUNS AND SAVE THE PERSONNEL

1 Toosey tapes, reel 7
2 Ibid.
3 Sir John Smyth, *The Life Story of Brigadier P J D Toosey*, p. 6
4 Toosey tapes, reel 8
5 Archie Crawford, letter to Sir John Smyth, 24 July 1972
6 Toosey autobiography, p. 12
7 Ibid.
8 Liddell Hart, *History of the Second World War*, p. 34
9 Toosey autobiography, p. 13

10 Ibid.
11 Ibid., p. 14.
12 Ibid.
13 Ibid., p. 16
14 Ibid.
15 Ibid.
16 Ibid., p. 18
17 Ibid.
18 Ibid., p. 19
19 Ibid.
20 Ibid., p. 21
21 Ibid., p. 23
22 Ibid.
23 Ibid., p. 24
24 Ibid.
25 Ibid., p. 20
26 Archie Crawford, letter to Sir John Smyth, 24 July 1972
27 Toosey autobiography, p. 25
28 Ibid.
29 Hubert Servaes, letter to Arthur Villiers, 18 November 1945
30 Toosey autobiography, p. 27a
31 Ibid.
32 Tom Brown, letter to the author, 19 December 2003
33 Toosey autobiography, p. 27a
34 Ibid.
35 Ibid.
36 Ibid., p. 28
37 Stephen Alexander, *Sweet Kwai Run Softly*, p. 27
38 Hubert Servaes, letter to Arthur Villiers, 18 November 1945
39 Toosey autobiography, p. 29
40 Ibid.
41 Geoffrey Pharaoh Adams, *No Time for Geishas,* p. 53
42 Alan Warren, *Singapore 1942*, p. 12
43 A. Iriye, *Origins of the Second World War in Asia and the Pacific,* p. 143
44 Alan Warren, *Singapore 1942*, p. 48
45 Toosey autobiography, p. 31
46 Churchill quoted in Alan Warren, *Singapore 1942*, p. 77
47 Toosey autobiography, p. 32
48 Ibid.

49 Stephen Alexander, *Sweet Kwai Run Softly*, p. 42
50 Toosey autobiography, p. 33
51 Stephen Alexander, *Sweet Kwai Run Softly*, p. 47
52 Toosey autobiography, p. 35
53 Ibid.
54 Ibid.
55 Hubert Servaes, letter to Arthur Villiers, 18 November 1945
56 Toosey autobiography, p. 44
57 Ibid.
58 Ibid., p. 46
59 Ibid., p. 47
60 Ibid., p. 48
61 Hubert Servaes, letter to Arthur Villiers, 18 November 1945
62 Toosey autobiography, p. 48
63 Ibid.
64 Alan Warren, *Singapore 1942*, p. 262
65 Ibid., p. 263
66 Ibid.
67 Ibid.
68 Ibid., p. 265

CHAPTER 4 – AN ODD AND CURIOUS PARTY

1 Bill Drower, *Our Man on the Hill*, p. 65
2 Charles Elston interview, 31 July 2003
3 Alan Warren, *Singapore 1942*, p. 267
4 Charles Steel, letter to Louise (in *Secret Letters from the Railway*, ed., Brian Best, pp. 23–4)
5 Ibid., p. 27
6 Roy Whitecross, *Slaves of the Son of Heaven*, p. 7
7 Ibid.
8 Charles Steel, letter to Louise (in *Secret Letters from the Railway*, ed., Brian Best, p. 23)
9 Toosey Camp Report, p. 2
10 Charles Steel, letter to Louise (in *Secret Letters from the Railway*, ed., Brian Best, p. 34)
11 Ibid., p. 49
12 Toosey Camp Report, p. 4

13 Ibid., p. 3

14 Charles Steel, letter to Louise (in *Secret Letters from the Railway*, ed., Brian Best, p. 40)

15 Stephen Alexander, *Sweet Kwai Run Softly*, p. 89

16 Ibid., p. 93

17 Stanley Pavillard, *Bamboo Doctor*, p. 52

18 Russell Braddon, *Naked Island*, pp. 208–9

19 Toosey Camp Report, p. 4

20 Ibid., p. 3

21 Stephen Alexander, *Sweet Kwai Run Softly*, p. 91

22 Ibid., pp. 91–2

23 Ibid., p. 91

24 Charles Steel, letter to Louise, February 1942 (in *Secret Letters from the Railway*, ed., Brian Best, p. 50)

25 Brigadier Duke, letter to Toosey, June 1942

26 J.H.H. Coombes, *Ban Pong Express*, p. 70

27 Capt. Robinson, diary

28 John Coast, *Railroad of Death*, p. 56

29 Capt. Robinson, diary

30 Charles Steel, letter to Louise, February 1942 (in *Secret Letters from the Railway*, ed., Brian Best, p. 53)

31 Toosey Camp Report, p. 4

32 Stephen Alexander, *Sweet Kwai Run Softly*, p. 103

33 E. E. Dunlop, *The War Diaries of Weary Dunlop*, 20 January 1943

34 Ibid.

35 Toosey Camp Report, p. 4

36 E. E. Dunlop, *The War Diaries of Weary Dunlop*, 20 January 1943

37 Toosey tapes, reel 21

38 Ibid.

39 F. S. Robinson diary, 27 October 1942

40 Toosey tapes, reel 21

41 Toosey Camp Report, p. 4

42 Peter Davies, *The Man Behind the Bridge*, p. 6

43 Toosey Camp Report, p. 4

44 Toosey tapes, reel 21

CHAPTER 5 – BUILDING BRIDGES ON
THE KHWAE MAE KHLONG

1 Joseph Gordon Smith, unpublished memoirs
2 Ibid.
3 David Boyle in conversation with Peter Davies
4 Toosey Camp Report, p. 7
5 Patricia Mark, email, 1 December 2004
6 BBC Timewatch, *The Man Behind the Bridge,* 1997
7 Toosey tapes, reel 49
8 Stephen Alexander, *Sweet Kwai Run Softly*, pp. 111–12
9 Ibid., p. 9
10 Warmenhoven Report, p. 13
11 Robert Hislop, letter, 3 October 1979, quoted in Peter Davies, *The Man Behind the Bridge*, pp. 103–104
12 Stephen Alexander, *Sweet Kwai Run Softly*, p. 116
13 Futamatsu, translated by Ewart Escritt
14 Toosey tapes, reel 21
15 Toosey Camp Report, p. 25
16 Ernest Gordon, *Miracle on the Kwai,* p. 66
17 Toosey tapes, reel 21
18 Ibid.
19 *Stanford Observer,* November 1982, p. 5
20 Toosey Camp Report, p. 7
21 David Boyle in conversation with Peter Davies
22 Ibid.
23 Stephen Alexander, *Sweet Kwai Run Softly,* p. 113
24 David Boyle in conversation with Peter Davies
25 Toosey Camp Report, p. 7
26 Toosey tapes, reel 49
27 Ibid., reel 49
28 Toosey autobiography, p. 61
29 Sibylla Jane Flower, *Captors and Captives on the Burma–Thailand Railway*, p. 243
30 Charles Steel to Louise (in *Secret Letters from the Railway*, ed., Brian Best, p. 59)
31 Toosey Camp Report, p. 25
32 J. Stewart, *To the River Kwai,* 1988
33 Ian Watt, quoted in the *Stanford Observer*, 1982, p. 5

CHAPTER 6 – ESCAPE TO THE JUNGLE

1 Stephen Alexander, *Sweet Kwai Run Softly*, p. 110
2 Toosey tapes, reel 21
3 Jonathan Moffat & Audrey Holmes McCormick, *Moon over Malaya,* pp. 194–5
4 Toosey Camp Report, p. 7
5 Toosey tapes, reel 51
6 David Boyle in conversation with Peter Davies, 1975
7 Colonel Nicholson, *The Bridge on the River Kwai*
8 Stephen Alexander, *Sweet Kwai Run Softly*, p. 117
9 BBC Timewatch, *The Man Behind the Bridge,* 1997
10 Toosey autobiography, p. 172
11 Toosey tapes, reel 21
12 Stephen Alexander, *Sweet Kwai Run Softly,* p. 118
13 Warmenhoven report
14 Quoted in *Secret Letters from the Railway*, ed., Brian Best, p. 74
15 Toosey Camp Report, p. 39
16 Warmenhoven Report, p. 3
17 Ibid.
18 Ibid.
19 Ibid., p. 34
20 Ibid., p. 6
21 Russell Braddon, *Naked Island,* p. 319
22 Diary of Louis Baume
23 Roy Whitecross, *Slaves of the Son of Heaven,* p. 42
24 Stanley S. Pavillard, *Bamboo Doctor,* p. 130
25 Russell Braddon, *Naked Island,* p. 328
26 Stanley Pavillard, *Bamboo Doctor,* pp. 136–7
27 E. E. Dunlop, *The Diaries of Weary Dunlop,* 28 April 1943
28 Patricia Mark, email, 1 December 2004
29 Stanley Pavillard, *Bamboo Doctor,* p. 18
30 Arthur Moon, letter to Sir John Smyth, 1972
31 *The Major Arthur Moon Collection* (the catalogue of an exhibition held in the Queen's Hall, Victoria, 1945), p. 4
32 Ibid., p. 5
33 Russell Braddon, *Naked Island,* p. 375
34 Ibid., p. 375
35 Toosey autobiography, p. 58
36 Report on Tamarkan P.O.W Hospital, Major A.A. Moon, A.A.M.C, p. 3

CHAPTER 7 – TAMARKAN BASE HOSPITAL

1 R. Burton, *Road to Three Pagodas*, pp. 121–2
2 Toosey autobiography, p. 58
3 Ibid., p. 59
4 C.F. Blackater, *Gods without Reason,* p. 115
5 Toosey autobiography, p. 59
6 Ibid.
7 L.L. Baynes, *The Other Side of Tenko,* pp. 122–3
8 C.F. Blackater, *Gods without Reason,* p. 117
9 Alec Young diary, May 1943
10 Jack Caplan, letter to the *Observer,* 1 September 1968
11 Alec Young, letter to Phil Toosey, September 1968
12 Private Lionel McCosker, letter to Toosey, November 1945
13 Toosey tapes, reel 13
14 Carel Hamel, *Soldatendominee,* p. 158
15 Ibid.
16 Ibid., p. 166
17 Ibid.
18 Ibid., p. 165
19 Ibid., p. 162
20 Ibid.
21 Ibid., p. 167
22 Dick Van Zoonen, note on Hamel translation
23 C.F. Blackater, *Gods without Reason,* p. 121
24 Report on Tamarkan P.O.W Hospital, Major A. A. Moon, A.A.M.C, p. 3
25 Toosey tapes, reel 27
26 E.P. Heath, written statement, 25 July 1945
27 Sibylla Jane Flower, Peter Heath obituary, *The Times,* 28 January 2003
28 Ibid.
29 Peter Heath, written statement, 25 July 1945
30 Peter Heath, interview with Peter Davies
31 Phil Toosey, letter to Peter Heath, 11 June 1943
32 Peter Heath, letter to Phil Toosey, 30 June 1943
33 Phil Toosey, letter to Peter Heath, 15 October 1943
34 C.F. Blackater, *Gods without Reason,* p. 120
35 Ibid., p. 122
36 Ibid., pp. 124–5

37 Ibid., p. 125
38 *The Argus Weekend Magazine*, 3 September 1949, p. 9
39 George Downes, letter to Sir John Smyth, 1972
40 Edwin Webster, 'A Man's a Man for a' that'
41 Clifford Kinvig, *River Kwai Railway*, p. 164
42 Warmenhoven Report, p. 7
43 Carel Hamel, *Soldatendominee*, p. 176
44 Alec Young diary, 20 September 1943
45 Nagase speaking to Toosey, September 1943, recorded by C.F. Blackater in his diary
46 Toosey tapes, reel 51
47 Ibid.

CHAPTER 8 – BY THE LIGHT OF THE BOMBER'S MOON

 1 Carel Hamel, *Soldatendominee*, p. 178
 2 Toosey Camp Report, p. 10
 3 Louis Baume diary, 27 August 1943
 4 Toosey Camp Report, p. 4
 5 Ibid., Appendix 'B', Major E.A. Smyth, p. 4
 6 Charles Wylie in conversation with the author, 1 December 2003
 7 Sherring in Toosey Camp Report, Appendix 'F'
 8 Ibid.
 9 Ibid.
10 Ibid.
11 Patricia Mark, *VJ Day*, chapter 4
12 Fergus Anckorn, undated letter to Norman Pritchard
13 Norman Pritchard, letter to the author, April 2004
14 John Smyth, *The Life of Brigadier P J D Toosey*, p. 109
15 Philip Buchan, letter to Sir John Smyth, 1972
16 Speech to be given at Ubon by Dr C.H. den Hertog, September 1945
17 Toosey Camp Report, Davidson, Appendix 'A', p. 27
18 Toosey Camp Report, Appendix 'B', Major E.A. Smyth, p. 5
19 Ibid., p. 8
20 Toosey Camp Report, p. 13
21 Ibid., p. 18
22 Louis Baume diary, June 1944

23 Ibid., June 1944
24 Toosey Camp Report, p. 13
25 Ibid., Appendix 'B', Major E. A. Smyth, p. 8
26 Louis Baume diary, 4 September 1944
27 Ibid.
28 Ibid., 6 September 1944
29 Ibid.
30 Toosey Camp Report p. 14
31 Louis Baume diary, 6 September 1944
32 Toosey tapes, reel 31
33 Charles Steel, letter to Louise (in *Secret Letters from the Railway* ed., Brian Best, pp. 23–4)
34 Toosey tapes, reel 31
35 John Smyth, *The Life Story of Brigadier P J D Toosey*, p. 113
36 Toosey, speech to a boys' school, 1972
37 Dick Van Zoonen, email, June 2004
38 Charles Steel, letter to Louise, November 1944 (in *Secret Letters from the Railway* ed., Brian Best, p. 106)
39 Mountbatten, letter to Phil Toosey, 6 September 1968
40 Toosey Camp Report, pp. 15–16
41 Louis Baume diary, 4 December 1944
42 Toosey tapes, reel 31
43 Charles Steel to Louise, 31 December 1944 (in *Secret Letters from the Railway* ed., Brian Best, p. 110)
44 Louis Baume diary, 4 December 1944
45 Ibid., 24 December 1944
46 Charles Steel to Louise, 24 January 1945 (in *Secret Letters from the Railway* ed., Brian Best, p. 112)
47 Toosey autobiography, p. 66

CHAPTER 9 – THE OFFICERS' MESS

1 Alec Young, letter to Phil Toosey, September 1960
2 Toosey Camp Report, p.18
3 Ibid., p. 20
4 Captain Robinson diary
5 J.H.H. Coombes, *Ban Pong Express*, p. 151
6 Rohan Rivett, *Behind Bamboo*, p. 299

7 Louis Baume diary, 30 January 1945
8 Ibid., February 1945
9 Cary Owtram, unpublished memoirs, p. 164
10 Ibid.
11 Louis Baume diary, 1 March 1945
12 Capt. Robinson, unpublished document, Imperial War Museum 99/31/1
13 Ibid.
14 Cary Owtram, unpublished memoirs, p. 161
15 Louis Baume diary, 28 February 1945
16 Arthur Knights, unpublished memoirs, p. 3
17 Louis Baume diary, March 1945
18 Arthur Knights unpublished memoirs, p. 5
19 Ibid., p. 6
20 Toosey Camp Report, p. 19
21 Louis Baume diary, 28 April 1945
22 Phil Toosey, letter to Harry Flower, 25 June 1974
23 Ibid.
24 Toosey Camp Report, p. 19
25 Ibid., p. 20
26 Bill Drower in conversation with the author, May 2005
27 Ibid.
28 Bill Drower, *Our Man on the Hill,* p. 65
29 Stanley Gimson diary, 28 April 1945
30 Louis Baume diary, 6 June 1945
31 Bill Drower, *Our Man on the Hill* p. 82
32 Cary Owtram, memoirs, p. 159
33 Toosey Camp Report, p. 20
34 Cary Owtram, unpublished memoirs, p. 169
35 Toosey autobiography, p. 67
36 Toosey Camp Report, p. 21
37 Stephen Alexander, *Sweet Kwai Run Softly,* p. 208
38 Toosey Camp Report, p. 21
39 Ibid.
40 Ibid., p. 22
41 Ibid.
42 Ibid.
43 Ibid.
44 Ibid.

45 Ibid.
46 Toosey Camp Report, p. 23
47 George Holland in conversation with the author, October 2004
48 Stanley Gimson diary, July 1944
49 Stephen Alexander, *Sweet Kwai Run Softly,* p. 212
50 Ibid.
51 Toosey Camp Report, p. 24
52 Stanley Gimson, *Behind the Bamboo Screen 'The Closing Days',* pp. 130–31
53 Toosey Camp Report, p. 23
54 Stanley Gimson, *Behind the Bamboo Screen 'The Closing Days',* p. 131
55 Louis Baume diary, 16 August 1945
56 Toosey autobiography, p. 74
57 Louis Baume, 17 August 1945

CHAPTER 10 – CLEAN SHIRTS AND SHORTS

1 Theo Newell, unpublished memoirs
2 Louis Baume diary, p. 190
3 Bob Sutliffe diary, 16 August 1945
4 Bill Drower, *Our Man on the Hill,* p. 82
5 Louis Baume diary, 26 August 1945
6 Toosey autobiography, p. 76
7 Louis Baume diary, 26 August 1945
8 Jonathan Moffat and Audrey Holmes MacCormick, *Moon over Malaya,* p. 215
9 John Smyth, *The Life Story of P J D Toosey,* p. 125
10 BBC *Timewatch*, 'The True Story of the Bridge on the River Kwai' 1997
11 Toosey autobiography, p. 77
12 Louis Baume diary, 4 September 1945
13 Ibid., 1 September 1945
14 Jack Leeman, *The Body Snatchers,* p. 88
15 Toosey tapes, reel 10
16 Peter Davies, *The Man Behind the Bridge,* p. 205
17 Carel Hamel, letter to Phil Toosey, April 1946
18 Louis Baume diary, 19 September 1945
19 Toosey autobiography, p. 78

20 Ibid.
21 Louis Baume diary, 20 September 1945
22 Dr C. den Hertog, unpublished speech, September 1945
23 Louis Baume diary, 24 September 1945
24 Toosey autobiography, p. 80
25 Toosey tapes, reel 7
26 Toosey autobiography, p. 81
27 Ibid., p. 82
28 Louis Baume diary, 9 November 1945

CHAPTER 11 – THE CAPTAIN REVIVED

1   Gillian Summers,19 January 2005
2   Patricia Mark, January 2005
3   Gillian Summers, 19 January 2005
4   Anon.
5   Anon.
6   Gillian Summers
7   David Bowie, 'Captive surgeon in Hong Kong: The story of the British Military Hospital Hong Kong 1942–45'.
8   Ian Mackintosh, letter to Barings' staff and families, 17 September 1942
9   Ibid., June 1943
10 Anon.
11 Ernest Gordon, *Miracle on the Kwai,* p. 179
12 Malcolm Northcote, letter to Phil Toosey, 27 November 1945
13 Ernest Gordon, *Miracle on the Kwai*, p. 182
14 Ewart Escritt, letter to Geoffrey Gill
15 Malcolm Northcote, letter to Phil Toosey, 27 November 1945
16 Arthur Osborne, letter to Phil Toosey, 3 December 1945
17 Evelyn B. Baring, letter to Alberto Dodero, 20 May 1946
18 Toosey, letter to Alan Tod, 1 June 1946
19 Toosey, letter to Evelyn B. Baring, 1 June 1946
20 Toosey, letter to Evelyn B. Baring, 1 August 1946
21 Ibid.
22 Ibid.
23 Dick Lockett, letter to Evelyn B. Baring, September 1946
24 Toosey's Africa diary, October 1949

25 Toosey autobiography, p. 9
26 Toosey, letter to Sir John Hobhouse, 1960
27 Arthur Moon, letter to Sir John Smyth, 1972
28 Ibid.
29 Toosey tapes, reel 47
30 Lord Ashburton interviewed, January 2005
31 Arthur White, interview 2004
32 John Smyth, *The Life Story of Brigadier P. J. D. Toosey,* p. 137
33 Roehampton Report, 'Neurological Disease', point 1
34 Gillian Summers, January 2005
35 John Smyth, *The Life Story of Brigadier P. J. D. Toosey,* p. 68
36 Ian Watt in the *Observer,* 1 September 1967
37 Toosey, letter to Ian Watt, 15 August 1967
38 'Myth and Reality in an Asian Jungle', *Sunday Tribune,* 1 September 1968
39 Alec Guinness, letter to Patrick Toosey, 26 April 1991
40 Ian Watt in the *Observer,* 1 September 1967
41 Ibid.
42 Toosey, letter to Ian Watt, 15 August 1967
43 Alec Young, letter to Phil Toosey, September 1968
44 Mountbatten, letter to Phil Toosey, 6 September 1968

EPILOGUE – BORROWED TIME

 1 Toosey tapes, reel 46
 2 David Hamilton in conversation with the author, 22 September 2003
 3 Toosey tapes, reel 46
 4 John Smyth, *The Life Story of Brigadier P J D Toosey,* p. 143
 5 Ibid., p.144
 6 Ibid.
 7 Toosey tapes, reel 51
 8 E. Forrester, letter to Phil Toosey, 17 June 1974
 9 Lord Mountbatten, letter to Phil Toosey, 16 June 1974
10 Joyce Boston, letter to Phil Toosey, 16 June 1974
11 W.L.C. 'Dum' Tweedy, letter to Phil Toosey, 18 June 1974
12 Patrick Toosey, letter to Phil Toosey, 9 June 1974
13 Toosey, letter to Peter Davies, 5 December 1973
14 Peter Davies in conversation with the author, August 2003

15 Toosey, letter to Peter Davies, 18 November 1975
16 Toosey, letter to Alex Toosey, 24 November 1975
17 Ibid., 29 November 1975
18 John Smyth, *The Life Story of Brigadier P J D Toosey*, p. 134
19 *Ocean Mail,* January 1976

BIBLIOGRAPHY

PUBLISHED SOURCES

Adams, Geoffrey Pharaoh with Popham, Hugh, *No Time for Geishas* (London: Corgi, 1974)

Alexander, Stephen, *Sweet Kwai Run Softly* (Bristol: Merriotts Press, 1995)

Barker, A.J., *Behind Barbed Wire* (London: B.T. Batsford Ltd, 1974)

Barker, Ralph, *One Man's Jungle* (London: Chatto & Windus, 1975)

Barber, Noel, *Sinister Twilight: The Fall of Singapore* (London: Collins, 1968)

Baynes, L. L., *The Other Side of Tenko* (Lewes: Book Guild, 1984)

Best, Brian (ed.), *Secret Letters from the Railway: The Remarkable Record of Charles Steel – A Japanese POW* (Barnsley: Pen & Sword, Military, 2004)

Blackater, C.F., *Gods without Reason* (London: Eyre & Spottiswoode, 1948)

Boulle, Pierre translated by Xan Fielding, *The Bridge on the River Kwai*, (New York: Bantam Books, 1954)

Braddon, Russell, *The Naked Island* (London: Bodley Head, 1952)

Brownlow, Kevin, *David Lean: A Biography* (New York: St Martin's Press, 1996)

Burton, R., *Road to Three Pagodas* (London: MacDonald, 1963)

Chalker, Jack, *Burma Railway Artist* (London: Leo Cooper, 1994)

Clarke, Hugh V., *A Life for Every Sleeper* (London: Allen & Unwin, 1986)

Coast, John, *Railroad of Death* (London: The Commodore Press, 1946)

Coombes, J.H.H., *Ban Pong Express* (Darlington: W. Dresser, 1948)

Davies, Peter, *The Man Behind the Bridge: Colonel Toosey and the River Kwai* (London: The Athlone Press, 1991)

Davies, Russell, *Ronald Searle* (London: Chris Beetles, 2003)

Drower, William Mortimer, *Our Man on the Hill: A British Diplomat*

Remembers (Berkeley: IGS Press Institute of Governmental Studies, University of California, 1993)

Dunlop, E.E. *The War Diaries of Weary Dunlop* (Wheathampstead: Lennard Publishing, 1987)

Fraser-Cavassoni, Natasha, *Sam Spiegel: The Biography of a Hollywood Legend* (London: Little, Brown, 2003)

Goh Chor, Boon, *Living Hell* (Singapore: Asiapac Books PTE Ltd, 1999)

Gordon, Ernest, *Miracle on the River Kwai* (London: Fontana Books, 1963)

Hamel, J.C., *Soldatendominee* (S. Gravenh age: NV Uitgeverij W. Van Hoeve, 1948)

Hardie, Robert, *The Burma–Siam Railway: The Secret Diary of Dr Robert Hardie 1942–45* (London: Imperial War Museum, 1983)

Hartley, Peter, *Escape to Captivity* (London: J M Dent and Sons, 1952)

Henderson, Lt. Col. W., *From China, Burma, India to the Kwai* (Waco: Texian Press, 1991)

Hersey, John, *Hiroshima* (London: Penguin, 1946)

Iriye, A., *Origins of the Second World War in Asia and the Pacific* (London: Longman, 1987)

Kinvig, Clifford, *River Kwai Railway* (London: Brassey's, 1992)

Kirby, Major General S. Woodburn, *The War Against Japan* (London: H.M. Stationery Office, 1969)

Liddell-Hart, *History of the Second World War* (London: Cassell & Company, 1970)

Lomax, Eric, *The Railway Man* (London: Vintage, 1996)

McGowran, Tom, *Beyond the Bamboo Screen* (Dumfermline: Cualann Press, 1999)

Miller, P.J. *Liverpool School of Tropical Medicine* (Liverpool: School of Tropical Medicine, 1998)

Moffatt, Jonathan and Holmes McCormick, Audrey, *Moon Over Malaya: A Tale of Argylls and Marines* (Stroud: Tempus Publishing Ltd, 2002)

Moore, Bob and Fedorowich, Kent (eds), *Prisoners of War and their Captors in World War II* (Oxford, Berg, 1996)

Morris, John, *The Phoenix Cup: Some Notes on Japan in 1946* (London: The Cresset Press, 1947)

Nelson, David, *The Story of Changi, Singapore* (Singapore: Changi Publications, 1974)

Orbell, John, *Baring Brothers & Co, Limited: A History to 1939* (London: Baring Brothers & Co Limited, 1985)

Pavillard, Stanley, *Bamboo Doctor* (London: Macmillan & Co, 1960)

Peachey, Philip R., *Jeweller's Rouge: Survival by the River Kwai* (Springfield Leisure Art Collection, 2002)

Piper, David, *I Am Well, Who Are You?* (Exeter: Anna Piper, 1998)

Power, Helen J., *Tropical Medicine in the Twentieth Century* (London: Kegan Paul International, 1999)

Read, Piers Paul, *Alec Guinness* (London: Simon & Schuster, 2003)

Rivett, Rohan D., *Behind Bamboo* (Sydney: Angus & Robertson, 1946)

Rayvern Allen, David, *Jim: The Life of E W Swanton* (London: Aurum Press, 2004)

Searle, Ronald, *Forty Drawings* (Cambridge: University Press, 1946)

Searle, Ronald, *To the Kwai – and Back: War Drawings 1939–45* (London: Collins, 1986)

Shennan, Margaret, *Out in the Midday Sun* (London: John Murray, 2000)

Sinclair-Stevenson, Christopher, *The Gordon Highlanders* (London: Hamish Hamilton Ltd, 1968)

Smiley, David, *Irregular Regular* (Norwich: Michael Russell, 1994)

Spencer Chapman, F., *The Jungle is Neutral* (Singapore: Times Books International, 1948)

Tamayama, Kazuo and Nunneley, John, *Tales by Japanese Soldiers* (London, Cassell, 2000)

Velmans, Loet, *Long Way Back to the River Kwai: Memories of World War II* (New York: Arcade Publishing, 2003)

Warren, Alan, *Singapore 1942: Britain's Greatest Defeat* (London: Hambledon and London, 2002)

Whitecross, Roy, *Slaves of the Son of Heaven* (Bath: Chivers, 1989)

Yardley, Richard, *The Amanohasidate or The Gate of Heaven* (printed in Abergavenny, 2003)

FILMS & DOCUMENTARIES

The Bridge on the River Kwai, directed by David Lean, produced by Sam Spiegel, Columbia Pictures 1957, remix June 2000

'The True Story of the Bridge on the River Kwai', written and directed by Paul Elston, *Timewatch*, 1997

'The True Story of the Bridge on the River Kwai', executive producer Charles Mathay, Greystone Communications Inc., 2000

ARTICLES

Fisher, Charles A., 'The Thailand–Burma Railway' *Economic Geography*, June/ July 1947

Grant, Rafael, 'A War Hero Named Boonpong' *Newsweek*, August 1973

Pritchard, Norman, 'Bamboo: A Survey of Building Conditions and Accommodation for Prisoners of War in Malaya and Thailand 1942–45' *The Architect and Building News*, 1 February 1946

Ramsey, Winston G. (ed.), 'The Death Railway', *After the Battle*, Number 26, published by Battle of Britain Prints, 1979

Swanton, E.W. 'A Cricketer Under the Japs', *Spectator,* 15 February 1992

Testro, Ron, 'Do Not Let Them Be "Forgotten Men"', *The Argus Weekend Magazine*, September 1949

Tsukamoto, Kazuyu (translated by C. E. Escritt), 'The Mae Khluang Steel Bridge: Built in the Battlezone', *Railway Fan,* December 1981

Watt, Ian, 'The Myth of the River Kwai', *Observer*, 1 September 1968

Watt, Ian, 'Humanities on the River Kwai', *Stanford Observer*, November 1982

MEDICAL REPORTS

Gill, G., Henry and Reid, 'Chronic cardiac beriberi in a former prisoner of the Japanese' *The Nutrition Society*, 1980, pp. 273–4

Gill, G., 'Study of mortality and autopsy findings amongst former prisoners of the Japanese'

——, 'Disease and death on the Thai–Burma railway', *Bulletin Liverpool Medical Historical Society,* 1995–6, vol. 8, pp. 55–63

Gill, G., and Bell, D., 'Strongyloides stercoralis infection in former Far East prisoners of war' *British Medical Journal*, 1979, BMJ/327/79

——, 'Persisting tropical diseases amongst former prisoners of war of the Japanese' *The Practitioner*, August 1980, vol. 224, pp. 801–3

——, 'The health of former prisoners of war of the Japanese', *Practice of Medicine*, April 1981, vol. 225, pp. 531–8

Moon, Dr A.A., 'Medical report on the hospital at Tamarkan', September 1945

Walters, Caplan and Hayward A., 'FEPOW survey', *Queen Mary's Hospital Roehampton,* 1971

UNPUBLISHED SOURCES

Annual Confidential Reports (Lieutenant Colonel P.J.D. Toosey), *War Department*, 1948, 1949, 1950

History of 359 (4th West Lancs) Medium Regiment RA (TA) 1859–1959, privately published by 359 (4th West Lancs), Edge Lane Liverpool, 1959

Baume, Lieutenant L.C., *Diaries 1945–45*, IWM 66/310/1-2

Beattie, Rod, War graves database at the Thailand–Burma Railway Centre 2005

Brett, Lt C.C., 'Confidential Report on the Thailand–Burma Railway', *Seatic Bulletin*, No. 246, IWM 93/14/4

Butterworth, A.K., collection, IWM 95/17/1

Coates & Neild, 'Up Country with "F" Force', Chronological Diary

Davidson, R.A.N., collection, IWM 92/35/1

Dunstan, Peter, The British Far East Prisoners of War graves' archives

Escritt, Ewart, Note on the 'V' Organisation, Oxford, November 1982 IWM

Escritt, Ewart, collection, IWM 93/7/1 & 2

Gimson, Stanley, *Diary 1942–1945*, IWM

Leaney, W.J., collection, IWM 84/45/1

Leeman, Jack, 'The Body Snatchers', January 1962

Knights, Lt. Col. A.E., Notes on the V-Organisation, IWM 97/23/1

Newell, Capt. T., collection, IWM P470

Owtram, Lt. Col. Cary, *Memoirs*

Pritchard, Norman, *Christmas Behind Bamboo*

Richardson, J.A., collection, IWM 87/58/1

Riley, W.G., collection, IWM 86/87/1

Robinson, Captain F.S., collection, IWM 93/31/1

Routley, Dr P.E.F., personal papers, IWM PJDT 21

Sharp, J.C., collection, IWM

Smyth, Sir John, *The Life Story of Brigadier P. J. D. Toosey*

Sutcliffe, Lt. R., *Diary*, IWM 93/14/1

Toosey, Philip John Denton, collection, IWM 93/14/5

Toosey, Philip John Denton et al., Camp Report, Ubon, September 1945

Toosey, Philip John Denton et al., *War Diary of the 135th Herts Yeomanry*, 1942

Toosey, Philip John Denton, unpublished autobiographical writings

Toosey, Philip John Denton, interviews with Peter Davies 1974–5

Toosey, Philip John Denton, interview for the RNIB, 1974

V-Scheme, IWM PP/MCR 179

Warmenhoven, Lt. Col. K.A., 'History of the Railway Siam–Burma', 1947, PRO 45564

Watt, Ian, 'The Humanities on the River Kwai: The Grace Adams Tanner Lecture in Human Values', 1981, PJDT 93/14/2

Webster, Edwin, 'A Man's a Man for a' that', 1968

Weir, D., collection, IWM 99/82/1

Young, Alec, *Diary*, IWM 75/124/1

All letters quoted come from the Toosey family collection, the Toosey scrapbook at the Imperial War Museum IWM 93/14/5 PJDT 98 and the Barings archives at ING Bank N.V. (London Branch).

PICTURE CREDITS

The numbers in italics refer to the pictures in the plate section.

Amornsri Subawahat: *28*
British Film Institute: *47*
Corbis Images: *46*
David Smiley: *40*, p. 298
Dick van Zoonen: *11*, *12*, *23*
Frederick Ransome Smith: *38*
Gresham's School, Norfolk: p. 38
Imperial War Museum, London, Toosey Album: *3*, *6*, *39*, p. 44
Imperial War Museum, London: *7*, *10*, *34*, *35*, *36*, p. 70, p. 263, p. 273
ING Bank, N.V. (London Branch): *2*
Jack Chalker: *8*, p. 188
Patricia Mark: *27*, p. 156
Peter Davies: *16*, *51*, p. 27, p. 109, p. 174, p. 224
Peter Dunstan: *9*, *41*, p. 248
Peter Jones: *26*, p. 206
Record of the Thailand Burma Railway courtesy Peter Davies: *17*, *20*
Ren-ichi Sugano and Thailand–Burma Railway Centre: *19*, *20*, pp. 26–7,
    p. 172
Rex Images: p. 21
Rod Beattie at the Thailand–Burma Railway Centre: p. 89
Ronald Searle: *25*, p. 116, p. 179
Stephen Alexander: *13*, p. 126, p. 139
The Estate of the late Stanley Gimson: *24*
The family of the late Norman Pritchard: *30*, p. 238, p. 300
The Ronald Grant Archive: *31*

Toosey Family Collection: *1*, *4*, *5*, *15*, *18*, *21*, *22*, *30*, *32*, *33*, *42*, *43*,
    44, *45*, *48*, *49*, *50*, p. vi, p. 143, p. 307, p. 318, p. 341, p. 375
William M. Drower: *37*

INDEX